ild your Resilience

About the Author

Donald Robertson is a UKCP registered psychotherapist, specializing in cognitive-behavioural therapy (CBT), clinical hypnosis, and other evidence-based approaches. He is also a Fellow of the Royal Society for Public Health (RSPH) and has delivered stress management and resilience training to many organizations, ranging from small charities to major corporations. He has been in practice as a therapist for over fifteen years and mainly treats clients with anxiety-related problems at his clinic in Harley Street, London. Donald is also an experienced trainer and workshop facilitator.

He is the author of dozens of articles in therapy journals and magazines and of the books *The Philosophy of Cognitive-Behavioural Therapy* (2010) and *The Practice of Cognitive-Behavioural Hypnotherapy* (in press). He is also the editor of *The Discovery of Hypnosis* (2009), the complete writings of James Braid, the founder of hypnotherapy.

Teach® Yourself

Build your Resilience

How to survive and thrive in any situation

Donald J. Robertson

Hodder Education
338 Euston Road, London NW1 3BH.
Hodder Education is an Hachette UK company.
First published in UK 2012 by Hodder Education.
First published in US 2012 by The McGraw-Hill Companies, Inc.
This edition published 2012.

British Library Cataloguing in Publication Data: a catalogue record for this title is available from the British Library.
Library of Congress Catalog Card Number: on file.

www.hoddereducation.co.uk
Cover image: © Pei Ling Hoo – Fotolia
Typeset by Cenveo Publisher Services.
Printed and bound by CPI Group (UK) Ltd, Croydon, CR0 4YY

Contents

Acknowledgements

Thanks to my lovely wife, Mandy, for her endless patience, love and support, while I was working on this book and to my beautiful baby daughter, Poppy Louise Robertson, for playing games with me and regularly providing some healthy diversion from work.

Thanks to our cat, Daisy 'Meepster' Robertson, for staying off my laptop this time and not stomping all over the keys.

Special thanks are due to Paul Young for reading the manuscript and providing feedback and suggestions for incorporation into the final version of the book.

References to classical texts follow the conventional system of letter number, or chapter and passage. Quotations from Marcus Aurelius are based upon Gregory Hays' translation, unless otherwise specified (Aurelius, 2003).

1

Introduction: what is resilience?

In this chapter you will learn:

- ***What is meant by 'resilience' in psychological research on the subject and a way of defining resilience in relation to pursuit of your personal values in life***
- ***What 'risk factors' and life events typically create increased vulnerability to stress-related problems***
- ***What 'protective factors' and coping strategies typically reduce the risk of stress-related problems***
- ***How to begin developing a personal resilience strategy or plan***
- ***How to use this book and* troubleshoot *common problems you may encounter while trying to build resilience.***

> ***You have power over your mind – not outside events. Realize this, and you will find strength.***
>
> Marcus Aurelius, *Meditations*

The importance of resilience

How can you improve your ability to 'thrive and survive' in any situation? What disadvantages, stresses or difficulties do you currently face? What future problems might you need to anticipate and prepare for? What strengths and assets have helped you to cope well with difficult events in the past? What can you learn from the way other people deal with life's challenges? These are all questions about psychological *resilience*. Building resilience is a way of improving your ability to cope with adversity or stressful situations in general.

We all need some degree of resilience in order to cope with the problems life throws at us. Indeed, research shows that resilience is normal and involves ordinary skills and resources. Everyone is capable of being resilient and becoming more so by developing appropriate coping strategies. The types of adversity that demand resilience can range from ordinary 'daily hassles' to major setbacks, stressful life events such as divorce, redundancy, bankruptcy, illness or bereavement, and perhaps even more severe trauma in some cases. Most people believe that they are at least moderately resilient. However, few people are as resilient as they could be in all areas of life, and there are always more aspects of resilience that can be developed.

This book differs from the vast majority of self-help books, which are normally assumed to serve a 'remedial' function by attempting to *mend a specific problem*, such as overcoming depression or managing anxiety. By contrast, the self-help approach you're reading about here aims to serve a more *general* and *preventative* function by improving resilience to both current and future adversities. Building resilience also tends to improve your wellbeing and quality of life by enhancing positive qualities like psychological flexibility, social skills and problem-solving ability. This book will therefore help you to expand beyond your 'comfort zone' and reach out towards new values and goals, by meeting challenges and opportunities that arise resiliently.

Exhibiting resilience does not mean completely eliminating anxiety and other forms of distress. Many resilient people experience strong emotions but cope well with them and overcome stressful problems anyway. Someone who is bereaved may naturally feel extreme sadness, for example, while still adapting well over time and avoiding developing more serious depression as a result. Resilience does not usually mean amputating or avoiding your emotions but rather, as we shall see, it may often involve *accepting* them while actively pursuing healthy goals and personal values.

Research on 'resilience' is a fairly specialized area that only really began to develop in the 1970s, and initially focused on factors that contribute to resilience during the developmental course of *childhood*. However, there has been increasing awareness that similar factors are relevant to the resilience of adults faced with adversity and research has also been conducted in this area. Established resilience-building programmes have now been used to help prepare schoolchildren and college students to cope with stress, while reducing the risk of depression and anxiety, to enhance the performance of athletes, parental skills, teachers' performance, and also to improve productivity, job satisfaction, and work–life balance among corporate employees (Reivich & Shatté, 2002, p. 11).

Whereas traditional stress management and therapy approaches generally target problems once they have arisen, resilience-building approaches train individuals to anticipate stress and prepare in advance to minimise its impact by weathering the storm.

Key idea: Psychological resilience

Resilience consists of *various processes*, ways of thinking and acting through which individuals adapt and cope well with adversity, without suffering from long-term harmful consequences due to stress. It has been defined by researchers in this field as consisting of 'patterns of positive adaptation during or following significant adversity' (Masten, Cutuli, Herbers & Reed, 2009, p. 118). Resilience employs fairly *ordinary* abilities such as problem-solving, assertiveness, and dealing with your thoughts and feelings, etc. It therefore reduces the impact of stressful life events while also enhancing general wellbeing and quality of life. However, there's some ambiguity about what 'adapting' or 'recovering' mean insofar as there's no set-in-stone definition of wellbeing. In this book, we'll use the approach known as 'values clarification' to help you define resilience in terms of remaining committed to living in accord with your personal values despite encountering challenges or setbacks. Whereas reduced anxiety and depression are seen as the ultimate goal in some traditional approaches to resilience-building, here we view these more as common internal barriers or obstacles to a more fundamental aim: living in accord with your personal values.

DEFINING RESILIENCE FURTHER

Various groups of researchers have found that there are certain individuals who tend to cope particularly well with even highly-stressful life events, such as poverty, divorce or trauma. These challenges have little impact on the ability of some people to function, such as their performance academically or at work, and don't lead to long-term stress-related or psychological problems such as anxiety or depressive disorders. The term 'resilient' is used to refer to such robust individuals. 'Resilience' is therefore the name of the dynamic, ongoing *process* whereby people cope well with stressful events.

What do we *ordinarily* mean by 'resilience'? The standard dictionary definition is derived from physics and engineering where it refers to the capacity of a material to automatically resume its original shape after being bent, stretched, compressed or misshapen in some way. For example, rubber is highly resilient to physical stress whereas glass is not. Resilience, in this sense, is linked to things like flexibility, pliability, suppleness, springiness and elasticity. The word ultimately derives from a Latin term, *resiliens*, meaning 'to spring forward', or leap back into position. By analogy, the term 'resilience' is used in biology and medicine to refer to the ability of an organism, such as a human being, to recover from stress, injury or illness.

For example, bywords for resilience include the following, relating to the ability to cope with stress and adversity:

> ***Hardiness, toughness, strength, fortitude, adaptability, flexibility, endurance, robustness, resourcefulness, etc.***

Resilience also encompasses the notion of an ability to recover from harm or setbacks, coping with the *consequences* of adversity:

> ***Buoyancy, bouncing back, recovery, getting back on your feet, return to form, etc.***

This aspect of resilience is also expressed as an ability for 'self-righting' by modern authors. It's sometimes said, for instance, that resilience is more associated with a 'survivor' mentality whereas lack of resilience is more associated with a 'victim' mentality.

In studies on children, surviving setbacks is understood in terms of achieving typical developmental goals, performance at school, etc. However, with adults it's less clear how we measure resilience, i.e., what constitutes 'bouncing back'. One answer to this is that we can define resilience as coping with challenges or setbacks in a way that allows you to remain committed to living in accord with your own core values. If you particularly value integrity, for example, resilience might involve retaining your integrity in the face of problems or recovering it following a temporary setback.

The opposite of psychological resilience, the inability to cope and 'risk' of harmful consequences, might be expressed as:

> ***Risk, vulnerability, susceptibility, weakness, helplessness, fragility, etc.***

Psychological or *emotional* resilience (the two terms are often used interchangeably) is the type of resilience focused on in this book. It has been formally defined by researchers as:

> ***Positive adaptation in the context of significant challenges, variously referring to the capacity for, processes of, or outcomes of successful life-course development during or following exposure to potentially life-altering experiences.***
>
> (Masten, Cutuli, Herbers & Reed, 2009, p. 119)

In plain English, the term 'resilience' is used by psychologists to refer to your ability to cope well with stressful events and their consequences.

Remember this: Resilience is normal

Research on resilience shows it's quite normal for people to cope well despite adversities and the skills and attitudes that help people to overcome even major setbacks tend to be pretty ordinary. You don't need *superpowers* to be resilient in the face of stressful situations, just qualities like confidence and some ability to problem-solve, interact well with other people, and handle unpleasant emotions, etc.

Coping with noise

CASE STUDY

Throughout this book we'll look at specific examples of resilient individuals but let's start with the example of a group who struggle with a stress-related problem... For the past few years, I've been involved in delivering and writing-up a series of Government-funded research studies in which people were taught CBT strategies, similar to some of the ones in this book, to cope with stress and improve sleep, despite problems with noise in their environment. Our participants had bother with noisy neighbours, traffic noise, or noise from plumbing or machinery, etc. This can cause a huge amount of distress and some people would say they felt as though the noise was 'driving them mad' at times. They often felt their quality of life had been ruined and many had developed stress-related symptoms such as headaches, insomnia or digestive problems. However, we soon realized that many of our participants also lived with partners or spouses who coped better with the noise, were less upset by it, and perhaps barely noticed it after a while. Somehow they were being more resilient, although their ability to 'get used to it' was probably just a fairly normal process of adapting to a noisy environment. The *Coping with Noise* studies produced statistical evidence showing that those who had initially struggled could be taught coping skills that reduced their stress, despite the noise. I worked closely with many of our participants and the ones who benefited the most, and acquired resilience to noise-related stress, typically described how they'd learned to *accept* the problem, let go of their struggle with it, and thereby became less preoccupied with it, which ironically led them to notice the sound less often. We'll return to this strategy of 'letting go' and 'acceptance' in much more detail later.

Assessing your own resilience

RISK FACTORS

Risk factors are basically the various problems in life that can cause stress-related symptoms or more serious mental health disorders and may impair quality of life. There are four main types of challenge that are typically seen as calling for resilience (Reivich & Shatté, 2002, p. 15):

1 *Overcoming childhood problems.* Resilience is required, in some cases, to overcome developmental problems that may be 'stacked against you', such as coming from an impoverished or broken home, experiencing neglect or even abuse, and other childhood disadvantages that might otherwise increase the risk of later psychological problems as an adult.
2 *Living with daily hassles.* Resilience is employed in coping with daily hassles, minor adversities that occur throughout life, such as arguments in various relationships, difficulties at work, and the challenges of everyday living.
3 *Recovering from major setbacks.* At some point in life, most people will encounter highly stressful or even traumatic life events that demand greater resilience, such as redundancy, financial problems, bereavement, relationship break-ups, serious illness, being the victim of violence or other serious crime or even more extreme situations such as natural disasters, war, terrorism, etc.

4 *Reaching out for greater meaning and purpose*. Resilience can also be seen as part of the process of expanding beyond our 'comfort zone' and reaching out toward new goals because it can be stressful and challenging to proactively seize opportunities in life as well as reactively coping with threats.

Often risk factors such as these have a cumulative effect. So that an individual may suffer from a series of challenges in life, each one building up the level of risk and threatening healthy functioning.

Key idea: Risk factors

Risk factors increase your vulnerability to long-term harm. They include childhood developmental problems and stressful life events ranging from ongoing daily hassles to major setbacks or even traumas. These problems challenge you to cope with some degree of resilience to avoid harmful consequences, such as long-term anxiety or depression, etc., and to remain committed to your personal values in life.

PROTECTIVE FACTORS

Protective factors reduce the risk of suffering more serious stress-related problems such as anxiety or depression in the future, and minimise the long-term impact of adverse events on your quality of life. They may be 'external', such as social support, or 'internal', such as your personal attitudes and coping skills. We'll summarize a handful of key protective factors that contribute to general adult resilience below.

Social support

The most consistently reported protective factors are relationships within the family or within the wider society that offer healthy emotional support and encouragement. That's probably the thing we know with most certainty about resilience. People who have a supportive family, good relationships with friends or even a positive connection to religious groups, community groups, or similar organizations will generally tend to exhibit more resilience in the face of adversity. Some of the benefits of healthy relationships include:

- Having positive role models to look up to and learn from
- Experiencing care and support from others that you love or trust

- Being able to disclose problems and share them with others who will listen appropriately
- Receiving appropriate encouragement and reassurance from others.

Moreover, acting *altruistically* by providing support to others has also been found to contribute to personal resilience in some studies. Perhaps helping others to be more resilient can also help you become more resilient yourself sometimes.

Closely related to the importance of social support is the finding that social skills often correlate with resilience. One might expect that individuals with good communication skills would tend to have healthier relationships and therefore more positive social support. Resilient people also tend to actively make the best use of the social support available, for example, by seeking help for certain problems, disclosing their feelings appropriately to friends or family, etc.

Remember this: Social support is a major source of resilience

Having social support is one of the most consistently reported sources of resilience. That might be support from within your family, from friends, or from some civic or religious group. However, being able to appropriately access that support is therefore important and may be linked to possessing certain social skills such as assertiveness and good communication style. Ask yourself how you might increase your access to appropriate social support over time. Joining groups, making friends and improving communication are long-range resilience-building strategies.

Individual characteristics

A number of similar characteristics of personal behaviour have been reported as contributing to resilience, which we might roughly summarize as follows:

- Healthy *self-esteem*, self-worth, or self-*acceptance*, and awareness of personal strengths and resources
- *Self-confidence*, belief in your ability to perform competently in the face of adversity
- Good *problem-solving ability*, the ability to make decisions and put plans into effect
- *Social skills*, such as assertiveness, empathy, communication skills, etc.
- Good '*emotional self-regulation*', the ability to appropriately handle your thoughts, feelings and impulses to action.

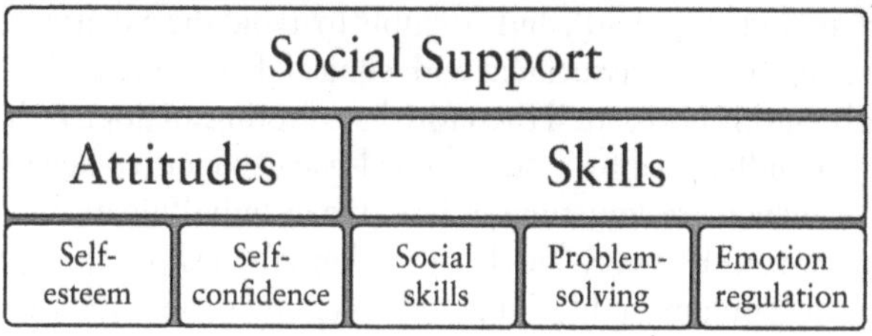

Figure 1.1

These are known to be attitudes and skills that can be developed through resilience-building training, similar to training methods used in stress management and psychological therapies, etc.

Key idea: Protective factors

Protective factors make people resilient by defending them against the risk of long-term problems due to adverse events. Research on resilience has generally pointed towards social support as being the most important protective factor. Attitudes such as positive self-esteem (or self-acceptance) and self-confidence tend to be protective. Also, coping strategies such as employing social skills, active problem-solving, and handling your emotions well, tend to protect against harm and contribute to resilience. In our approach, some of these older concepts are revised. The concept of 'self-confidence' is understood largely as a willingness to fully accept unpleasant feelings, like anxiety, while acting in accord with your most important personal values. 'Self-esteem' is likewise replaced by the notion of developing a more direct non-verbal awareness of yourself, as the observer of your experiences, acting in accord with your values.

EXPERIENTIAL AVOIDANCE

Traditionally, stress management and resilience-building have tended to focus on the idea of *controlling* stressful thoughts and feelings and replacing them with more positive ones. However, more recently researchers in the field of psychotherapy have increasingly favoured the conclusion that the effort to eliminate unpleasant experiences, called 'experiential avoidance', may often contribute to more serious problems over the long-term. For example, the specific belief that 'anxiety is bad', and attempts to avoid the experience of anxiety, appear to be associated with clinical depression and anxiety. Throughout this book we'll therefore be adopting an approach that's more influenced by modern 'third-wave' cognitive-behavioural therapies, which are sometimes referred to as 'mindfulness and acceptance-based' approaches because they emphasize acknowledging unpleasant thoughts and feelings and accepting them, rather than trying to eliminate or avoid them.

Remember this: Resilient people feel distress

It would be a mistake to assume that being resilient means being 'perfect' or never feeling upset or frustrated. Resilient people experience unpleasant thoughts and feelings but handle them in ways that prevent them escalating into more serious, long-term problems such as anxiety and depression.

Self-assessment: Evaluating your resilience

As a rough initial guide, rate yourself in terms of the following ingredients of resilience:

1 I have plenty of support from other people in life (/10)
2 I am able to accept myself for who I really am (/10)
3 I am confident in my ability to cope with adversity (/10)
4 I am good at communicating and interacting with others in times of stress (/10)
5 I am good at facing challenging problems in life and solving them systematically (/10)
6 I cope well with my emotions in the face of adversity (/10)

Rather than looking at your total score, consider each answer individually. For each item above, if you rated it more than zero, ask yourself why. Also, what could you do to increase your score on each item, making it closer to ten?

Approaches to resilience-building

So how is resilience built? The American Psychological Association (APA) has published its own research-based public information leaflet entitled *The Road to Resilience*, developed by a team of six psychologists working in this area. Their ten recommendations for developing and maintaining resilience can be paraphrased as follows:

1. Maintain good relationships with family, friends and others.
2. Avoid seeing situations as insurmountable problems and look for ways forward where possible.
3. Accept certain circumstances as being outside of your control, where necessary.
4. Set realistic goals, in small steps if necessary, and plan to work regularly on things that are achievable.
5. Take decisive action to improve your situation rather than simply avoiding problems.
6. Look for opportunities for personal growth by trying to find positive or constructive meaning in events.
7. Nurture a positive view of yourself and develop confidence in your ability to solve external problems.
8. Keep things in perspective by looking at them in a balanced way and focusing on the bigger picture.
9. Maintain a hopeful and optimistic outlook, focusing on concrete goals, rather than worrying about possible future catastrophes.
10. Take care of yourself, paying attention to your own needs and feelings and looking after your body by taking healthy physical exercise and regularly engaging in enjoyable, relaxing and healthy activities, perhaps including practices such as meditation.

Throughout the rest of this book you will learn specific techniques and strategies to help you develop these attitudes and skills, and learn other resilient ways of thinking and acting. Some of the most common methods of resilience-building, which form the basis of this book albeit with some modifications, are described below.

COGNITIVE-BEHAVIOURAL THERAPY (CBT)

Cognitive-Behavioural Therapy (CBT) and its precursor Rational-Emotive Behaviour Therapy (REBT) are psychological therapies that target thoughts and beliefs (cognitions), and also behaviour, in order to deal with emotional disturbance. CBT is the basis of most resilience-building approaches, which take evidence-based techniques used with clinical anxiety and depression and adapt them for use in managing general stress. Michael Neenan has written an excellent self-help book entitled *Developing Resilience: A Cognitive-Behavioural Approach* (2009), which explores at length the role of challenging unhelpful attitudes. Throughout this book, we'll also be drawing on modern CBT as a source of methods for resilience-building.

PROBLEM-SOLVING TRAINING (PST)

Problem-Solving Therapy, or Training (PST), is a simple cognitive-behavioural approach first developed in the 1970s, which has accumulated support from many studies for a wide-range of stress-related problems, but particularly the treatment of clinical depression. Several forms of resilience-building, such as Neenan's CBT approach, specifically include elements of problem-solving training. However, the problem-solving mode of thinking can itself become a threat to resilience if it doesn't know when to stop. We need to learn to balance problem-solving with acceptance, particularly where fruitless attempts at problem-solving are themselves becoming part of the problem.

PROGRESSIVE AND APPLIED RELAXATION

Progressive Relaxation is an old approach that dates back to the 1920s but has been continually developed and incorporated into different forms of CBT. Although used for therapy it has also been used *preventatively*, to build physical and emotional resilience to future stress and illness. Progressive Relaxation and a modern variation of it called Applied Relaxation are therefore used in established resilience-building approaches.

SOCIAL SKILLS TRAINING AND ASSERTIVENESS

The earliest form of social skills training was probably *assertiveness* training, which originated in the 1950s as a form of behaviour therapy. Social skills, including assertiveness, empathy and communications skills, are widely used as part of resilience-building approaches. We've seen that social support is frequently reported to be one of the most important factors contributing to resilience. A focus on developing social skills can help you protect, enhance and access appropriate sources of social support.

THE PENN RESILIENCY PROGRAMME (PRP)

It may also help to briefly summarize the contents of an established resilience-building package before outlining the revised approach described in this book, and explaining the reasons for making it slightly different. The Penn Resiliency Programme (PRP) is perhaps the best example of an established resilience-building approach. It was developed initially as a means of minimizing depression over the long-term with schoolchildren, based on Martin Seligman's earlier work on 'learned optimism' and adapting the techniques of standard cognitive therapy to serve a *preventative* rather than *remedial* function. It has been supported by compelling evidence showing its effectiveness as preventative treatment for depression and also, in some studies, for anxiety. For example, up to two years after undergoing classes in resilience-building, children considered at risk of depression were found to be about half as likely to have actually developed it as their peers in 'control' groups, who did not receive any resilience training (Reivich & Shatté, 2002, p. 11). In schoolchildren, for whom this approach was originally designed, research found that 'conduct problems', their behaviour, also improved as a result.

The version of the Penn Resiliency Programme (PRP) described by Reivich and Shatté (2002) consists of 'seven key skills':

1. *Monitoring your thoughts*: Learning to catch your unhelpful thoughts as they occur and to understand how they influence your feelings and actions.
2. *Spotting 'thinking errors'*: Spotting common errors (or 'thinking traps') among your thoughts such as excessive self-blame or jumping to conclusions, etc.
3. *Identifying unhelpful beliefs*: Identifying unhelpful underlying ('core' or 'iceberg') beliefs and evaluating them.
4. *Challenging unhelpful beliefs*: This includes *problem-solving* as well as learning to dispute faulty 'Why?' beliefs, or rumination, about the causation of problems that can get in the way of solving them.
5. *Challenging catastrophic worries*: Dealing specifically with 'What if?' thinking, or unrealistic worry, by challenging catastrophic beliefs about consequences of problems and focusing instead on the most likely outcomes ('decatastrophizing' or 'putting things in perspective').
6. *Rapid calming and focusing strategies*: Coping skills for use in real-world situations, consisting of a simplified form of Applied Relaxation (Reivich & Shatté, 2002, pp. 192–196) and coping imagery used to 'calm' stressful emotions and distraction ('focusing') techniques to quickly manage intrusive thoughts, worry and rumination.

7 '*Real-time resilience*': This involves using a much-abbreviated version of the disputation skills (4 and 5) above to challenge unhelpful thoughts more quickly and replace them with resilient ones in specific situations by completing the 'tag lines' or self-statements: 'A more accurate way of seeing this is...', 'That's not true because...', and 'A more likely outcome is... and I can... to deal with it' (Reivich & Shatté, 2002, pp. 206–210)

Seligman's more recent resilience training programme is designed not for children but for adults in the military. The Master Resilience Training (MRT) programme is based upon the PRP approach but extends it to include additional components influenced by wider issues in Positive Psychology (Seligman, 2011, pp. 163–176):

- Keeping a gratitude journal, recording positive events and their personal meaning to enhance mood
- Identifying personal signature strengths and putting them into practice more regularly
- Building stronger relationships by developing an active, constructive responding style, praising specific behaviours, and through assertiveness training.

Positive Psychology began to develop in the late 1990s. It focuses on directly cultivating positive *strengths* rather than remedying weaknesses as a way of improving quality of life and general wellbeing, which has the benefit of increasing resilience to future difficulties.

MINDFULNESS AND ACCEPTANCE-BASED APPROACHES

These and other similar approaches draw heavily on established CBT methods used in the treatment of clinical anxiety and depression, which are modified for use with a normal (non-clinical) population and to serve a more preventative function. They emphasize the importance of your *attitude* towards adversity and coping with stress, your 'thinking style', as the main factor determining emotional resilience. For example:

> ***Your thinking style is what causes you to respond emotionally to events, so it's your thinking style that determines your level of resilience – your ability to overcome, steer through, and bounce back when adversity strikes.***
>
> (Reivich & Shatté, 2002, p. 3)

However, in recent decades, CBT itself has changed, and a 'third wave' of therapies has evolved, which adopt a different emphasis. 'Mindfulness and acceptance-based' approaches, as these are known, interpret research findings in the field of psychology as suggesting that it's not so much the *content* of our thoughts and attitudes that matters as our *relationship* with them, i.e., how we respond to them. As the name suggests, these approaches generally recommend relating to unhelpful thoughts with mindfulness and acceptance rather than challenging and disputing their content. This fundamentally differs both from traditional CBT and from resilience-building approaches like PRP.

The key question here is whether the best way to build resilience is to gather evidence and dispute the logic of unhelpful thoughts, like traditional CBT, or simply to acknowledge them and distance ourselves from them, without getting into an internal struggle, like mindfulness and acceptance-based approaches now recommend. Some authors believe that we can both dispute thoughts and learn to detach from them, whereas others find these approaches may sometimes conflict. Both traditional CBT and more recent mindfulness and acceptance-based approaches agree that certain changes in behaviour, such as acting in accord with values, solving practical problems, developing social skills, and perhaps even learning to let go of muscular tension, are important and beneficial ways to improve our functioning and quality of life. This book adopts an integrative approach to resilience-building that can probably be best described as a form of 'Acceptance-Based Behaviour Therapy' (ABBT) (Roemer & Orsillo, 2009).

THIS BOOK'S APPROACH

The self-help approach to resilience-building described in this book therefore draws upon established resilience training programmes but also incorporates many elements from more recent research on mindfulness and acceptance-based approaches to the treatment of common psychological problems. The specific form of acceptance-based therapy most relevant to resilience-building is perhaps Acceptance and Commitment Therapy (ACT), which later chapters will discuss in more detail. The central goal of ACT is increasing general 'psychological flexibility', a concept quite similar to psychological resilience.

Subsequent chapters will look at the ACT approach to psychological flexibility and resilience and how more traditional cognitive-behavioural skills can be incorporated with a mindfulness and acceptance-based approach. Their contents might be summed-up as follows:

1. Psychological flexibility skills (Mindfulness and valued living):
   a. Clarification of personal values
   b. Commitment to valued action
   c. Defusion of unpleasant or unhelpful thoughts
   d. Willing acceptance of unpleasant feelings
   e. Awareness of the self as observer
   f. Connection with the present moment.
2. Additional skills and strategies
   a. Worry postponement
   b. Progressive muscle relaxation
   c. Applied relaxation
   d. Problem-solving
   e. Assertiveness and other social skills.

Some of these headings may seem a little cryptic at first but they'll become clear as you read the following chapters. In a nutshell, this approach shares certain elements with established resilience-building approaches. The main difference is that it places greater emphasis upon your relationship with unhelpful thoughts and beliefs rather than attempting to dispute them. It also emphasizes the role of clarifying and acting in accord with personal values, which is similar, however, to the emphasis on 'signature strengths' adopted in Seligman's more recent work in this area.

In the final chapter, we'll also be looking at perhaps the oldest Western system of resilience-building, the classical Graeco-Roman school of philosophy known as 'Stoicism', which is derived from the teachings of Socrates and inspired the development of modern CBT (Robertson, 2010). The Stoics are, in a sense, the ancient forebears of most modern resilience-building approaches. Indeed, Epictetus, the Stoic philosopher who has most influenced the field of psychotherapy, has been described as 'the patron saint of the resilient' (Neenan, 2009, p. 21).

DEVELOPING A PERSONAL RESILIENCE STRATEGY

A good way to start resilience building consists of reviewing your past experiences to identify what you can learn about coping with stress and developing a personal resilience plan or strategy for the future. This approach is recommended by the APA in their guidance on resilience and similar exercises have been used in CBT for resilience-building.

Try it now: Evaluate your previous resilience strategies

Identify a specific time in the past when you have shown resilience in the face of adversity or coped well with stressful life events.

1. What was your goal?
2. What was the actual outcome?
3. What obstacles did you have to overcome?
4. What unpleasant thoughts and feelings do you remember having in that situation?
5. Who, if anyone, did you receive external help or support from?
6. What specific attitudes or skills helped you cope with the situation?
7. How would you rate your resilience in that situation (0–100%)?
8. Why wasn't it 0%? What strengths and personal qualities helped you?
9. If it wasn't 100%, how could your resilience be improved during similar situations in the future?
10. Based on your experience, how might you advise someone else to cope with a similar problem in the future?

If you want, repeat the process above for about three situations in total and look for patterns in your problems and ways of coping.

Hopefully, this will help you start reflecting on your existing strengths and how you can develop them further in the course of building resilience.

Try it now: Develop your personal resilience plan

Now, based on your answers, consider how you could develop your own resilience and cope better with similar stressful events in the future:

1. What would be the most helpful attitude to adopt towards similar problems in the future?
2. What skills and strategies would it help to develop and use?
3. What personal strengths or social resources do you have that might help you show resilience in the future?
4. How can you improve these resources and make better use of them?

Start thinking about your needs in terms of resilience-building. This book will provide some useful information and techniques but there may be other things you need to address in order to become more resilient. Try to develop your own plan of action.

How to use this book

Most of the following chapters assume that the topic being learned can be broadly divided into three stages:

1. *Understanding* the subject of the chapter and how to assess yourself in relevant ways
2. *Learning* the specific resilience strategies being discussed
3. *Applying* the strategies in practice and following through with them to build long-term resilience.

All three stages are usually important. Don't make the common error of reading a self-help book without actually putting the techniques into practice as you'll get minimal benefit that way. However, also avoid acting impulsively; read the information in the chapters and consider the strategies carefully, planning how you're going to make use of them systematically if possible. It's normal to encounter difficulty and setbacks along the way, that's part of expanding beyond your comfort zone and challenging yourself to learn and grow. Your very first step in learning resilience, therefore, is probably going to be preparing to deal with problems during resilience-building and applying the contents of this book to your life. So let's begin by anticipating common problems and planning how to cope with them.

TROUBLESHOOTING

There's part of the book I don't understand

I've tried to make this book as readable as possible but some of the concepts derived from modern therapy are necessarily quite challenging and subtle. If you're stuck, try reading the rest of the book and coming back to the part you don't understand later. Otherwise try searching for information online. If you're really not sure about something feel free to contact me, the author, with your questions at: donald@londoncognitive.com

I've tried one of the strategies but it's not working

First of all, make sure you understand the technique. Re-read the chapter and look elsewhere for additional information. Second, it's often a case of perseverance or 'trial and error' learning with self-help. Be patient and give it a fair trial before you abandon a technique. Also be sure not to throw the baby out with the bathwater. Maybe it's working partially but not perfectly, in which case you might want to persevere and perhaps modify your approach over time. However, if it's just not going to work for you then try strategies from elsewhere in the book. There are plenty of options provided but you shouldn't expect everything on the 'menu' of strategies provided to be equally relevant and helpful for every individual. Some things will suit you better than others. Be selective and focus on the parts of the book you find most helpful.

I'm struggling with my self-discipline and motivation

Motivation is integral to self-help. There are, fortunately, many ways that you can try to develop your motivation – it's not a fixed quantity. Some of the chapters actually contain exercises that may help to motivate you or to develop more structure and self-discipline. For example, the chapter on values clarification may help you to tap into potential sources of motivation by planning action in accord with your most cherished values and priorities in life. Another common strategy is to draw up a list of the 'pros and cons' of change (or applying some resilience strategy) and then a similar list of the 'pros and cons' of doing nothing. The chapter on commitment to valued action will help you to decide how to cope with different 'barriers to action', some of which can be problem-solved whereas others, such as unpleasant feelings, may need to be accepted in the service of developing resilience. The chapter on acceptance will even give you strategies for accepting, and moving beyond, feelings of frustration or discomfort in the process of pursuing your goals.

I'm not sure whether it's working or not

People often say this when they're rushing things. As a rule of thumb you should persevere with most strategies at least once per day for at least two weeks in order to be able to properly evaluate their effect. Don't necessarily expect a quick fix or miracle cure. You're engaged in a learning process that requires practice, like learning to play a musical instrument or drive a car. Rome wasn't built in a day. The other reason for this problem is that people set ambiguous goals that can't be measured. Try to set SMART goals (see Chapter 4) that are specific and measurable enough for you to be able to properly monitor your progress. Keep regular (daily) records of your use of strategies and try to focus systematically on one strategy and goal at a time, so that you can give it a fair trial.

I seemed to be making progress but then encountered a setback

That's so common as to be the norm. You can only really 'fail' by giving up. It's normal to encounter setbacks along the way but part of resilience is picking yourself up and carrying on. Most setbacks are temporary and people who have already developed some skills and made some progress tend to recover more quickly from setbacks than they would otherwise. You can lose a battle but still win the war. As Coué, a Christian and one of the fathers of self-help once said, even Christ stumbled and fell, more than once, on the road to Calvary. The chapter on commitment to valued action has some advice on re-commitment to action following lapses or setbacks.

I'm experiencing more serious psychological problems

If you feel you're struggling with more serious psychological, emotional or behavioural problems, such as psychosis, or *clinical* anxiety or depression, then you should seek help from an appropriately qualified professional. In the UK, the first port of call should normally be your General Practitioner (GP), who will be able to advise you further on any mental health problems you're experiencing. If you are suffering from any *diagnosable* mental health problems, you should not use this book except under the supervision of an appropriate therapist. In some cases, for example if you are receiving CBT, your therapist may wish to recommend this book, or parts of it, as self-help homework to be used as an adjunct to psychological therapy.

I've encountered another problem not mentioned here

Think now, at the outset, about what else you could do to cope with each of the common problems mentioned above. Also consider what other problems you might encounter that I've not mentioned. The chapter on problem-solving will provide you with a flexible, systematic way of generating solutions to any problem and planning how to put them into action.

Try it now: Anticipating problems and solutions

This is perhaps the most important exercise in the whole book! Start as you mean to go on by anticipating possible problems and trying to prevent them from becoming obstacles to your use of this self-help guide:

1. Make a list of problems you might encounter while reading this book and trying to build resilience. Consider problems you may have encountered in the past using self-help guides, if appropriate.
2. Take a moment to brainstorm as many possible solutions to each problem as possible, writing them down in a notebook.
3. When you've exhausted all the solutions you can think of, try asking yourself some questions to prompt more. What would you advise someone else to do if they encountered the same problem? What do you think a resilient person would do in the same situation? What do you think an expert, or someone who knows you well, would advise you to do?

4 Consider which possible solutions would be easiest to put into practice and most likely to succeed, and mark them with an asterisk.
5 Keep a record of your responses for future reference, so that you can return to them if you do encounter any problems while trying to use the strategies in this book to build your resilience.

You may want to get a notebook to use as a 'resilience-building journal', recording your answers to other questions in this book and what you learn along the way.

FOCUS POINTS

The main points to remember from this chapter are:

- Resilience is ordinary not extraordinary; most people exhibit some degree of resilience in life.
- They do so using ordinary attitudes and skills that anyone can learn to develop, thereby building resilience.
- Existing resilience-building programmes draw heavily on cognitive-behavioural therapy (CBT) and have been supported by research on the prevention of depression and related problems.
- This book adopts a similar approach but also incorporates more recent 'mindfulness and acceptance-based' approaches that change the way you relate to unpleasant thoughts and feelings rather than trying to directly change their content.
- Resilience involves coping with adversity in a way that preserves your *wellbeing*, which we can define in terms of your ability to live a life committed to your most important personal values.

NEXT STEP

The following chapters will now begin to explore many specific concepts and strategies that you can use to build resilience. First of all, though, we'll have to tackle the problem of 'experiential avoidance', one of the main obstacles to developing psychological flexibility and resilience.

Further reading

Neenan, M. (2009). *Developing Resilience: A Cognitive-Behavioural Approach*.

Reivich, K. & Shatté, A. (2002). *The Resilience Factor*.

Seligman, M. E. (1995). *The Optimistic Child: A Proven Program to Safeguard Children against Depression and Build Lifelong Resilience*.

The American Psychological Association's *The Road to Resilience* guidance leaflet is currently (at the time of writing) available online at this address: www.apa.org/helpcenter/road-resilience.aspx

2

Letting go of experiential avoidance

In this chapter you will learn:

- *How struggling to control unpleasant thoughts and feelings ('experiential avoidance') can backfire*
- *How* unworkable *efforts at change often maintain suffering in the long term and prevent feelings following their natural course*
- *How experiential avoidance impairs quality of life by interfering with valued activities*
- *That controlling unpleasant experiences sometimes* does *work, especially for milder problems, but not when it's done too rigidly or excessively*
- *The importance of* letting go *of these old habitual ways of coping, if they're not working out, and embracing psychological flexibility instead in the form of mindful acceptance and valued action.*

> *The human soul degrades itself above all, when it does its best to become an abscess, a kind of detached growth on the world. To be disgruntled at anything that happens is a kind of secession from Nature...*
>
> Marcus Aurelius, *Meditations*

> *Is control controlled by its need for control?*
>
> William Burroughs, *Ah Pook is Here*

The importance of undermining experiential avoidance

ACCEPTANCE AND COMMITMENT THERAPY (ACT)

Does trying to control and avoid unpleasant experiences (like pain, anxiety, depression and anger) work for you in the long term? Will it really help you solve your problems or is this 'solution' just another part of the problem? Is it even possible to completely control automatic thoughts and feelings? How can you completely avoid unpleasant thoughts and feelings if they're such a common part of human experience? The term 'experiential avoidance' is used in modern therapy to refer to unhelpful efforts to suppress, control or avoid unpleasant experiences. By 'unpleasant experiences' we mean thoughts, feelings, memories, bodily sensations or urges to act in certain ways.

Acceptance and Commitment Therapy (ACT) is one of the most influential of several modern mindfulness and acceptance-based therapies. These approaches derive from research on older cognitive and behavioural therapies and also draw, to some extent, on Buddhist meditation practices and philosophy. ACT is particularly well-suited to general resilience-building because it assumes that most psychological problems, although they take many forms, are due to the same handful of core processes, collectively termed '*experiential avoidance*'. Hence, ACT emphasizes the importance of letting go of experiential avoidance, rigid patterns of behaviour driven by feelings of aversion, and cultivating 'psychological flexibility' instead, a concept similar to psychological resilience. Psychological flexibility can be described as consisting of an *open, centred*, and *engaged* style of responding to events. The approach adopted throughout the rest of this book therefore combines elements of ACT with traditional cognitive-behavioural approaches to resilience-building.

Key idea: Acceptance and Commitment Therapy (ACT)

ACT (pronounced as the word 'act') is based on a growing body of basic psychological research called Relational Frame Theory (RFT), which was first developed in the 1980s by Steven Hayes and his colleagues based upon earlier concepts in behavioural psychology. ACT is defined in terms of six 'core processes' which combine to maintain overall 'psychological flexibility', a concept similar to resilience. Recent literature has tended to group these six processes under the heading of three 'response styles' as follows:

- Open responding
  - Acceptance
  - Cognitive defusion
- Centred responding
  - Self-as-context
  - Contact with the present moment
- Engaged responding
  - Values
  - Committed action.

Some of these headings might seem a bit mysterious at the moment but we'll be exploring them in detail later. However, before developing these positive aspects of psychological flexibility, ACT approaches often recommend first explicitly undermining and letting go of experiential avoidance, so that's where this chapter begins.

WHAT IS EXPERIENTIAL AVOIDANCE?

Psychiatric problems are *not abnormal*. That may seem like a paradoxical statement but the National Comorbidity Survey in the USA, for example, reported that almost 50 per cent of people met criteria for at least one psychiatric diagnosis at some point in their life. This makes having a history of mental health problems statistically quite normal. Having a history of mental health problems is more common, for example, than having blue eyes or being left-handed. Depression and anxiety, even when quite severe and disabling, appear to be part of the human condition, to some extent. Moreover, *everyone* can probably expect to experience milder ('subclinical') symptoms of anxiety and depression many times throughout their life. Human life is tough, and psychologically more demanding than most animal life. Research on thought content has actually shown that in the normal population a large percentage of thoughts that occur throughout the day are quite negative or unpleasant. People suffer more emotionally than is perhaps given away by their external appearance. Paradoxically, the USA and

UK, despite their power and affluence, have notoriously high rates of prescription for antidepressants. People often keep quiet about or conceal their internal distress and research has shown that many people with mental health problems do not seek treatment. Rates of anxiety, depression, and other forms of distress are probably far more common than people normally assume. When you ride a bus or train, for example, the chances are that several people around you are currently suffering from clinical depression or anxiety, although you won't know this from their outward appearance.

If periodic anxiety and depression are virtually the norm, can psychological *resilience* really consist in permanently *eliminating* them? Probably not. In fact rather than offering a *solution* the underlying assumption that we should try to eliminate unpleasant feelings, which is part of our cultural heritage, may be a fundamental *problem*. You should ask yourself what you can learn from your own experience about how workable these efforts are in the long term, rather than what you assume *should* be happening when you try to control your automatic reactions. Sometimes this is expressed as saying that in the *external* world the rule we tend to follow is 'if you don't like something then get rid of it' whereas in the *inner* world of thoughts and feelings, this rule doesn't work, and instead things operate according to the rule 'if you aren't willing to have it then you've got it' or perhaps 'if you struggle with something then you'll get more of it'. By analogy, when our immune system, which normally protects us, becomes over-active we can develop health problems such as *allergies*. The tendency to view painful internal experiences themselves as threats and problems-to-be-solved has been described as a kind of 'allergic reaction' to certain unpleasant thoughts and feelings (Hayes, Strosahl & Wilson, 2012, p. 19). Or to put it another way, trying to eliminate internal distress is a bit like shooting the messenger rather than addressing the real problem, which is often a failure to act in valued directions.

ACT makes a distinction between 'clean' and 'dirty' discomfort, to help illustrate the role of acceptance. 'Clean discomfort' refers to the painful experiences that life deals us and which animals, infants and our pre-human ancestors allowed themselves to experience naively and naturally, and evolved to adapt to. 'Dirty discomfort', or emotional suffering, occurs when we refuse to accept painful thoughts and feelings and struggle with them instead, compounding the problem, creating a kind of second-order 'discomfort about discomfort'. We can remain at the level of natural, clean discomfort when we willingly accept our unpleasant experiences for what they are, allowing them to follow their natural course, without adding any further suffering and becoming more and more ensnared by our attempts to control them.

Key idea: Experiential avoidance

At the heart of ACT is the observation that psychological suffering is common and therefore cannot realistically be avoided. Although we might be able to avoid certain external events, our attempts to avoid or control painful internal experiences often backfire and simply compound and prolong our emotional suffering, consuming a lot of time and energy in the process. They also tend to get in the way of living life more fully, by interfering with valued activities and damaging our quality of life. It's a bit like a man who digs holes for a living and one day falls into one. He looks around for some tool to help get him out and finds only his spade, so he does what he knows best and starts digging. What often works in the rest of life, trying to control and avoid external problems, we're naturally inclined to try in the internal world of thoughts and feelings, where it's often simply the wrong tool for the job. Moreover, thoughts and actions that are driven by experiential avoidance tend to become more narrowly defined, rigid, and insensitive to changing situations, leading to many behavioural problems.

Paradoxically, avoidance can be seen as a subtle form of *attachment* to an experience or a way of becoming ensnared by it. You may even end up feeling your life is defined by your struggle to avoid or control certain unpleasant experiences. Put crudely, to avoid an internal experience, we need to first think about it and pay attention to it, which creates a contradiction. Experiential avoidance is therefore a deeply *ironic* process because it tends to fuel the very unpleasant experiences being avoided, which, of course, simply increases the urge to avoid them, creating a deeply vicious cycle.

In his cognitive-behavioural guide to resilience, Neenan notes that the concept of Low Frustration-Tolerance (LFT), 'I can't stand it!', appears to be one of the key attitudes that undermines resilience. High Frustration-Tolerance is the willingness to endure short-term pain or discomfort for long-term gain. Low Frustration-Tolerance is similar to the concept of experiential avoidance, except that the term 'tolerance' isn't used in ACT because it might be taken to imply a *begrudging* acceptance rather than something more wholehearted. Hence, we might say that resilience often requires some *tolerance* of frustration, anxiety and pain, or rather a willingness to accept these experiences, within certain limits, in the course of pursuing important goals in life.

Remember this: Sometimes control and avoidance work

Attempts to avoid or control unpleasant experiences *sometimes do work*, especially if the feelings are not too intense or if they're relatively short-lived. For example, it might be perfectly appropriate to distract yourself briefly during a painful medical procedure, although this may be difficult to maintain if pain is chronic or recurring. The main thing to consider is whether your current way of coping is really *workable* or not, both in terms of the long-term effect on the problem itself and any cost in terms of your quality of life in general and pursuit of personal values.

RESEARCH AND APPLICATIONS

An impressive collection of modern research studies have provided evidence for the correlation between experiential avoidance and a wide variety of clinical problems. Likewise, laboratory studies have shown that individuals asked to accept their feelings tend to report less distress following exposure to stressful tasks than those instructed to try to avoid their feelings by suppressing them. Indeed, researchers have reported that belief in the statement 'anxiety is bad' is associated with a wide range of psychological problems, which arguably provides a clear example of the role of experiential avoidance in mental health. People who assume anxiety is dangerous or abnormal may be more prone to struggle with it and to suffer more severe long-term problems as a result, whereas individuals who accept anxiety as relatively harmless and normal may fare better. Psychological inflexibility and experiential avoidance have been found by researchers to correlate with distress during experimental tasks and to predict long-term problems in the real world. Experiential avoidance predicts poorer resilience in the face of stressful life events whereas its opposite, greater psychological flexibility, appears to mediate the effect of coping strategies used to deal with stress (Hayes, Strosahl & Wilson, 2012, p. 367). Likewise, in a review pooling statistics from 21 randomized studies ACT has been shown to be effective for a wide range of different problems among different populations, despite its focus on a handful of common processes (Hayes, Luoma, Bond, Masuda & Lillis, 2006).

EXPERIENTIAL AVOIDANCE AND RESILIENCE

Although ACT is a somewhat recent and innovative approach, Steven Hayes, its founder, has already published a detailed review of its use in resilience-building and the *prevention* of psychological problems (Biglan, Hayes & Pistorello, 2008). He and his colleagues conclude that numerous recent research studies show that acceptance-based strategies are beneficial for a wide range of problems and have the potential to improve the effectiveness of other preventative and resilience-building approaches. They point out that the emphasis on increasing action in accord with personal values and improving quality of life in this approach, rather than simply reducing symptoms of distress, makes it particularly relevant to the field of prevention, where you may be functioning 'normally' and not *currently* experiencing particularly stressful life events or pronounced emotional suffering. Indeed, we can define resilience in terms of your ability to remain committed to living in accord with your personal values, rather than in terms of eliminating unpleasant experiences.

The diverse *range* of problems acceptance-based therapies have been found effective in treating, both clinical and non-clinical, is put forward as a major reason for concluding that they target *common factors* fundamental to the prevention of future stress-related problems.

> ***It is this breadth of perspective that endows ACT with a special opportunity to function as a unified model of both human suffering and human resiliency.***
>
> (Hayes, Strosahl & Wilson 2012, p. 28)

ACT attempts to undermine the underlying desire to control or avoid unpleasant thoughts and feelings, through experiential avoidance. As Hayes points out, a range of studies suggest that experiential avoidance increases the risk of developing a wide variety of physical and mental health problems. It's possible either that experiential avoidance causes a host of problems *itself* or that it increases vulnerability to stressful life events, which in turn cause physical and mental health problems. Hayes points out evidence from certain studies suggests that rather than being 'immune' or numb to emotional pain, resilient individuals do experience unpleasant feelings, like anxiety or depression, but nevertheless continue to function well, without being overwhelmed by suffering. This is broadly consistent with the idea that resilience may involve being less avoidant of unpleasant feelings and more willing to accept and make room for them, without allowing them to become barriers to valued action or normal functioning. Hence, the specific way you cope with stressful situations may be less important to resilience than your underlying willingness to accept unpleasant experiences that arise while acting in accord with your personal values.

Research has provided direct evidence, for example, showing that psychological acceptance is associated with greater resilience and quality of life in the elderly. Likewise, another study found that acceptance was one of the main factors that predicted resilience among those adjusting to death and loss. Moreover, creativity and problem-solving ability, which are typically considered integral to resilience, have also been found to correlate with openness to experience, a concept very similar to what ACT means by 'acceptance', and an 'open' response style. Hayes and his colleagues therefore conclude that in relation to resilience-building,

> ***These interconnections suggest that prevention researchers may be able to inoculate people against many types of adversity by increasing their openness to distress that naturally arises from adversity.***
>
> (Biglan, Hayes & Pistorello, 2008, p. 13)

In other words, the evidence suggests we should be able to build resilience to stressful events by undermining experiential avoidance and cultivating psychological flexibility and acceptance instead. Hayes argues that acceptance-based strategies should therefore be incorporated into existing resilience-building approaches such as Seligman's cognitive-behavioural approach to preventing depression, the basis of the Penn Resiliency Programme. In general, this would involve replacing the emphasis on disputing irrational beliefs and thoughts in many approaches, particularly CBT, with a greater emphasis on mindfulness and acceptance of thoughts in the service of a valued action.

CASE STUDY

Letting go of experiential avoidance

Tom was a therapy client who sought help because he had become preoccupied with his health, a problem called 'health anxiety' or 'hypochondriasis'. He suffered from back pain, which he focused on regularly throughout the day, continually changing his posture and trying to relax his muscles to alleviate the discomfort. He also spent a lot of time in bed, lying down, trying to avoid the discomfort of back pain. Sometimes he would drink alcohol to try to cope. Unfortunately, all of his efforts seemed only to make him more tense, frustrated, and acutely aware of his bodily sensations. We agreed that 'learning to live with' back pain might be the best approach and he was surprised to discover that shortly after he stopped trying to suppress the pain and discomfort, he noticed that he was automatically paying less attention to it. Over time, ironically, he also became less physically tense as a result and the symptoms diminished. Although his back still caused discomfort sometimes, he was able to accept the sensations and carry on with physical activity, without letting it get in the way. By giving up the struggle to eliminate pain, he found it intruded less into his awareness. It's likely that his excessive preoccupation with his body previously had actually been *causing* more and more muscular tension and this now decreased as he learned to simply let go and do nothing to control or suppress the internal experience of discomfort.

The unworkable change agenda

The desire to control or avoid unpleasant thoughts and feelings ('experiential avoidance') is sometimes also referred to as the 'unworkable' change agenda. It's often found to be problematic, especially when dealing with more intense thoughts and feelings, or looking at the long-term consequences of avoidance in terms of quality of life and your ability to pursue your personal values in life. In fact, it can be said that psychological pain or discomfort only turns into genuine emotional suffering when combined with a fundamental unwillingness to accept the experience for what it is and gets overlaid with a constant futile struggle to control or avoid it instead.

Try it now: Turning control up and down

Close your eyes and imagine that you have an 'effort to relax' dial that goes from 0–10, and is currently set in the middle, at the number 5. Gradually turn your dial up to 6 or 7, and imagine what it would be like to feel a stronger desire to control your body and relax the muscles. Notice how your body reacts to this increased concern about relaxation. If you like, turn the dial all the way up to 10, one number at a time, and notice what you experience in response to extremely intense desire to relax. (You may notice that a very strong desire to relax actually makes you feel more tense, ironically, or creates other internal reactions.)

Now slowly turn your dial back down to 5, and notice what changes. If you like, slowly turn your dial, one number at a time, all the way down to 1 or even 0, and imagine letting go completely of any effort, or even desire, to relax. Notice how your body responds to this radical letting-go. An alternative is to focus on increasing and decreasing the desire specifically to relax your *breathing*. Experimenting in this way should help you learn from experience what it means to radically let go of any effort to control your feelings.

It's not so much that you have *no* control whatsoever over your thoughts and feelings, just that you have much *less* control than over your physical actions, speech and movement, etc. Ironically, the best way to 'control' them may sometimes be to stop trying, abandon the struggle for control, accept them, and allow them to come and go naturally over time. By analogy, many people who suffer from insomnia lie awake at night, tossing and turning, worrying about lack of sleep, and trying to force themselves to drop off. In doing so, they often appear to be fuelling the very problem they're trying to solve. When these individuals stop struggling and willingly accept that they're lying awake in bed, paradoxically, they often fall asleep more quickly.

The whole 'control and avoidance' agenda, although ultimately unworkable in most instances, is very deeply entrenched in our culture, and taken for granted by many people. Hayes identifies several reasons for this:

- Control and avoidance often works quite well as a form of practical problem-solving in terms of coping with *external* situations and events, such as avoiding hitting your thumb with a hammer when putting in nails – although if you do hit your thumb, it might be harder to control your *internal* reactions, your automatic thoughts of frustration and feelings of pain.
- Experiential avoidance strategies, such as drugs or distraction, often do reduce unpleasant experiences in the *short-term* and the sense of relief reinforces our urge to use them again in the future – although they may not work so well over the long-term.
- We learn from our family and society that we're expected to be able to control our thoughts and feelings, e.g., 'Boys don't cry', 'Don't be scared', etc.
- Other people *appear* to be quite successful at controlling or avoiding unpleasant thoughts and feelings, because they don't always show distress publicly – although they might say the same about you!
- Our society frequently assumes that it's healthy and natural to avoid unpleasant feelings, e.g., by using drugs, alcohol, comfort foods, etc., as ways of 'feeling better'.

Of course, sometimes, you may find that your attempts to control automatic thoughts and feelings actually do work. In that case, you may be well-advised to continue using them. However, you should at least consider an alternative approach if:

- Your current ways of coping appear to work temporarily but the problem keeps recurring, so they don't really solve things in the longer-term
- Your attempts to control unpleasant experiences cause additional problems or get in the way of your quality of life and pursuit of personal values

- You're trying to control things excessively or becoming overly-preoccupied with the struggle
- You take coping strategies that sometimes work and use them at times when they're no longer relevant or helpful.

Experiential avoidance often takes on a compulsive quality and can actually be physically very harmful, for example, attempts to control unpleasant experiences by abusing illegal or prescription drugs, alcohol abuse, self-harm, or suicide attempts, are obviously dangerous. However, avoiding discomfort by frequently 'comfort eating' or avoiding exercise may also be quite physically harmful in the long-term. A common analogy for this is that it's like being engaged in a prolonged tug-o'-war contest with a monster, over a bottomless pit. Acceptance means letting go of the rope, and stopping the futile struggle, so that you can get on with doing what's really important to you in life. Struggling with painful experiences often simply *escalates* them into more serious psychological suffering.

Try it now: Thought-suppression experiment

Here's an experiment to help you understand one of the main reasons why experiential avoidance is believed to often be unworkable and counter-productive over the long term.

Try, right now, not to think of an elephant. The fewer pink elephants you think of the better. Keep trying. In fact, close your eyes and keep trying for at least one minute. Notice what happens during this experiment and also whether the thought returns afterwards. Whether or not you succeeded, you can probably recognize the problem. Trying not to think of anything is tricky because we usually have to think about something, paradoxically, in order to try not to think about it. Sometimes, moreover, the thoughts will rebound and occur more frequently afterwards, when you stop trying. This is especially problematic when people try to suppress upsetting thoughts during periods of intense emotion, as the thoughts become likely to automatically rebound when the emotion is next experienced.

Trying to forcefully suppress upsetting automatic thoughts, or worry, can backfire in the same way. In fact, thought-suppression tends to become even harder when *strong emotions* are involved. For example, imagine that someone had your brain attached to a mind-reading machine that would set off a loud alarm immediately should you even have the slightest thought of an elephant. Pretend that it's really *important* that you don't think of elephants and that doing so is very dangerous – a life or death matter. An evil mastermind has you prisoner, closely monitoring your thoughts, and has a gun pointed at you so that he can pull the trigger and shoot you immediately at the first sign of any thoughts about elephants. Suppose, in addition, he has you wired to a very sensitive stress-monitoring device, like a 'polygraph', that measures your heart rate, sweat glands, breathing, etc., and will set an alarm bell ringing at the slightest sign of stress or anxiety. Close your eyes for about one minute and imagine this scenario: that it's a matter of life-or-death, highly important, that you completely avoid either *thinking* of elephants or *feeling* any trace of anxiety. What happens?

Now, what if, instead of having to control your thoughts or feelings, your captor was simply interested in your actions and asked you to remain silent and hand over your wallet to avoid being shot? That would be pretty easy to do by comparison, wouldn't it? Your physical actions are much easier to control than your automatic thoughts and feelings and trying to do so doesn't tend to backfire in the same way.

LETTING GO OF THE UNWORKABLE CHANGE AGENDA

ACT also refers to a willingness to abandon the 'change agenda' of experiential avoidance as 'creative hopelessness'. That doesn't mean *feeling* hopeless or seeing *yourself* as hopeless but rather finding the whole struggle to control your thoughts and feelings to be hopeless in the long term, part of the problem rather than the solution. In therapy sessions, one of the first steps often involves identifying the client's current ways of coping with problems and asking: 'How's that *working out* for you?' This usually highlights the cost and ineffectiveness, especially over the long term, of the behaviour involved. People may spend a lot of time and energy in futile attempts to control unpleasant thoughts and feelings, which are ultimately unhelpful or even positively harmful. It's not you, though, that's 'hopeless', it's (perhaps) the attempt to control unpleasant emotions and automatic thoughts. Creativity comes from abandoning that rigid strategy and thereby opening up to a whole new flexible way of responding to problems. The alternative being commitment to valued action, in the present moment, and willing acceptance of thoughts and feelings that try to get in the way, although this allows for a broad repertoire of different responses and increased psychological flexibility.

Remember this: Letting go of experiential avoidance

Ironically, when we abandon attempts to control unpleasant experiences and learn to willingly accept them in the service of following our values, emotional suffering and distressing thoughts often tend to reduce significantly. However, the experts in this area counsel against simply regarding strategies such as acceptance and defusion as themselves forms of (indirect) experiential control. If you sneakily think of accepting your pain as a roundabout way to eliminate it over time you're perhaps not fully letting go of your emotional self-control agenda and keeping one eye fixed on your pain rather than allowing your attention to roam freely.

There are many different types of experiential avoidance and you should ask yourself in what ways you currently try to tolerate, avoid, control, cope with or escape from unpleasant thoughts or feelings. Some common examples include:

- Drinking alcohol or using illegal or prescription drugs
- Comfort-eating to quell negative feelings

- Avoiding certain situations, people or activities
- Procrastinating or putting things off
- Escaping or trying to leave certain situations quickly
- Becoming withdrawn from life or sleeping too much
- Watching television, browsing the internet, etc., as forms of distraction
- Trying to suppress or block upsetting feelings
- Trying to argue with yourself or think positively
- Trying to force yourself to relax or using other therapy or self-help techniques excessively if they aren't working for you in the long-term
- Venting anger, complaining, crying, apologising, etc.
- Performing ritualistic, repetitive or superstitious behaviours as a way of neutralizing anxiety or warding-off danger
- Prolonged worrying, unproductive problem-solving or planning, over-analysing things, or ruminating about the past, i.e., thinking-too-much as a way of avoiding your feelings
- Seeking reassurance or support excessively from other people
- And countless other things…

What thoughts, feelings or urges do you usually try to avoid experiencing? What's the possible cost to you of attempting to avoid these things, over time? The more you try to suppress, control or avoid painful experiences in these ways the more you're likely to experience their *presence* over the long term, because these strategies tend to backfire in many cases. Perhaps worse, using these unhelpful ways of coping is likely to cause you to suffer further because of the increasing loss or *absence* of vitality and personal meaning that comes from them getting in the way of valued activities.

Self-assessment: Experiential avoidance ('How's it working out for you?')

Pick a problem that you've been struggling with for a while. List the main ways you have of coping with unpleasant experiences such as stress, anxiety, depression, anger, pain, etc. You might want to mark these 'A' or 'C' to indicate whether these appear to be 'acceptance' or 'control' strategies. Then record the particular experiences being avoided. Finally, rate the 'workability' of each strategy (0–100%), meaning how helpful it actually is in terms of avoiding, reducing or controlling unpleasant experiences and living in accord with your values, over the *long term*.

For example, someone who drinks alcohol (strategy) to cope with social anxiety (experience) might rate the workability of that quite low, perhaps 10% as a long-term way of avoiding aversive feelings and perhaps 0%, in relation to their value of exhibiting self-discipline and a healthy lifestyle. Rating workability is like asking the question commonly used in therapy: 'How is that working out for you?' Emotional avoidance sometimes appears to 'work' in the short-term, by making you feel temporarily better, but it often leads to little benefit in the long term. Moreover, these strategies are probably not in line with your core values, and the disadvantages or *unworkability* of them in this regard will also tend to become more obvious when you consider the long-term consequences of using them.

		Long-term workability	
Coping strategies	Unpleasant thoughts/ feelings	Avoiding distress (%)	Achieving values (%)

The alternative to experiential avoidance is creative hopelessness leading to the adoption of a more psychologically flexible way of responding, through mindfulness and willing acceptance of unpleasant experiences in the service of commitment to valued action. Acceptance, in this sense, denotes a fundamental willingness to completely *let go* of the whole unworkable agenda of avoidance and control. Willing acceptance is difficult, not because it requires effort, ironically, but because it requires letting go of certain efforts that have probably become deeply habitual. We'll therefore be looking at the components of mindful acceptance and the 'open response style' shortly.

Maintaining resilience through creative hopelessness

Look at all the different ways you respond to unpleasant experiences and see how many of them can be subsumed under the same broad heading of 'experiential avoidance'. The term 'creative hopelessness' refers to abandoning that whole way of coping, in its many different guises. Look out for signs that you may be engaging in experiential avoidance, such as:

- Worrying or ruminating about a problem
- Struggling or fighting with your thoughts or feelings
- Having a strong urge to defend yourself against painful experiences
- Suppressing or blocking thoughts or feelings
- Using substances or doing activities that distract you or numb your feelings
- Seeking reassurance or support from other people unnecessarily.

Immediately ask yourself, 'How's this working out for me?', 'Is this helpful or unhelpful?', or 'What fundamental value does this serve?' Experiment with letting go of unworkable, unhelpful strategies where possible. The subsequent chapters will help you learn how to let go more effectively of experiential avoidance by using mindfulness and acceptance-based strategies instead.

FOCUS POINTS

The main points to remember from this chapter are:

- 'Experiential avoidance' refers to the common tendency to try to control, suppress or avoid unpleasant internal experiences, including thoughts, feelings, and urges to act in certain ways, etc.
- Acceptance and Commitment Therapy (ACT) places particular emphasis on identifying the role of experiential avoidance.
- Sometimes control and avoidance of unpleasant feelings can work, perhaps in the short-term, so it's important to evaluate how 'workable' it truly is in terms of your long-term wellbeing and quality of life.
- Undermining and letting go of experiential avoidance is bound to be difficult at first, in many cases, but the strategies you learn in subsequent chapters will make it easier.

NEXT STEP

Once you've assessed and started to let go of the unworkable change agenda, and gone through 'creative hopelessness', the next step involves building greater psychological flexibility. Challenging yourself to move out of your comfort zone and pursue your most important values in life will usually mean handling difficult thoughts and feelings that stand in your way. The chapters on mindfulness and acceptance will help you to find a new way of responding to unpleasant experiences, without trying to control or avoid them.

Further reading

Harris, R. (2008). *The Happiness Trap (Based on ACT: A revolutionary mindfulness-based programme for overcoming stress, anxiety and depression)*.

Hayes, S. C. (2005). *Get Out of Your Mind and into Your Life: The New Acceptance and Commitment Therapy*.

3

Values clarification

In this chapter you will learn:

- *That 'values', in this sense, describe ways of acting or fulfilling some role in life ('virtues', if you like) that you perceive as* intrinsically *rewarding*
- *The difference between 'values' and 'goals' in relation to action*
- *The profound contrast between a life driven by avoidance of unpleasant experiences* versus *a life motivated by the pursuit of your most important values*
- *How to clarify and assess your deepest values, your philosophy of life, and the importance of doing so for emotional resilience*
- *That resilience can be defined as the ability to remain committed to your personal values in the face of adversity, despite experiencing stressful thoughts and feelings.*

> ***Ambition means tying your well-being to what other people say or do.***
> ***Self-indulgence means tying it to the things that happen to you.***
> ***Sanity means tying it to your own actions.***
>
> Marcus Aurelius, *Meditations*

The importance of commitment to valued action

How seriously have you considered, recently, what's *most important* to you in life? Can you put your deepest values into words? How *consistent* is your daily routine with your fundamental personal values? What stops you from acting in line with your core values right now, from moment to moment, even in the small things that you do each day? At the present moment, *fundamentally*, what direction are you actually taking in your life? *Quo vadis?* Where are you going? What sort of person do you want to become? These are all questions about your fundamental direction and values in life.

So what *are* values? The word has acquired a specific meaning in the psychological approaches we're drawing upon here. Values are basically expressed in very general statements about what you have chosen to see as an ideal or important way to behave throughout life: 'Acting wisely', 'To be creative and learn from life', etc. Values sum up in a few words the personal standard you seek to measure your own actions against. They've been described as the 'verbal glue' that helps to organize our goals and actions coherently, in a way that's experienced as meaningful and potentially fulfilling. They give us a sense of direction and define our philosophy of life. The use of verbs (dynamic, 'doing' words) rather than nouns or adjectives (static, 'being' words) may better encapsulate the role of activity. Hence, some authors have more recently taken to speaking of the process of 'valued living', or acting in the service of values. 'Living or acting wisely', in other words, might be a better statement of the value of wisdom than 'being wise' or 'having wisdom', because it's phrased in terms of *action*.

Values such as acting with 'integrity' therefore can't be possessed like an object or achieved in some final sense. Rather they are chosen 'life directions' that can be continually exhibited in the quality of our actions. Acting in accord with your values is a constant challenge, an ongoing *process* throughout life, rather than some *outcome* or end-point that you can achieve once-and-for-all, allowing you to rest on your laurels. 'Being a good friend', for example, never really ends. Likewise, values such as these are ways of acting that are within your control rather than consequences that are, in part, down to external factors or up to chance. 'Acting with generosity' is a personal value that you could live by at any given moment, whereas 'being rich and famous' is a potential outcome that depends to a large extent upon your environment – it's more in the hands of fate. Moreover, our values are fundamental *choices* that underlie and guide our judgements. We don't really arrive at our deepest values through a process of reasoning: they are even more *fundamental* than that. When we reason about things we're already taking certain values for granted.

Ancient Greek philosophy explicitly valued four cardinal virtues: wisdom, justice (or integrity), temperance and fortitude. The ideal was to be perfectly wise, just, self-disciplined and courageous. The Greek word for 'virtue' (*arête*) is tricky to translate but it's perhaps more accurate to say it means 'excellence' or 'strength', a positive quality that someone or something would be admired for possessing, or that's 'valued', in other words. Socrates, and many ancient Greek and Roman philosophers, arrived at the conclusion that the most important human virtue of all was 'wisdom' (*sophia*). That's why they chose the Greek word for 'philosophy' (*philosophia*), which literally means 'love of wisdom' or *valuing* wisdom, to describe what they dedicated themselves to doing. The ancient cardinal virtues of wisdom, justice, temperance and fortitude are an integral part of early Western civilization and they may be similar to what you find important in your own philosophy of life or you may hold quite different values. You may even find it difficult at first to put your core values into words. It often takes time and effort to clarify what your authentic personal values truly are and they may not be your first answers. Ask yourself, though: what difference would it make if I were much clearer about the most important things in life?

'Values clarification' is not a new idea. Socrates was famous for his penetrating dialogues concerning the meaning of 'the good' and the essence of different virtues. A modern approach, based upon the work of Louis Raths, was described in the book *Values Clarification* (Simon, Howe & Kirschenbaum, 1972), which contains 76 different strategies for exploring values. However, clarifying and enacting values is also an integral part of two modern 'mindfulness and acceptance-based' forms of behaviour therapy: Behavioural Activation (BA) and Acceptance and Commitment Therapy (ACT). The typical steps, in modern approaches, are:

1 Values clarification and assessment
2 Goal-setting and action-planning based on values
3 Maintaining a more general and long-term commitment to valued living, by dealing with barriers to action.

ACT in particular treats valued living as the overall purpose of therapy to which other strategies, including addressing unpleasant experiences, can be seen as adjuncts, playing a supporting role. From our perspective, values are important because they help to define what it means for you to be psychologically resilient. To be resilient is to remain committed to following your personal values despite facing adversities, including unpleasant experiences such as pain and anxiety, and to regain your commitment whenever it falters.

Key idea: 'Values' in action

The term 'value', in mindfulness and acceptance-based approaches to therapy, such as ACT, has quite a specific meaning, not unlike the ancient philosophical notion of 'virtue'. Values are defined as verbal statements of what's most important to you, which provide long-term and stable sources of personal meaning, purpose and vitality. For example, 'The most important thing to me is to act with compassion', would be a clear statement of value. Following a value, such as living with compassion, is not something you can ever *finish* doing, not a goal you can finally achieve. Rather it's a standard by which your actions can continually be measured, a direction in life, a never-ending process. Values are like a compass direction guiding you, rather than a destination you're going to arrive at. Developing clear values allows you to experience relevant actions as more intrinsically rewarding, often giving a sense of greater meaning and vitality to life.

APPLICATIONS AND RESEARCH

There's not much research on values clarification *itself* because it's seldom used alone but it forms an important component of ACT and similar approaches, which are supported by various studies. It's been used as an approach to help people make important decisions, concerning their career choices, etc., but more recently values clarification has also been used in the treatment of clinical depression and other problems, where it helps to provide a source of motivation and to foster a greater sense of fulfilment in the present moment, preventing morbid rumination about the past or worry about the future.

VALUES CLARIFICATION AND RESILIENCE

Values clarification is perhaps the best way to begin self-help work if there's no crisis to deal with and no obvious *current* problem, such as stress, anxiety or depression. Almost everyone can identify areas in which, to some extent, they could be acting more in accord with their personal values. By definition, values clarification helps to give you a sense of direction and identify healthy goals for you to work towards. Acting in the service of your values will often mean facing emotional challenges, which the other techniques in this book can help you to cope with. Learning to be guided by your values instead of your automatic thoughts and feelings will help you cope with daily hassles and weather more serious adversity when it arises.

Perhaps more importantly, values clarification can help define what 'resilience' actually means for you in practice. To be resilient means to cope with adversity in a way that preserves your wellbeing, but how do we define what's normal and healthy for you? We can understand wellbeing in terms of living in accord with your personal values. Resilience therefore consists of your ability to remain on course, committed to your personal values, despite facing adversity, challenging events, and even setbacks. By clarifying your underlying values you therefore help to define more specifically what it means for you to be psychologically resilient in life.

Values clarification

CASE STUDY

Jim sought therapy because he was having a tough time coping at work. Clarifying his values, particularly by picturing his funeral and the eulogies he'd like to receive, helped him very quickly to realize that he was in the wrong job. The fundamental value he placed on 'creativity' just wasn't being served by his current lifestyle. However, rather than immediately changing careers, which wouldn't have been very practical, he began looking first for small opportunities to be creative in his daily routine, such as developing a screenplay he was working on for at least ten minutes each day, something he'd previously 'put on the back burner'. Even a few minutes each day of doing something he fundamentally valued was better than nothing and started a process of connecting with his values and exploring how they related to the rest of his work. Over time, he continued to reflect on his values, clarify them, connect with them more deeply, and experiment with actions based upon them. Eventually an opportunity arose for him to take a new job that made even more use of his creative potential and provided him with a greater sense of satisfaction.

Value clarification and assessment

WHAT IS 'VALUED LIVING'?

In a sense, clarifying your personal values is pointless unless you begin to act more in accord with them, and we'll look at strategies for doing that shortly. However, some people benefit immediately from gaining clarity regarding core values, which may have been long-overlooked and neglected. When values clarification is working well, it's experienced as a process of 're-connecting' with your fundamental priorities in life, getting back in touch with what's genuinely important to you.

We're going to begin by considering the nature of values before asking some quite penetrating questions that are designed to be contemplated very deeply over time. Don't worry if answering the questions below doesn't give you perfect clarity right away. The main thing is that you start the process of working on your values. Think of it as a work in progress. Sometimes only by trying to live in accord with your personal values will you truly begin to understand what they are and you may even feel that you're changing your values somewhat as a result of trying to put them into practice.

Values *versus* goals

It's important to make a clear distinction from the outset between *values* and *goals*. They're very different things and often confused, which is thought to contribute to common psychological problems. *Goals* are specific outcomes or results that you might try to achieve, such as washing all the dishes before going to bed. *Values* are more fundamental ideals that give meaning and importance to individual goals, and a sense of direction to your actions, such as being a clean and tidy person or a good husband. 'Am I done yet?' is a question that you can ask about achieving goals but not values. Goals are achievable but values are never finished, they're a lifelong pursuit. If your focus is on achieving the goal of being praised by others, you may have to wait for a long time to succeed. If your focus is on living in accord with the value of generosity, in a sense, you experience success *immediately*, as soon as you totally commit to acting in a generous way.

Hence, focusing too much on goals takes your attention away from the here and now. As John Lennon wrote, 'Life is what happens to you while you're busy making other plans'. Valued living means 'holding goals lightly' and paying more attention to the quality of the journey than to the destination, although you'd better know roughly where you're heading. In ACT this is illustrated using the metaphor of skiing. Imagine that you kept climbing up a mountain to ski down it but every time you reached the top someone picked you up in a helicopter and gave you a lift back down to your destination below, spoiling your chance to ski. Skiing is about how you get down the slope, it's not just about reaching the destination. Living, like skiing, is about valuing the quality of your actions, how you get there, not just focusing on the ultimate goals and destinations you're heading towards.

For our purposes, it's most useful if you try to define your values in terms of qualities that you might exhibit in your behaviour, i.e., personal virtues or strengths you value. These may often be associated with fulfilling certain roles well, such as being a 'good father' or a 'good friend', etc. One helpful values clarification exercise you might try involves identifying the roles that are most important to you in life and writing down a description of how you act when fulfilling them well, for example, what does it mean to you to be a 'good friend'?

Intrinsic *versus* extrinsic value

Modern behaviour therapists emphasize the distinction between more 'extrinsic' rewards, consequence of an activity, and the possibility of 'intrinsic' reward, experiencing the activity *itself* as rewarding insofar as serves core values. Activities are said to have 'intrinsic value' when we pursue them for their own sake, like creating music or playing a game just for the sake of it, as an end-in-itself. Activities have '*extrinsic* value' when they're pursued for the sake of some outcome or consequence that may or may not follow. For example, playing football has *intrinsic* value if we choose to do it just for fun but playing football professionally may be more about the *extrinsic* values of earning wealth and achieving fame.

A dearth of intrinsically valued activities, from moment to moment, can make life seem empty even when pursuing seemingly important goals. Worse still, living a life devoid of intrinsic value can become an unhealthy long-term habit that leads to anxiety, depression, and other problems over time. The end does not justify the means, in terms of our quality of life. Bear in mind that some people pin all their hopes on achieving happiness in the future, forgetful of the present moment, and then die before they even achieve their goals. Life is more like playing a game or a piece of music, a process or 'journey' to be valued each step of the way rather than simply a means to an end. Hence, focusing on values should lead you to become more centred and mindful of the present moment whereas focusing on goals tends to do the opposite by leading you into concern about the future.

What happens if you shift your focus onto intrinsic values instead of extrinsic goals? You might value integrity very highly and act in a way that you're satisfied exhibits this virtue yet still find that people respond negatively, in a way that you didn't expect. Does that constitute success or failure? If your priority is to achieve the goal of getting them to respond positively then you've failed. However, if your priority is to act with integrity, whether or not people respond positively, then you've succeeded. Whether or not you achieve extrinsic goals or outcomes is often partly down to chance and less directly under your control than the way you go about doing things, i.e., whether or not you act in accord with your values.

Hence, it's considered better for mental health to act in a way that's guided primarily by your personal core values rather than by external goals, which may succeed or fail. This helps to increase the perceived *intrinsic* value of the present moment, focusing attention on the here and now rather than ruminating about the past or worrying about the future. However, in order to help you act more consistently in the service of your values, over the long term, you will probably need to plan your actions, and setting short- and long-term goals can help you do that. Remember, it's better to have goals that are subservient to your values than ones that sneakily replace them. Think of the miser who starts acquiring money because it allows him to enjoy life but ends up seeing it as an end-in-itself and gathering wealth obsessively for its own sake.

Remember this: 'I don't have any values!'

Short answer: Yes, you do! They just need to be clarified. In the sense we're interested in, it's virtually impossible not to hold any values. However, many people, especially when feeling depressed, will tend to say that they don't feel as though they have any values, they can't see any point to anything. This is best understood as a lack of awareness of personal values, being out of touch with them. Look to your actions instead of your feelings. Almost all human action is purposeful, to some extent, and you choose to do some things, and avoid doing other things, literally all day long. So what clues do your actions give you about your underlying values? You may find that your actions are driven by avoidance (an 'away from' orientation) rather than the pursuit of personal values (a 'toward' orientation). Avoidance isn't a genuine value, so ask yourself what avoidance prevents you from doing – what would you do in life if you felt able to accept the experiences you're currently avoiding and they ceased to be barriers? to action?

Demands and experiential avoidance

Something to watch out for is experiential avoidance masquerading as valued action. Pursuing control of your feelings can be easily confused with the pursuit of your true values. Feeling relaxed or avoiding feeling anxiety isn't usually an authentic value, though. You can always ask yourself: 'What am I doing that in the service of?' or 'If I were relaxed, what would that allow me to do differently in life?' Moreover, feelings are often not directly under your voluntary control, so you run the risk of valuing something that's controlled by your environment, thereby making yourself a *slave to fortune*. Worse still, direct attempts to suppress or avoid unpleasant feelings like anxiety often backfire in the long run, making them more of a problem. Accepting and tolerating unpleasant feelings, ironically, is often more likely to reduce the suffering caused by them over time. Hence, it tends to be more helpful to consciously value ways of *acting* rather than *feeling*. We'll return to this issue in later chapters when discussing the role of 'mindfulness' and 'acceptance' in resilience-building.

It also helps to distinguish values from *demands*, expressed as 'I must…', 'I should…', 'I have to…', which are generally less helpful ways to maintain actions. Demands are more *coercive* than values and tend to imply the threat of *aversive* consequences, for example, 'I must do this otherwise something awful will happen'. They're often just *experiential avoidance* in disguise. In fact, demands are often rigid in ways that bear the hallmark of 'fusion', a concept we'll discuss in later chapters. Demands like 'I must pass my exams' can be seen as valued goals that are taken more seriously and literally than is absolutely necessary, and have become irrationally absolute and inflexible. It's healthier in general to act in ways that move *towards* positive values rather than in ways that attempt to get *away* from negative experiences, such as attempts to avoid anxiety or feared catastrophes. It's better to spend your life running towards your goals, or running in step with your values, rather than away from your problems or fears. Make sure your values are *authentic* and not just what you assume your family or society put pressure on you to treat as important.

Remember this: 'Values' are not goals or demands

Values are not goals and it's absolutely essential to distinguish between the two. Values describe the overall direction you take in life, whereas goals are specific destination points along the way. If you focus on achieving goals, you place attention on the future. Focusing on values means paying more attention to the here and now and the quality of your current actions from moment to moment.

Values are also not demands. Demands tend to imply the threat of punishment, or social pressure. Compliance with, or rebellion against, social demands often masquerades as following values. However, your *authentic* values are things you personally choose as important, regardless of what other people might think.

VALUES CLARIFICATION QUESTIONS

One way of clarifying your underlying values is simply to pick something, more or less anything, that you freely choose to do, and ask yourself: 'What am I doing it for?', 'What's so important about that?', 'What's the value of that?', and so on. This works best if you pick something you actively chose to do, requiring effort. The philosopher Aristotle was one of the first people to describe how the purpose of any behaviour can be analysed by repeatedly asking a chain of questions such as: 'What is this being done *for the sake of*?' For example, suppose I make an effort to go to work: what am I doing it for the sake of? To earn money? And for the sake of what do I earn money? To support my family, to be a good husband and parent, so perhaps that's my underlying value. Take time now to really ask yourself this and perhaps also some of the typical values clarification questions below:

- What's *ultimately* the most important thing in life to you?
- What do you *really* want your life to stand for, or be about?

- What would you most like your life to be remembered for after you've died?
- What sort of things do you *most* want to spend your life doing?
- What sort of person do you *most* want to be in your relationships, at work, and in life generally?
- If you knew for certain that you only had one month left to live, how would you want to spend the remaining time before you died?
- If you didn't have to struggle with problematic thoughts or unpleasant feelings, what would you *choose* to spend your time doing? What would you do if you were free from any worries or anxieties?
- What would you choose to do if you were *guaranteed to succeed* and knew you couldn't fail in any situation?

Ask yourself also about the qualities you most appreciate in others, as these are probably also relevant to your personal values for living:

- Which specific individuals (real or fictional) do you most admire?
- What sort of people in general do you most admire?
- What do you admire most about them? How would you label their strengths?

When clarifying your values, it helps to write them down as if nobody else will ever read them, focusing on your own personal priorities not what you think other people would expect you to value. Also, imagine that anything is possible, don't be constrained by your environment, write down what you really care about, what your life would be like in an ideal world.

Try it now: The eulogy exercise

This well-known exercise has long been common in self-help literature. The purpose is to help you get in touch with and clarify your values.

Imagine that you're deceased and looking down on things from the afterlife, observing your own funeral.

Ask yourself what, ideally, you'd like people to say about your life, at its conclusion. What would you want them to remember you for and say about you in your eulogy?

Alternatively, imagine that what your life stood for is summed up in a sentence or two on your tombstone. What would you want it to say? Write an extract down on paper from the obituary you'd like to have if it helps to clarify your values. What does this thought experiment tell you about what's most important to you in life?

You might further explore your values by reviewing them periodically, discussing them with other people, or writing about them in more depth.

Assessing values across domains of life

Values assessment often begins by completing a detailed assessment form to provide a more comprehensive overview across different domains. The simplified questions below cover similar areas.

Self-assessment: Values in different life domains

Try to identify what aspects of each domain are important to you, and how you would summarize your values. Not everyone has values in all of these domains so don't worry if you struggle because it's okay to leave one or two blank. If it helps, ask yourself what sort of person you would like *to be*, in relation to each domain.

Domains	*Values*
Relationships Including intimate relationships, with your spouse or partner; family relationships of other kinds, e.g., children, parents or siblings; friendships and social relationships, etc.	
Work and study Including work, education, study and learning, etc.	
Self-care Including physical and mental health, appearance and wellbeing, etc.	
Lifestyle Including leisure activities and hobbies; finances, household; daily routine, etc.	
Other (please specify): For example, spiritual, religious, or philosophical views; community, citizenship, or political activities	

In concluding your initial values clarification, it may help to ask yourself: 'What's missing from my values?', 'Could these values be improved in any way?' This may help to identify *additional* values that have been overlooked. Once you've developed a sense of your main values, across different areas of life, the next step is normally to evaluate which ones you should focus on living more in accord with, which will be covered in the next chapter.

Remember this: Make sure they're your own values

We all have values that we've inherited from our family and culture but they're not necessarily our authentic personal values. You might *genuinely* agree with the values of your family and culture. However, you should try to check whether your values would still remain the same in the absence of any influence or control from your family or culture. You can do this, to some extent, using thought experiments, such as imagining yourself spending the rest of your life on a deserted island. Would permanently and completely removing your family and culture from your environment alter your values in any significant way? If nobody else knew you were living according to your values, would you still pursue them all?

FOCUS POINTS

The main points to remember from this chapter are:

- 'Values', in this sense, like *virtues*, are about ways of acting that are important to you and constitute the type of person you want to be in life.
- Focusing on values leads to being centred in the present moment, whereas focus on goals tends to fuel concern about the future.
- Values are *intrinsically* rewarding in contrast to goals which are about *extrinsic* rewards; you gain immediately from valued action rather than having to wait.
- Values often become vague but 'values clarification' methods can get you back in touch with them.
- Values clarification and valued activity form a good basis for developing psychological resilience in general.

NEXT STEP

Once you've clarified your values sufficiently, the next step is to begin planning how you can act more consistently with them and overcome any 'barriers to action' that you encounter along the way. The next chapter will explore the idea of setting goals and scheduling actions based on your values and making a commitment to valued living in general.

Further reading

Harris, R. (2008). *The Happiness Trap (Based on ACT: A revolutionary mindfulness-based programme for overcoming stress, anxiety and depression).*

Hayes, S. C. (2005). *Get Out of Your Mind and into Your Life: The New Acceptance and Commitment Therapy.*

Simon, Sidney B.; Howe, Leland W. and Kirschenbaum, Howard (1995). *Values Clarification: A Practical, Action-Directed Workbook.*

4

Commitment to valued action

In this chapter you will learn:

- ***That commitment to valued action can be seen as central to our definition of emotional resilience***
- ***How to set goals and schedule activities based on your core values***
- ***How to be mindful of acting in the service of your core values***
- ***How to begin dealing with barriers or obstacles to valued living***
- ***How to remain committed to progressively larger patterns of valued action.***

> ***The mind adapts and converts to its own purposes the obstacles to our acting. The impediment to action advances action. What stands in the way becomes the way.***
>
> Marcus Aurelius, *Meditations*

The importance of commitment to valued action

Do you have more freedom to control your internal *feelings* or how you *act* by moving your arms, legs and organs of speech? What happens to that free choice if you always act how your automatic, habitual thoughts and feelings are telling you to? Do you assume that unpleasant thoughts and feelings, by their nature, create barriers to action? The pursuit of values can provide the overall framework within which other resilience techniques are employed, when 'barriers' or apparent obstacles to valued living arise. We will therefore begin by looking at commitment to valued action in resilience-building and then explore the role of mindfulness and acceptance in later chapters.

What would your life actually be like if you *always* acted according to your automatic thoughts and feelings? What would it be like, by contrast, if you always acted according to your core values? Since the time of ancient Greek philosophers, the choice presented from moment to moment has been expressed metaphorically as a fork in the road between 'vice and virtue' – albeit not terms psychologists would use today. This was sometimes called the 'Pythagorean Fork' or 'Choice of Hercules'. In a famous parable, recounted by Socrates, the hero Hercules is portrayed, in his youth, as stumbling across a forked path in the forest and, ultimately, choosing the path of the goddess Virtue (*arête*) and ignoring that of her rival Vice (*kakia*). In ACT something similar is expressed as the continual choice between 'acceptance and commitment' *versus* 'control and avoidance', the life of valued action *versus* the life of internal struggle against unpleasant feelings.

Allowing your feelings to drive your actions can mean abandoning control of your life's direction. Moreover, trying to control automatic thoughts and feelings directly can sometimes backfire as we've seen when discussing 'experiential avoidance'. Sometimes people don't pursue their core values because they've become withdrawn, passive, or lack a sense of direction. However, it's also very common to find that people who appear very 'busy' are spending all their time doing everything *except* pursuing their underlying values in life, often because they're allowing the battle with negative feelings to run their lives. Trying to avoid unpleasant experiences can become a 'full-time job', while valued living, meaningful activity, is put permanently on hold. However, perhaps you neither have to do what your thoughts and feelings are telling you *nor* spend your life fighting to control or avoid them. You can commit to acting in accord with your values, *despite* what thoughts and feelings are put in your way. Changing your behaviour in a constructive direction often brings about more healthy and stable changes in internal experiences over time. In behaviour therapy, this is sometimes called the strategy of changing from the '*outside* in'.

APPLICATIONS AND RESEARCH

Behavioural Activation, which involves planning valued goals and actions, has acquired particularly strong support from modern research studies as a treatment for clinical depression. At present this is its main application, although similar strategies are used with a wide range of different issues. Indeed, research on ACT has suggested that its basic concepts and techniques, including commitment to valued living, may be effective across the board with a very wide variety of different problems.

VALUED ACTION AND RESILIENCE

Acting in accord with your core values requires resilience because it presents one of the main challenges of life. Indeed, we can *define* resilience in terms of your ability to remain committed to your personal values despite challenges and setbacks in life. Moreover, embracing your values more fully means reaching out for greater purpose and meaning in life by going beyond your comfort zone, which is both exciting and anxiety-provoking. Nevertheless, by making a commitment to valued living and shifting your focus away from extrinsic goals and onto the intrinsic value of your own actions you focus attention on what are most under your control in life, your own intentions and behaviour.

Making valued action your priority and learning to take external goals lightly will help you become more resilient to stress. Researchers have argued that focusing too much on extrinsic goals in life can both cause anxiety over uncertainty whether they will be achieved and depression over the prospect of failure (Borkovec & Sharpless, 2004, p. 230). Shifting your priorities so that you place more importance and focus upon the way you go about doing things, the quality of your current actions, appears to alleviate this stress as well as improving quality of life in other ways. Moreover, as the Stoics advised many centuries ago, placing too much importance on external goals puts your emotions in the hands of fate, because you never have total control over the outcome. Whereas making it your priority to act in accord with your fundamental values, or at least to make the commitment to doing so, is always within your power.

CASE STUDY

Valued living

Angela suffered from a chronic, severe form of anxiety called Generalized Anxiety Disorder (GAD). She had a strong sense of personal inadequacy because she hadn't achieved certain external goals in life, relating to material and social success. She constantly compared herself 'upward' to other, more successful people, which inevitably made her feel anxious, depressed and frustrated. (She didn't balance this by comparing herself 'downward' to the many people she could be grateful for being better off than.) As a consequence, she continually worried about how she could catch up with other people and make her life a success, putting herself under enormous pressure to achieve, leading to emotional and physical exhaustion.

After clarifying her values she learned to systematically make time for small valued actions each day, such as reading novels she cherished or contacting someone and showing friendship and support to them. These progressively became more frequent, until commitment to her core values became part of her lifestyle in general, reducing the demands she placed on herself to achieve external success, leading to a reduction in worry and a more balanced sense of self-esteem.

Assessing valued goals and actions

Consider which of your values are most important to you. Which are you living most consistently with and which are you most neglecting? This will lead you naturally to begin considering which you'd most benefit from attending to from now on in life.

Self-assessment: Deviation from values

This is a common ACT exercise. Use the table format below to help you assess where you currently stand in relation to your personal values and what areas you might benefit from prioritizing work on.

1 List your main values, identified in the preceding exercises, in the first column.
2 In the 'consistency' column, rate the extent to which your actions over the past week have been consistent with your personal values (0–10).
3 Some values are more important than others. In the next column, rate how important each value is to you (0–10).
4 Finally, subtract the 'consistency' score for each value from its 'importance' score and record the result under 'deviation' to estimate how far you may recently have deviated from or neglected activities that involve your most important values.

The values with the highest deviation scores may be the ones you wish to prioritize working on, although this is only a rough guide and you can feel free to use other criteria to decide where to begin making changes.

Values	*Consistency*	*Importance*	*Deviation*

To begin with, focus on just one or two core values and domains of life, where you've perhaps not been as consistent with your values as you'd have liked. You can widen your scope to address other values and areas of functioning later, one step at a time.

Try it now: Planning initial valued actions

It may also help to begin by simply drawing up a rough table like the one below, to generate a list of example activities that would be consistent with your core values and the type of person you want to be, distinguishing between general strategies and more specific tactics for the main value you're looking to work on.

Value	*General strategies*	*Specific tactics*
Being a good parent	1 Spend more time with my children	Teach them to paint Take them to the beach Ask them questions
	2 Set a good example	Stop smoking Mind my language Stop complaining about things in front of them

Ask yourself what small or easy actions you could begin to take, in line with your most important values. Sometimes you may find that valued actions are just ends-in-themselves, like playing music or being creative for its own sake, whereas other actions may naturally be linked to certain goals, in the service of values, like finishing the draft of an essay, trying to pass a college course, in the service of valuing learning.

GOAL-SETTING

Setting goals can help you to live in accord with your values, so long as goals don't begin to eclipse values. Goal-setting is best approached as an ongoing process through which the process of valued living starts to become the real underlying goal. From this perspective, goals are not *inherently* valuable but only means to the end of living, moment-to-moment, according to your core values. The problem is that our goals are always too far away, we perceive ourselves as lacking ('wanting') the things we want. We can never be satisfied so long as we're completely goal-focused whereas placing the primary value on our way of life allows us to continually embody what we value, from moment to moment.

Studies have shown that when people write down their goals clearly they're more likely to take steps to achieve them and it also helps to give you more time to think them over and refine them. (So remember it's important to actually *do* these exercises and write things down!) It often helps to phrase them in terms of specific, achievable outcomes, e.g., using the 'SMART' acronym as a guide. Goals should generally be chosen in the service of your core values, so think carefully about their relevance to your underlying priorities in life.

Key idea: Setting SMART goals

There are several different versions of the SMART acronym, which is widely used in business and life-coaching, as well as behaviour therapy. However, this version fits well with the concept of valued living. SMART goals should be:

- Specific enough to be clear and unambiguous
- Measurable enough for you to know for sure if and when you've achieved them
- Achievable, realistic, and within your sphere of control
- Relevant to your core values, which they serve
- Time-limited, to be achieved by a specified deadline, or with a certain frequency.

Where possible, goals should also be phrased positively, in terms of the *presence* of what you're trying to achieve rather than the absence of what you're trying to reduce or avoid. For our purposes, goals may be either individual outcomes, like painting the living room, or a series of smaller recurring achievements, such as tidying up at the end of each day.

Goals are very useful ways to check that you're on track in the pursuit of your values. For example, successfully completing a difficult essay might be a measure of how well you're acting in accord with the value of 'exercising scholarship and learning'. What's most important, though, is acting according to your value rather than whether or not you achieve your goal of finishing the essay. So goals are best taken 'lightly'; in valued living, values take priority over goals.

Try it now: Setting SMART goals

Once you've identified the most important core values and areas of your life to work on, try to identify specific, achievable goals (outcomes) that are consistent with them.

Values

(For example, being a good husband.)

Corresponding SMART goals

(For example, tell my wife at least once per day that I love her and say something complimentary to her.)

Once you've set specific goals that relate to your core values, you'll probably need to break them down into smaller sub-goals, and identify the specific practical steps required to achieve them. Action-planning is therefore the next thing to consider.

Applying goals and actions

ACTION-PLANNING AND ACTIVITY SCHEDULING

You may find it useful to use the table format below to begin breaking down your valued goals into more specific actions. Summarize the main values you're working on, your long-term goals, short-term goals ('sub-goals'), and the first steps you plan to take.

Values	*Long-term goals*	*Sub-goals*	*First steps*

Try it now: Scheduling valued actions

If you want to take a more thorough approach, brainstorm a list of activities that would potentially serve your key values and goals, including both small, easy steps and larger or more difficult activities. (See the chapter on 'problem-solving' for more advice on generating alternative solutions for achieving goals.)

Consider things that you used to do in the past but may have reduced or stopped doing, and whether they might serve your personal values. Rate each one in terms of the anticipated difficulty of *performing* the activity (0–100%), not how likely it is to achieve your goals. Finally place your activities in rank order from the most to the least difficult.

Now simply choose activities from your list and schedule them, noting down when you plan to attempt them, what values they are intended to serve, what goals they might help achieve, as well as your anticipated difficulty rating. After completing each task, you can also note down how difficult it *actually* was and any useful observations or reflections. Which activities should you choose first? Some activities may genuinely be more *urgent* than others, for example, you may have a deadline by which to complete an essay or apply for a job. That will obviously influence your scheduling. However, as long as it's not an excuse for procrastinating about the bigger tasks, it's generally better to start with the *easier* activities first and then work your way up the hierarchy to the most difficult ones. Start with small steps and take bigger ones later. Some activities will be 'one off' items, such as mending a broken chair, whereas others might be more frequent or recurring, such as going to the gym three times a week. If an activity is to be done repeatedly you can save space by making it one entry on your list.

Activity scheduled	*Value to be served*	*Goal to be served*	*Anticipated difficulty (%)*	*Actual difficulty (%)*
1 Mend broken chair Monday evening	Being pragmatic and organized	Tidying house	50%	10%
2 Go to gym Mon, Tues, Thurs	Looking after health	Lose half a stone by April	60%	70%, 50%, 30%
3				
4				
5				
6				
7				

Moving beyond barriers to action

ANTICIPATING BARRIERS TO ACTION

The main reasons for failing to complete a valued activity are usually that you either forget your action, or encounter specific obstacles or 'barriers to action'. Barriers can be *internal* or *external.* You may experience unwanted, unpleasant thoughts or feelings, internally, such as worry or anxiety. You may also find the external consequences of your actions or other people's responses problematic, for example, you may encounter practical difficulties or other people may oppose you.

Key idea: Barriers to action

Barriers to action are simply 'obstacles' that appear to get in the way of your goals and valued actions. You can make a fundamental distinction between 'external' or practical barriers and 'internal' barriers, such as unpleasant thoughts and feelings. External barriers can usually be addressed using problem-solving methods whereas internal barriers are best addressed using the mindfulness and acceptance-based strategies described in other chapters. Although we can talk about 'overcoming barriers to action' it might be more accurate to say that problematic thoughts and feelings can often be accepted and 'moved through' or 'lived with' rather than overcome or eliminated. In a sense, they are only really 'barriers' or 'obstacles' as long as we try to avoid or control rather than accept them.

Make a record of activities that you're at risk of failing to complete and note down the anticipated barriers to action you might encounter. Mark barriers 'I' for internal or 'E' for external and note down possible strategies for getting beyond them. Treat this as a rough initial plan. As you go through the rest of this book you can return to your record and re-evaluate it as you learn new ways of responding to both internal and external barriers. The format below could be used to record the activities.

Valued activities	*Barriers to action*	*Strategies*

FORGETTING SCHEDULED ACTIVITIES

One of the simplest and most common reasons for failing to complete a scheduled activity is that you forget to do it. Behaviour therapists call this a problem of 'stimulus control' because you've probably failed to arrange suitable reminders that might prompt you by acting as a cue or stimulus for the activity. We use reminder cues every day, from the alarm going off in the morning, to the shopping-list we take to the store. The first thing is simply to ask yourself: 'How can I make certain that I remember to do this activity?' Writing things down on an activity schedule form like the one above will help, especially if you make a point of reading it every morning, or placing it somewhere you're bound to notice it frequently enough. Telling other people that you're planning to do something can help, especially if they're likely to remind you. Placing sticky notes with reminder messages in prominent places is a popular strategy or setting an electronic reminder on your computer, phone, or some other device. Arranging your environment to remind you is the key. It's common to use reminder cues such as sticky notes saying 'Remember what's important' or photographs of loved ones, to stimulate awareness of core values. So don't forget to use reminders!

MENTAL REHEARSAL OF VALUED ACTION

Sometimes people also find that mentally rehearsing an activity beforehand, by picturing themselves doing it at a certain point in time, can help them remember the task. Moreover, one of the central problems of engaging in valued action is being able to recall your values and remain mindful of them during activity. Some authors suggest that you might want to set aside time in the mornings to contemplate your core values and prepare yourself by committing to act in their service during the day ahead. Picture the setting in which the activity is to be performed and the specific steps involved. Imagine completing the task, as realistically as possible, while accepting any internal barriers that arise and continuing to focus on your values and acting accordingly. The ancient Stoic philosophers would do something similar each morning by mentally rehearsing how they planned to act in accord with the cardinal virtues and the precepts forming their personal philosophy of life.

Try it now: Mental rehearsal of valued action

Close your eyes and vividly imagine yourself taking the steps required to achieve some valued goal. As you do so, keep your focus on the intrinsic value of what you're doing. Rather than imagining things going perfectly, if your goal is challenging, imagine things realistically. Allow yourself to encounter barriers to action in your mind, such as uncomfortable thoughts or feelings. Practise accepting them willingly, while continuing to commit to your underlying values. Imagine feeling scared, for example, and experiencing doubts, but taking a step back from them, accepting them, and continuing to act in line with your values and towards your goal anyway, instead of allowing your thoughts and feelings to control your actions.

EXTERNAL BARRIERS: SKILLS DEFICITS AND PROBLEM-SOLVING

'External barriers', practical obstacles to valued action, include lack ('deficit') of resources (time, money, support), skills, knowledge, etc. Acquiring specific skills and knowledge, or creatively and systematically problem-solving, are the main approaches employed in the face of external barriers. If an external barrier arises you should normally just treat overcoming it as a new goal to be set.

Another reason for failing to complete a task is simply lacking the skills or knowledge required to do it. The simplest solution to this is to reformulate your plan of action so that the first activity becomes the task of *preparation*, i.e., acquiring the missing skills or knowledge. For example, you might plan to be more assertive with a noisy neighbour but fail because you can't find the right words when the time comes. If you lack assertiveness skills then you might want to plan an activity first that would help you develop them, for example, read a book on assertiveness, attend a class, write down what to say beforehand and rehearse it in the mirror, etc., treating this preparation as the first activity to be completed. Where you have difficulty figuring out how to accomplish some goal, the specific methodological approach to 'problem-solving' used in CBT may be helpful. (See the chapter on 'problem-solving' for more details.)

INTERNAL BARRIERS: THOUGHTS AND FEELINGS

'*Internal* barriers', psychological obstacles, consisting of automatic thoughts and emotional reactions, are generally more of a problem than external obstacles. The main strategy of mindfulness and acceptance-based approaches is to learn to commit to valued action while accepting, and making room for, such barriers along the way. Some of the therapeutic strategies discussed elsewhere in this book, such as *mindfulness*, *defusion*, and *acceptance*, may be required to deal with such potential obstacles. According to ACT, internal barriers to action pose the question: 'Are you willing to have this experience and yet act in a way consistent with what you value?' That means being willing to accept uncomfortable thoughts and feelings and remain committed to valued action *despite* them. Who is more resilient: someone who experiences no stress, no unpleasant experiences such as worry and anxiety, or someone who *does* feel stress but willingly accepts it and acts according to their values anyway?

The main strategy for responding to internal barriers in ACT is active 'willingness' to make room for them in the service of continued commitment to valued living. A good example would be the discomfort or even pain and exhaustion caused by exercise, if you're not used to it. The best answer to this internal barrier to exercise, when it arises, is to learn to willingly accept it, make room for it, and experience it in the service of the value of self-discipline and the goal of improving health and fitness. Trying to distract yourself from discomfort, suppressing it, may simply backfire by drawing more attention to it, and away from the value of your actions. One reason to willingly accept unpleasant experiences is that they're just not under your control and you'll never completely eliminate them from your life. It's better therefore to learn how to live with them while maintaining your goals and values.

If this seems challenging, don't worry. In the following chapters you'll learn how internal barriers, and unpleasant thoughts and feelings in general, can be experienced in a more *open* and *centred* way. This involves strategies of acceptance, defusion, awareness of yourself as observer and greater connection with the present moment.

Maintaining resilience through valued living

Maintaining a more general commitment to valued living involves a number of processes. For example:

- Making a public commitment, taking a stand, and sharing values with others as appropriate
- Reminding yourself to focus primarily on the *intrinsic value* of your behaviour, from moment to moment, as distinct from extrinsic goals in the near or distant future
- Systematically planning more specific goals and actions in accord with important values
- Willingly accepting certain unpleasant experiences in the service of valued living
- Persistently *renewing* your commitment to valued action whenever you falter, lapse or fail.

Making a *public* commitment to your goals and values can be a useful way of helping you to make a stronger private commitment to them. For example, tell your friends and family that you're going to make specific goals and values more of a priority in your life and perhaps even that you'd like their support.

RENEWING COMMITMENT

When setbacks occur, you should be prepared for them. Don't allow lapses or setbacks to be taken as a signal to give up completely. Quite the opposite: these are simply opportunities for you to repeatedly recommit to your core values. Even if you simply failed day after day to 'act with integrity', for example, you could still remain genuinely committed to acting with integrity as a core value. In fact, you can only fail if you assume your goal is to achieve some outcome, rather than to commit from moment to moment to following your chosen values because it's always within your power to choose that commitment, whether or not your actions succeed. This is like the ancient Stoic philosophical view that the wise man can never fail in life because he only aims to do what is under his control, to actively will himself to act with virtue, according to his values, from moment to moment, and to accept the consequences, whether success or failure ensues. (See the chapter on 'philosophy' for more discussion on this point.)

The main points to remember from this chapter are:

- Valued living *defines* what it means for you to be resilient, in terms of your ability to cope with potential barriers to valued goals and action.
- Setting goals, if approached 'lightly', can be a good way of living more in accord with your values.
- Scheduling specific valued activities can lead to a more rewarding life.
- Problem-solving is typically used to deal with *external* barriers to action, or practical obstacles to your goals.
- Strategies described throughout this book, particularly mindfulness and acceptance, are used to deal with *internal* barriers to action, unpleasant thoughts and feelings, etc.

NEXT STEP

Following your values will almost inevitably lead you to an encounter with specific barriers to action. The following chapters will show you how to overcome external (practical) barriers using problem-solving and specific skills like assertiveness. You will also learn how to use mindfulness, acceptance and other strategies to deal resiliently with internal barriers, mainly unpleasant experiences such as automatic thoughts and aversive feelings.

Further reading

Harris, R. (2008). *The Happiness Trap (Based on ACT: A revolutionary mindfulness-based programme for overcoming stress, anxiety and depression).*

Hayes, S. C. (2005). *Get Out of Your Mind and into Your Life: The New Acceptance and Commitment Therapy.*

Simon, Sidney B., Howe, Leland W. and Kirschenbaum, Howard (1995). *Values Clarification: A Practical, Action-Directed Workbook.*

5

Acceptance and defusion

In this chapter you will learn:

- *That psychological flexibility and resilience involve 'mindfulness', which can be understood as* openness *to experience and* centeredness *in the present moment*
- *An 'open' way of responding involves two processes, termed 'acceptance' and 'defusion'*
- *What's meant by willing 'acceptance' of unpleasant experiences, why it's important, and how it differs from passive resignation*
- *About the illusion of 'cognitive fusion' inherent in language and how it fuels experiential avoidance and problems in living*
- *Different strategies for 'defusing' thoughts and regaining an awareness of them as psychological processes that can be more easily accepted and made room for in the name of valued action.*

> *The mind is the ruler of the soul. It should remain unstirred by agitations of the flesh – gentle and violent ones alike. Not mingling [i.e., fusing] with them, but fencing itself off and keeping those feelings in their place. When they make their way into your thoughts, through the sympathetic link between mind and body, don't try to resist the sensation. The sensation is natural. But don't let the mind start in with judgements, calling it 'good' or 'bad'.*
>
> Marcus Aurelius, *Meditations*

> *He who knows how to suffer suffers less. He accepts the trouble such as it is, without adding to it the terrors that preoccupation and apprehension produce. Like the animal, he reduces suffering to its simplest expression; he even goes further; he lessens the trouble by the thought, he succeeds in forgetting, in no longer feeling it.*
>
> Paul Dubois, *Self-Control & How to Secure it*, 1909

The importance of acceptance and defusion

So far, you've explored 'valued action' and the role of changing your behaviour in the service of a more rewarding life. This will inevitably lead you into an encounter with certain barriers to action, particularly the obstacle of unpleasant *thoughts* and *feelings* such as worry and anxiety, and *urges* to act in ways that clash with your values. This chapter looks at the role of mindfulness and acceptance-based strategies in resilience, drawing on several modern evidence-based psychological therapies such as ACT. This chapter probably includes more *jargon* than the others (like 'defusion' in the title). That's because some of the concepts are particularly subtle and easily misunderstood, so specific terms have to be introduced to try to make the self-help instructions clearer and easier to follow. We're dealing with your relationship to your own private experiences, something nobody else can directly observe and therefore something that can at times be tricky to put into words. You'll therefore find it much easier to follow this chapter if you're actually doing most of the exercises described and studying your own experiences closely.

In the approach we're adopting here, mindfulness and acceptance are seen primarily as strategies in the service of valued living. Acceptance in this sense is not just passive 'giving up' but quite the contrary, a willingness to experience painful thoughts and feelings in the process of acting, living in accord with important personal values. Commitment to acting in accord with your values will almost inevitably lead you out of your 'comfort zone' and into an encounter with various 'barriers to action'. These are often external (practical) problems to be solved, but more often they will be *internal* thoughts and feelings, such as anxiety and worry, depression and rumination, or anger and brooding, and strong urges to act in certain ways, etc. 'Defusion' refers to the process of responding to thoughts as events in the mind rather than taking them literally and becoming engrossed in their meaning. As we'll see below, experiences are easier to accept when thoughts are seen for what they are in this way. Together, defusion and acceptance form what's termed an 'open' response style.

Do you remember what was said earlier about 'experiential avoidance'? Acceptance is the complete *opposite* of experiential avoidance, being fully open and present to your internal experiences. Unlike more conventional styles of therapy and self-help, it's not so much about 'feeling better' as becoming 'better at feeling', better at fully and directly experiencing life. That includes the whole repertoire of human emotions from happy to sad, and so on. This notion of workable acceptance is difficult to fully understand at first, it takes time to try it out in practice and learn from the experiment.

As negative thoughts and feelings are a normal part of life then what matters most may be how we *respond* to them and live with them, perhaps minimizing their *impact* on our ability to function when they inevitably occur. For example, the word 'patience', which derives from the Latin *pati*, 'to suffer', can perhaps be seen as another way of describing the virtue required to accept certain forms of suffering. To be patient and willingly accept unpleasant feelings is to suffer *well* rather than compounding our suffering by impatience and internal struggle.

If this sounds grim, it may be reassuring to discover that, *ironically*, when distress is accepted it appears to reduce anyway and perhaps in a more elegant and natural way than when we try to fight against our feelings. However, notice that if you deliberately approach acceptance as a way of eliminating unpleasant thoughts and feelings then you risk turning it into *non*-acceptance: 'I'm only accepting this feeling to get rid of it!' That often doesn't work very well so it's better just to forget completely about controlling unpleasant experiences and focus instead on accepting them more wholeheartedly, by allowing them to both come and go freely.

RESEARCH AND APPLICATIONS

In recent decades, the field of Cognitive-Behavioural Therapy (CBT) has increasingly shifted towards the view that *acceptance* of unpleasant thoughts and feelings may be a healthier long-term strategy, rather than trying to control or eliminate them. Acceptance, as opposed to experiential avoidance, has been found to correlate with better outcomes in therapy. Likewise, many different studies have demonstrated the effectiveness of acceptance-based approaches for a range of problems (Hayes, Luoma, Bond, Masuda & Lillis, 2006).

ACCEPTANCE AND RESILIENCE

Insofar as experiential avoidance appears to constitute a risk factor for future stress-related problems, acceptance is likely to constitute an important ingredient of psychological flexibility and emotional resilience. Learning to accept unpleasant thoughts and feelings means *letting go* of unhelpful efforts to control or avoid internal experiences. Acceptance is therefore a byword for abandoning the unworkable change agenda, which entails reducing the impact of avoidance and other unhealthy coping strategies. It seems natural to expect that abandoning attempts to avoid or control internal experiences would contribute to general resilience over the long term, especially as many of these behaviours, such as abusing alcohol or engaging in prolonged worry, are problematic in themselves and tend to damage our quality of life and ability to engage in valued action. Acceptance can also be viewed as letting go of *excessive effort* and thereby conserving your energy in life, increasing emotional resilience by reducing emotional fatigue and exhaustion.

CASE STUDY

Accepting social anxiety

Keith was a businessman who became very distressed at his level of anxiety during meetings at work and similar situations, such as interviews. He'd tried many methods to control his anxiety from deep breathing to various forms of psychotherapy and self-help. He'd learned to try to visualize himself as 'the world's greatest speaker' as a way of boosting his confidence. However, when asked 'How's this working out for you?' he had to admit that it wasn't. Although he could sometimes manage his anxiety by relaxing and boost his confidence with mental imagery and positive self-talk, this didn't last very long and he soon continued to worry and struggle with nerves in meetings.

We decided to try a different strategy and began by discussing the role of anxiety. Keith hadn't realized that it's quite natural for the heart rate to increase slightly when speaking to an audience and that his body was probably, quite rightly, producing more adrenaline to help him project to a room full of people. In fact, the physical symptoms of anxiety are largely indistinguishable from those of *excitement*. Keith realized that his struggle against anxiety was creating a vicious circle. The more he worried about looking anxious, the more anxious he became. He acknowledged that in situations where he didn't care whether or not he felt anxious, such as with his friends or when alone, he felt 'normal' and acted freely.

Although he was *desperate* to avoid feeling anxious, it was obvious to him that if he could 'forgive himself' and accept anxiety as harmless and nothing to be ashamed of, then he would, ironically, feel less anxious as a result. His desire to avoid looking anxious was the main *cause* of his anxiety. He was willing to try reversing this strategy and actively accepting feelings of anxiety, letting go of any attempts to suppress or conceal them when talking to others. Although difficult at first, he found with practice that this 'took the pressure off' and allowed him to feel 'normal' in the presence of others, including when talking in meetings. He still felt some 'nerves', which is fairly normal, but didn't dwell on it or allow it to affect his concentration or performance. Instead, he willingly *accepted* the feelings and focused on getting his ideas across instead, freeing him up to focus attention externally and respond more flexibly to the task at hand.

Cultivating psychological flexibility

Modern western culture, including most approaches to psychotherapy, tends to define mental health primarily in terms of the reduction of unpleasant experiences (or symptoms) such as anxiety and depression. In quite a radical departure from this perspective, ACT defines mental health in terms of 'psychological flexibility', understood in terms of the six core processes described earlier, namely, awareness of your self-as-context, defusion of your thoughts from reality, and willing acceptance of unpleasant experiences in the service of commitment to valued action in the present moment. In brief, psychological flexibility and resilience consists in mindfulness and commitment to valued living as opposed to experiential avoidance.

Self-assessment: Acceptance of internal experiences

Rate how strongly you believe each of the statements below (0–10):

1 Unpleasant feelings like pain, sadness, or anxiety are generally harmful (/10)

2 I feel the need to control unpleasant feelings or get rid of them when they occur (/10)
3 To help get rid of them, I should think in depth about what my unpleasant feelings mean and where they come from (/10)
4 Being unable to control unpleasant thoughts and feelings is a sign of weakness that reflects badly on me as a person (/10)
5 To be healthy and happy, I would have to eliminate unpleasant thoughts and feelings (/10)

Don't worry about adding up your total score, but just look at the individual ratings you gave. Take a moment to imagine what your life would be like, over the months and years to come, if you rated belief in each item 10 out of 10, the maximum. Now take a moment to imagine what your life would be like in the future if you adopted the opposite viewpoint and were able to rate each item as zero. Consider what changes in attitude might be worth testing out in practice.

COGNITIVE DEFUSION

ACT and other modern therapies have increasingly shifted the focus away from the *content* of thoughts on to their *function*. It's not *what* you think; it's the *way* that you think it. The truth or falsehood of thoughts is less important than how we respond to them. ACT was originally called 'Comprehensive Distancing' because it places particular emphasis upon a technique called 'distancing' in cognitive therapy. In 'distancing', thoughts are viewed in a detached way, as if you've taken a 'step back' from them and also see them as mere hypotheses rather than facts, as separate from the reality they claim to represent. The term 'cognitive defusion' is now used to describe a similar, but slightly more sophisticated, way of responding.

Key idea: Cognitive fusion

Cognitive fusion refers to the tendency to respond to thoughts as if they were the things they represent. Humans appear to suffer emotionally more than animals because in addition to the pain caused by real events, we also respond with distress to unpleasant thoughts and images. We're able to morbidly ruminate about the past and worry about the future because we can fuse our thoughts with reality and respond to them as if the events being imagined were really present, here and now. Fusion can be perfectly healthy, such as when we lose ourselves, becoming engrossed in a story, while reading a novel or watching a film. Becoming fused with morbid worry or rumination, however, is a recipe for greater emotional suffering and impaired quality of life.

'Cognitive fusion' refers to the tendency to respond to thoughts in terms of their literal content, sometimes described as 'buying into thoughts' as opposed to merely 'having thoughts'. This is a kind of *illusion* due to the fact that our thoughts refer to and represent things *beyond* themselves. Fusion means treating our thoughts as if they *are* what they *mean*. The word 'cat' is not the same as the animal it refers to, it merely symbolizes it. However, a severe cat phobic may respond with anxiety even when the word is mentioned, almost as if a real cat were present. Fusion is essentially the main cause of experiential avoidance and a potential barrier to willing acceptance. Most human suffering occurs in response to our thoughts rather than real physical threats in our immediate environment. Fusion allows verbal constructs to eclipse our direct sensory experience of the world, so that we increasingly respond to ideas rather than the concrete reality of the present moment. It often seems as though we're living more 'in our heads', the more we become fused with chains of thoughts, such as worry or rumination.

ACT is based on the assumption that language cannot perfectly represent human experience and therefore that confusion (or 'fusion') between thoughts and the concrete experiences they describe, as well as the person doing the thinking, is a common source of psychological difficulty. Defusion means experiencing thoughts *as thoughts*, mental activities, rather than what they represent. Magritte's famous painting of a smoker's pipe carrying the text 'This is not a pipe' perhaps illustrates the concept of defusion quite well – it's *not* a pipe, it's just a *painting* of a pipe.

Figure 5.1 This is not a sad face.

Our thoughts generally attempt to represent reality but we are prone to forget that they are *just* representations and not the real thing. In other words, fusion involves looking at things *through* your thoughts, and confusing them with reality, rather than looking *at* your thoughts, from a more detached perspective. 'The map is not the terrain' as Alfred Korzybski, one of the forerunners of CBT, put it many decades ago. Thoughts are not facts. Another way of putting that is that in fusion we become more focused on the *content* of thoughts, their meaning, rather than the *process* of thinking, the fact we're using words in certain ways. Our direct experience is of the thought as a mental process, words and pictures in the mind; we go beyond our experience when we treat our thoughts *as if they were facts* about the real world or about our essential character. This is the intrinsic *illusion* of words, the bewitchment of our consciousness by means of the language we use. In the same way, there's a fundamental difference between listening to a story by becoming completely absorbed in its meaning, or instead listening to the process of storytelling and watching the behaviour of the storyteller.

Hence, when thoughts become fused with experiences, we respond as if the things they represent were present. The word 'lemon', or even the mental image of biting into a lemon, doesn't *necessarily* make you salivate unless you become absorbed in its meaning to some extent, fusing it with the thing it represents, in which case you may physically react 'as if' tasting the juice of a lemon. In the same way, catastrophic worries about the future might be experienced as just a string of words or, a story we tell ourselves about feared catastrophes, if we're swept along by them into a state of fusion, they may become highly anxiety-provoking as if the feared event were actually happening. In some ways, fusion can resemble a kind of autosuggestion or self-hypnosis, where thoughts dominate the mind and evoke reactions (Braid, 2009). Hence, it's not our unpleasant thoughts that are the problem so much as our fusion with them.

It's useful to learn to spot the 'early warning signs' of fusion, noticing when you become hooked by unhelpful thoughts, so that you can take action immediately to defuse from them. For example, distressing, fused thoughts may be experienced as follows:

- Thoughts seem *true*, like facts, and we respond as if they're happening now.
- They seem serious or *important* and we focus our attention on them.
- They seem *compelling*, as though we have no choice but do what they're telling us we have to do.
- They seem *threatening*, as if we need to do something to get rid of them.
- They reflect negatively on our *essential character* rather than being seen as superficial and automatic.

Although fusion is related to the amount of belief you have in a thought, they're not quite the same thing. For example, most people *believe* 100 per cent that they are going to die one day. However, some people worry about this and feel death-anxiety, even when dying is a distant prospect. The concept of death in more vivid and, in a sense, confused with present-moment reality for those who become fused and ensnared with it. Mindfulness approaches therefore attempt to change the way we make use of and relate to such thoughts rather than challenging our belief in their content.

Several quite insidious problems are associated with fusion. First of all, when evaluative judgements (e.g., 'This is awful!') are confused with descriptions and treated as literal properties of the thing evaluated, this often causes suffering. Second, when thoughts are taken as literal descriptions of the self (e.g., 'I am stupid!'), this leads to an artificially rigid concept of who you are, linked to a myriad of other problems. We will return to the problem of self-conceptualization later when we discuss the alternative, the experience of 'self-as-context', perspective, or *observer* of experiences.

Another common problem is 'reason-giving', where fused thoughts are treated as causes of action, reasons (or excuses) why you 'must' behave in a certain way. In ACT this is highlighted by replacing the word 'BUT' in reason-giving with the word 'AND'. 'I want to speak in public but I feel anxious' becomes 'I want to speak in public and I feel anxious'. Feeling anxious isn't necessarily a reason why you 'cannot' perform the action as it's possible to accept feelings of anxiety while speaking. When you practise defusing your 'reasons' for action, you'll often discover a greater sense of flexibility and freedom in your behaviour, which may be essential for valued living to stand a chance.

Key idea: Cognitive defusion

Cognitive defusion occurs when we stop confusing thoughts with reality and view them as what they are, mental events in the here and now, rather than what they say they are, i.e., what they symbolize. When we defuse thoughts, we experience them as *just* words and pictures rather than taking their meaning too literally. We might also see them as the automatic or habitual products of our minds, flotsam and jetsam thrown up by our personal history, rather than anything particularly meaningful that we've *chosen* to think. Defusion causes thoughts to lose their automatic evocative quality and it helps to prevent us from becoming lost in thoughts that cause unnecessary emotional suffering.

One of the most obvious consequences of cognitive defusion strategies is that evaluative words tend suddenly to seem more arbitrary and meaningless. Value judgements such as 'I am such a *bad* person' or 'this situation is *awful*' frequently masquerade as literal descriptions of fact. Likewise, demands, *prescriptions* such as 'I must get things right' or *proscriptions* such as 'I must not make mistakes', are often adopted in a rigid, absolute and literal sense. When defusion strategies are used, such as saying the words repeatedly in a silly voice, these types of statement tend to feel especially meaningless and arbitrary. Defusing them, therefore, contributes to psychological flexibility and a more open and creative attitude towards problems.

Acceptance *depends* on defusion, because we aim to accept our internal experience, not at face-value, perceived *literally*, but as it is in reality, as a psychological process. You can accept the fact that someone disagrees with you without accepting that they're right. In a similar way, you might accept the fact that you're worrying about the future without accepting the content of your worries as real. Typically defusion entails the use of strategies that make problematic words and sentences lose some of their perceived meaning, so that they can more easily be accepted as mere *thoughts* rather than experienced as facts about reality. For example, some strategies used for cognitive defusion include:

- Repeat the words unusually quickly, for about 30 seconds.
- Repeat the word slowly, paying attention to the process of producing the sound, noticing even the smallest muscle movements or changes in breathing involved.
- Say the words in another voice, perhaps like a cartoon character or sounding as if spoken by a squeaky little mouse, a sleepy sloth, a quacking duck, etc.
- Sing the words along to some incongruous tune, like *Daisy, Daisy* or Happy Birthday.
- Label thoughts, explicitly, as thoughts, e.g., 'I am now having the thought that "I can't cope!" or 'My mind is telling me the same old story about me being stupid.'
- Saying 'Thank you, mind!', like it's another person, as if your mind and thoughts were *separate* from your observing consciousness.
- Reminding yourself that thoughts are just meaningless automatic reactions, like 'background noise' in consciousness or a radio playing in the room.
- Imagine each individual thought that passes through your mind is attached to a leaf floating past on a stream, written on placards being carried past by marching soldiers, written on clouds floating past in the sky, or being projected onto the screen of an empty cinema, while you watch from a distance.

However, these techniques are all merely aids to the underlying process of defusion, which you may eventually be able to do without any gimmicks. With practice you'll learn to defuse certain thoughts immediately just by seeing them as arbitrary mental events distinct from the reality they refer to. Defusing thoughts from reality is important because it makes them easier to willingly accept and helps prevent them getting in the way of valued action.

Try it now: Basic defusion techniques (labelling and milk, milk, milk)

Take a thought that's mildly distressing to you and focus on it, believing it, for about ten seconds, in a state of fusion. Notice what you experience. What thoughts or feelings are evoked automatically when you fuse with this idea? Now repeat the same thought again for about ten seconds, saying it slowly, but add the words 'I'm having the *thought* that…' in front and observe what happens. Speak a bit more slowly and pause between the words. Finally you might want to extend the sense of defusion further by adding 'I *notice* that I'm having the *thought* that…' and observing what happens.

Try saying the word 'milk' to yourself and focus on what the word conjures up: *its meaning*. Take a moment to notice all the different sensations, images and other associations evoked by the word 'milk'. Now try repeating the word over and over again, quickly, for about 30 seconds. What happens to your experience of its *meaning*? (This technique, although common in ACT, was first described by the psychologist Titchener way back in 1916.)

Try the same thing with a *mildly* distressing thought or idea. Sum it up in a single word or short phrase. For example, if you're perfectionistic and worry about failure, you might try using the word 'failure' or 'succeed'. Notice first what feelings and other associations it normally evokes. Now repeat it to yourself, quickly, for about 30 seconds. What happens to the sense of meaning? Do your feelings change? Did it become boring or start to sound a bit like a meaningless noise? Sounds without meaning can seem like the noises made by animals rather than human language.

According to Hayes, recent experimental research on this technique has shown that 20–45 seconds is the optimum duration and that 95 per cent of people report a reduction in the believability of the thought as a result.

Remember this: Defusing unhelpful thoughts

When a distressing thought occurs, ask yourself whether the process of thinking it is actually *helping* or not. In particular, is it consistent with your most important values for living or does it get in the way? If it's unhelpful or gets in the way of valued living, you might want to defuse it, accept what you're experiencing, and commit to valued action in the present moment. Cognitive defusion technically involves altering the *function* of thoughts without trying to change their content or prevent their occurrence. It can be applied to automatic thoughts, worry, reasons, excuses, beliefs, and whole 'stories' your mind tells you about yourself, your life, other people, your past, the future, and so on.

ACCEPTING AND LETTING GO

In the language of ACT, psychological flexibility consists in willingly accepting our experience of the present moment, defused from our thinking, and seen from the perspective of the self-as-observer, in the service of a commitment to living in accord with our authentic personal values. More concisely, it involves an open, centred and engaged way of responding to experiences. Accepting unpleasant experiences, paradoxically, also means letting go of any underlying attachment to them, by abandoning your struggle to avoid or control them and allowing yourself to experience them as they are, in the here and now.

When we refuse to accept an unpleasant experience, unfortunately, we tend to force our mind to pay more attention to it, until we potentially become overly preoccupied. Although acceptance requires paying attention to unpleasant feelings, that part is temporary, and accepting an experience will often mean that you find yourself paying far less attention to it in the long term. However, acceptance does require practice and you may have to spend five minutes per day, for example, learning to accept certain feelings in order to make progress, as well as applying these skills throughout the day whenever unpleasant internal experiences arise.

Key idea: Acceptance and letting go

Acceptance has been defined in ACT as: 'the voluntary adoption of an intentionally open, receptive, flexible and non-judgemental posture with respect to moment-to-moment experience' (Hayes, Strosahl & Wilson, 2012, p. 272). 'Willingness' is sometimes used specifically to mean putting yourself in the presence of experiences that need to be accepted, in the first place. Willing acceptance therefore means confronting painful experiences and experiencing them more fully for what they actually are, while letting go of any effort to control or eliminate them. In ACT, it has been compared to:

- Holding a delicate flower in your hands
- Sitting patiently with someone who has a serious illness
- Contemplating an exhibit in a museum or art gallery
- 'Being there' for a crying child.

It often requires something resembling compassion towards yourself to do this properly with your own upsetting thoughts and feelings, making room for things you normally feel compelled to avoid experiencing.

Would you be willing to accept queuing for ten minutes in the cold and rain, something normally quite aversive, to meet the person you most admire in the world? Would you just begrudgingly 'tolerate it' or would it seem acceptable or even trivial as a means to an end, despite the fact it's something you might normally avoid doing unless you have to? If you will the *end* you must also will the *means*. Acceptance means actively and consciously embracing internal experiences, thoughts and feelings, without struggling unnecessarily to change their frequency or content by trying to avoid or control them. Some authors prefer the term 'expansion' to acceptance, meaning 'opening up' psychologically and flexibly making room for unpleasant experiences that you're having.

Key idea: Combining acceptance and defusion

Acceptance also has to be understood as following on from defusion. It's acceptance of experience *as it is* that is being referred to rather than acceptance of experience as the mind initially represents it when thoughts are fused with reality. If the mind is constantly telling stories, it's the process of storytelling we accept not the literal content or meaning of the stories. This is important because cognitive fusion is a major source of suffering and so acceptance does not mean wallowing in negative thoughts fused with reality. Implicit in it is the assumption that the experiences accepted are relatively harmless and normal, that it's ultimately worthless trying to struggle with or analyse them, and that they may come and go naturally over time, if left alone. The sense of threat tends to narrow attention and make responses rigid and stereotyped. By contrast, an attitude of willing acceptance is associated with the broadening of attention and a sense of flexibility, creativity and openness.

Try it now: Accepting unpleasant experiences (holding your breath)

Don't do this if you have any medical problems that might make it inappropriate to hold your breath for a prolonged period. If you're okay with this sort of thing then get ready to time yourself holding your breath. You're going to try to cope by *avoiding* paying attention to your thoughts, feelings and urges to exhale. When you're ready, just close your eyes, take a deep breath and hold it for as long as possible, while observing your thoughts and feelings. How long did you last? What did it feel like? What thoughts went through your mind? What happened when you tried to avoid paying attention to difficult or unpleasant experiences? How easy was it to avoid noticing the urge to exhale? Did it become harder to ignore?

Now do the same thing again, but this time focus on willingly accepting your thoughts and feelings and keep waiting a bit longer before you exhale, detaching your actions from your feelings. Accept the urge to exhale but do nothing, patiently distancing yourself from any thoughts that occur.. Also view the exercise as something that you value learning from. How long did you last this time? What happened when you focused on mindful acceptance? What's the difference between trying to suppress the urge to exhale and just accepting it? How does it influence things if you place value on the experiment?

Try it now: Accepting by physicalizing

This technique has also been incorporated into modern acceptance-based approaches from Gestalt Therapy, a much older approach that developed in the 1950s.

1 Think about something that evokes mildly unpleasant feelings for you. Notice what the feelings are like and where they're manifested in your body.
2 Now imagine (symbolically) turning the feeling into a shape or object and taking a step back from it, putting it (temporarily) outside of your body, so that you can observe it from a distance of several feet away.
3 Patiently take note of its various properties. What colour, shape, texture and size is it? Does it move or change? Take time to notice each of its different properties in turn.
4 What happens to your response when you view it in this way? Can you willingly accept the experience from this perspective, letting go of any struggle to control or avoid it?
5 If you have a sense of resistance to accepting the experience, just treat that response in the same way. Put your original feelings over to one side and turn your resistance into a second object that you can put out there beside the first one. Again, notice its properties, then let go of any struggle you have and willingly accept it. How does letting go of the struggle affect the original object/feeling?
6 Can you welcome both objects back inside again and continue to willingly accept the experience, in the service of following your values? Continue to view these feelings as merely objects, contents of consciousness, quite distinct from your observing consciousness.

Sometimes it becomes easier to accept an unpleasant experience if you can dissect it into its component parts or ingredients. This is often done by dividing it into thoughts, actions, feelings, etc., and actively accepting each individual ingredient in turn. For example, when anxious, people often tense their muscles and feel their heart rate going up, their breathing becoming more rapid and shallow, etc., as they notice fearful thoughts and images cross their minds. Being aware of the individual ingredients of an unpleasant experience and focusing on accepting and defusing them one at a time can be easier than treating them as one big lump. People who suffer from clinical anxiety and depression tend to do the opposite and see their emotions as a single thing rather than composed of many different elements that change over time.

Try it now: Disassembling the experience

In ACT, the metaphor of a 'tin-can monster' is used to illustrate the value of disassembling complex experiences in order to defuse and accept them. It's as if we're facing a gigantic monster but when we take him apart, he's just made from old tin cans, bits of string, and wire; nothing special.

1 Cast your mind back to a pleasant time when you were a child and take a moment to relive that memory. Notice that although things were different there's some continuity between 'there and then' and 'here and now', your consciousness of things. Stay in touch with that sense of yourself as pure conscious observer, beyond the contents of consciousness. (We'll return to this experience of self-as-observer in more detail in the next chapter.)

2 Now pick a mildly unpleasant experience to work on. (Don't pick anything that's likely to be overwhelming or traumatic for you, without the aid of a therapist.) You're going to explore its different ingredients in turn

and work on using defusion and acceptance strategies on one part at a time. It's quite arbitrary how you divide things up but we'll follow the convention of distinguishing between thoughts, actions, feelings, etc.

3 Remaining connected to that sense of yourself as pure consciousness, focus on the experience you want to accept and begin by paying attention purely to the bodily sensations associated with it. If there are several, focus on one at a time. Allow yourself to willingly accept one sensation at a time, letting go of any struggle with it as completely as possible before continuing. Notice where sensations are focused and also the more subtle feelings at the periphery of these areas. Experience it with detached curiosity, consider where it begins and ends if you were to draw an outline around it, etc.
4 Now do the same for any emotions associated with the experience and when you're ready, continue to work on accepting any behavioural urges, thoughts or memories, in the same way, one at a time, letting go of any struggle and just being open and present to each part of the experience in turn.
5 Once you've learned to divide the experience into various small parts and accept them in isolation, you can combine them and focus on accepting the whole experience at once, gently welcoming each of its ingredients in turn as you do so.

Remember this: Acceptance is neither 'resignation' nor 'wanting'

The term 'acceptance' has become widely used in modern behaviour therapy for a willingness to experience the presence of unpleasant experiences, without necessarily wanting or liking them. Acceptance, in this sense, is active and not a passive resignation, partly because it's usually in the service of valued action. The term 'willingness' is sometimes used in an attempt to overcome unhelpful connotations of the word 'acceptance' such as the notion that it involves reluctant tolerance, an attitude of 'grin and bear it', etc. Willing acceptance of unpleasant experiences encountered when attempting to act in line with one's personal values is seen as the opposite of and main alternative to 'experiential avoidance'.

Maintaining resilience through acceptance and defusion

To maintain *resilience* through the skills of defusion and acceptance it's going to be important to integrate them properly with the various elements of psychological flexibility, discussed in the other chapters of this book. Fortunately, with practice, this will become obvious to you as most of these processes are very closely related and intertwining. For example, it's primarily fusion that allows us to become engrossed in worry about the future or rumination about the past, by reacting as if what we're thinking about was actually present and losing contact with the present moment. However, although our thoughts can be *about* 'there and then', the past or future, our thinking always *takes place* here and now. As soon as we defuse thoughts about the future or past, therefore, we're left with an awareness of the thought as thought, a process we're engaged in here and now. Mindfulness of the present moment is therefore intimately bound up with the defusion of such thoughts.

Frequently using defusion and acceptance skills in different settings and in response to a wide variety of thoughts and feelings will help 'generalize' the skills, until they potentially become part of your overall lifestyle. The more generalized the skills become the more resilient you will be to a wider variety of future stressors. To use the skills frequently, you will probably want to progressively abbreviate some of them. It's possible to learn to defuse thoughts quickly, during daily activity, by a variety of methods. For example, labelling unhelpful, fused thoughts using a single word that you quickly repeat three times, such as 'thoughts, thoughts, thoughts…' or 'worry, worry, worry…', can become a way of rapidly defusing them during daily activity.

Use a daily record like the one below to keep a log of your emotional suffering before and after attempts to cope with, control, or avoid unpleasant thoughts and feelings. When a situation arises that makes you upset, record your initial thoughts and feelings ('clean discomfort') and rate its intensity (0–100%), then what you did in response. Finally rate how distressed you were after responding to the initial problem ('dirty discomfort'). Mark your responses 'A' for acceptance or 'C' for control to help monitor any difference that results from accepting your initial reactions instead of struggling to control or avoid them.

Date/time Situation	*Initial thoughts & feelings*	*Initial suffering (%)*	*Responses (Accept/ Control)*	*Subsequent suffering (%)*

We'll see that the Stoic philosophy, in particular, emphasizes acceptance of events outside our direct control, on a grand scale. In fact, the sage Epictetus said that being educated in Stoic philosophy 'is precisely learning to will each thing just as it happens', in a nutshell.

Remember this: Acceptance and defusion are part of 'psychological flexibility'

The skills of acceptance and defusion closely complement each other, as fusion regularly gets in the way of acceptance. Moreover, these skills combine with two others, awareness of the present moment and of the self-as-context, in ACT's definition of 'mindfulness'. It's primarily our experience of the 'here and now' that has to be accepted in the service of valued living and our self-concept is a powerful barrier to action.

When two more ingredients, values clarification and commitment to action, are integrated, they lead to the goal of 'psychological flexibility' that's essentially ACT's definition of psychological resilience. If psychological vulnerability to stressful life events, to a large extent, is due to cognitive fusion and experiential avoidance then the opposing processes, of defusion and acceptance, would appear to be integral to psychological resilience and flexibility.

The main points to remember from this chapter are:

- Psychological flexibility, the alternative to experiential avoidance, consists of mindful acceptance of unpleasant experiences in the service of valued living.
- Mindfulness, in this sense, combines 'open' and 'centred' styles of responding to experience; this chapter described how the 'open' response style consists of acceptance and defusion strategies.
- Defusion involves experiencing your thoughts less literally, noticing that they are events in your mind rather than becoming too absorbed in their meaning or content.
- Acceptance means letting go of any struggle and allowing yourself to fully experience something, as if you were patiently studying an exhibit in a museum or art gallery.
- Acceptance and defusion are closely related because we must normally defuse thoughts to accept them, accepting the fact the thought is occurring rather than what it is trying to say about reality.

NEXT STEP

We've looked at part of what ACT means by mindfulness, the 'open' response style, and in the next chapter, you'll learn what it means to adopt a 'centred' response by connecting more fully with the present moment as well as with pure consciousness of thoughts and feelings, the 'context' in which they take place.

Further reading

Harris, R. (2008). *The Happiness Trap (Based on ACT: A revolutionary mindfulness-based programme for overcoming stress, anxiety and depression).*

Hayes, S. C. (2005). *Get Out of Your Mind and into Your Life: The New Acceptance and Commitment Therapy.*

6

Mindfulness and the present moment

In this chapter you will learn:

- *That psychological flexibility and resilience consists also in a 'centred' style of responding, in relation to your sense of self and the present moment*
- *How to become more mindful of your present-moment environment and the task-at-hand, as opposed to losing touch with your experience and functioning on 'autopilot'*
- *How to connect with yourself as the conscious 'context' or observer of your individual thoughts and feelings, and let go of fusion with your self-concept*
- *How to systematically intersperse mindfulness throughout your daily routine.*

> *Time is like a river, made up of the events which happen and a violent stream; for as soon as a thing has been seen, it is carried away, and another comes in its place, and this will be carried away too.*
>
> Marcus Aurelius, *Meditations*

> *If you can cut free of impressions that cling [i.e., fuse] to the mind, free of the future and the past – can make yourself, as [the pre-Socratic philosopher] Empedocles says, 'a sphere rejoicing in its perfect stillness', and concentrate on living what can be lived (which means the present) … then you can spend the time you have left in tranquillity. And in kindness. And at peace with the spirit within you.*
>
> Marcus Aurelius, *Meditations*

The importance of being centred

What are you actually doing right now? How are you using your mind and body? Who are you right now? What part of your experience do you identify with? Who is doing the identifying? Where is 'here' for you? Are you your thoughts and feelings? Or are you able to be aware of viewing your own stream of consciousness from a distance? Where exactly is your 'I' located? Are you the observer or the thoughts observed? What makes you the same person you were as a small child? What continuity is there between your awareness of yourself over the years? Have you ever been so preoccupied with your thoughts that you missed something important happening?

These questions all relate to your awareness of being *centred* in the here and now, as a self-aware or mindful observer of your own experiences. Although I talk about 'mindfulness' and meditation quite a lot in this chapter, I'm neither assuming nor excluding anything particularly *spiritual* or *mystical*. To be mindful of the present moment is to stop and 'smell the roses'.

Mindfulness meditation practices are extremely common in modern evidence-based psychological therapies because of their proven ability to help cultivate psychological flexibility and control attention. Moreover, research has shown that you don't need to be a Zen master: even short mindfulness exercises can be of some benefit in many cases. Flexible attention to the present moment allows you to learn to experience even unpleasant thoughts and feelings mindfully, with detachment, without them narrowing and monopolizing your attention. Being centred in this way allows you to connect with your sense of perspective and what's important in the present moment, your values and how to act upon them here and now.

WHAT IS MINDFULNESS?

The concept of 'mindfulness', familiar to many people from Buddhist meditation practices, is central to several modern approaches to therapy, each of which has a slightly different conception of what it means. Following on from previous chapters, we shall be using the definition of 'mindfulness' adopted in ACT, which conceptualizes it in terms of two key ingredients called the 'open' and 'centred' response styles. Having looked at the 'open' response style, in terms of strategies of acceptance and defusion, we're now ready to discuss the role of being 'centred'. A 'centred' response style consists of two ingredients also: present-moment awareness and a sense of 'self-as-context', being aware of yourself as observer of your own experience. We shall also explore the ways in which these processes interact and closely combine with each other to constitute an attitude of mindfulness and psychological flexibility.

Key idea: Mindfulness

Mindfulness provides an alternative and more flexible way of responding to thoughts. One of the most fundamental features of anxiety is that it involves a sudden *narrowing* both of attention and behaviour, attention becomes *automatically* more focused on potential sources of danger and behaviour becomes rigid and stereotyped, we feel compelled to *fight*, *freeze* or *flee*, etc. However, anything that allows us to respond differently to distressing events, apart from avoidance or safety-seeking, may tend to reduce distress. Mindfulness, as understood here, involves two closely related styles of flexible responding:

1 'Open' responding, consisting of defusion of thoughts and willingly accepting internal experiences.
2 'Centred' responding, consisting of an awareness of the present moment and the self as observer or 'context' of thoughts and feelings, etc.

RESEARCH AND APPLICATIONS

Similar to the preceding chapters, the processes discussed here are integral to ACT and have been employed in research on a range of problems. However, increasing mindful awareness of the present moment has been emphasized, in particular, in research on clinical depression and generalized anxiety disorder (GAD), where it plays an important role in mindfulness and acceptance-based treatment approaches. Mindfulness meditation techniques have also been found effective for general stress reduction. A recent review ('meta-analysis') that pooled statistical data from 39 different studies found that on average mindfulness-based approaches had treatment effect sizes classed as 'moderate' for symptoms of anxiety and depression across the board, and 'large' effect sizes for individuals with diagnosable anxiety or mood disorders (Hofmann, Sawyer, Witt & Oh, 2010). By contrast, a comprehensive review of the research on self-esteem has found that, contrary to popular belief, attempts directly to boost it potentially backfire and seldom provide any psychological benefits (Baumeister, Campbell, Krueger & Vohs, 2003). As we shall see, mindfulness often entails a sense of self-acceptance and detachment that directly contrasts with the popular notion of maintaining 'self-esteem'.

Part of the reason for the broad range of problems affected by mindfulness is that emotional suffering often involves rumination about the past or worry about the future. When attention is grounded in the present moment, it limits the frequency and duration of certain types of morbid thinking, and that appears to help reduce the impact of anxiety, depression, and related problems. Learning to control your attention so that you're able to focus more flexibly on the present moment, and your field of awareness, in a centred way, is therefore likely to serve a preventative function helping to make you more resilient to future adversities.

MINDFULNESS AND RESILIENCE

Attention to the present moment and to the self as observer of internal experience contributes to psychological flexibility and resilience. Meditation techniques of the kind described here are widely employed in general stress management as well as for more serious clinical problems. One of the key advantages of mindfulness is that it's a simple and generic approach that can be used at any time and easily becomes part of a general lifestyle. It can easily be used *preventatively*, in the absence of any major upsets, or remedially, following on from highly stressful life events. Being centred in your awareness of yourself as observer in the present moment also makes it easier to be aware of the connection between your actions and your personal values. It's therefore eminently suited to general resilience-building, particularly a self-help approach like the one presented here.

CASE STUDY

Mindfulness meditation

Duncan was suffering from a spell of mild depression, a problem which tended to come and go periodically for him. He'd tried a number of therapeutic and self-help approaches over the years and had grown weary with the effort to change his self-image, attitudes, and behaviour, etc. He seemed to be in a constant struggle with his feelings. Eventually, while staying at a Buddhist retreat centre, he decided to give up the battle and simply accept his depressed thoughts and feelings instead, while practising mindfulness regularly throughout the day. To his surprise, this appeared to work where other strategies had failed. It didn't dramatically transform his feelings but immediately alleviated the strain caused by battling against them and, with patience, the thoughts and feelings became less overwhelming and persistent.

In subsequent therapy, he learned to practise more regularly, sitting formally in meditation for about 15 minutes each evening and introducing shorter periods of mindfulness throughout his daily routine. As he continued, he noticed that in general, upsetting thoughts and feelings seemed less powerful and easier to accept. He was aware of experiencing a richer variety of thoughts and feelings as the old depressive thoughts tended to monopolize his attention less. His mood improved and he was able to get on with life in a more satisfactory way. When setbacks occurred in the future he was more able to cope with them resiliently by centring his attention to the here and now rather than ruminating about the meaning of his problems.

Connecting with the present moment

Making more contact with your environment, encountering it directly through your senses, and connecting more fully with *where* you are and *what* you're actually doing, from moment to moment, is integral to all mindfulness approaches. Fritz Perls, the founder of Gestalt Therapy, used to say, 'Lose your mind and come to your senses'. He meant that by stopping over-thinking, worrying about the future, and ruminating about the past, etc., we can learn to be more fully aware of the present moment, something that leads to a richer and more fulfilling experience of living. Mindfulness training therefore often involves learning to remain more in contact with your actions and environment in the *here and now*. The present moment is like the 'face' of the universe, at any given time, it's the only place action can begin. The future doesn't exist yet and the past has already gone. Everything else is *absent* except the here and now that currently faces you.

One important aspect of mindfulness of the present moment is that by noticing exactly what you're doing, your thoughts and actions, you'll more easily distinguish between workable and unworkable patterns of behaviour. In other words, if you act mindlessly, forgetful of yourself, you'll tend to overlook many *subtle* opportunities to learn from the consequences of your actions. Learning from your own direct experience tends to lead to more flexible and adaptive behaviour compared to following verbal rules learned from other people. In other words, studying your own experience as it happens and learning from it can fundamentally contribute to psychological flexibility and resilience to future adversity. Sometimes merely *slowing down* can help achieve this, by making you more aware of experiences that otherwise speed past before you can fully acknowledge them. Many mindfulness exercises therefore involve shifting awareness slowly and patiently, registering different aspects of experience in turn.

How is it even possible for someone to lose touch with the reality of the present moment? Cognitive *fusion* is one of the main sources of alienation from the here-and-now of our experience. Many thoughts, particularly distressing ones, tend to refer to the past (rumination) or future (worry), and to thereby take us away from the present moment. Hence, defusing thoughts can contribute to contact with the present moment. Although your thoughts frequently *refer* to the past or future, they must always *take place* in the present moment. Only by fusing thoughts with reality can we 'travel through time' in our imagination, away from the present moment. Likewise, focus on the concrete experience of the present-moment may, in turn, shift our attention away from abstract concepts, such as value-judgements, and on to greater attention to the sensations of specific physical events we experience in the here and now, such as our own breathing, the way we use our muscles, sounds around us, or the shapes and colours in our environment, etc.

It's often said that the central 'skill' in meditation is the ability to spot awareness straying and to recover by re-attending to the present moment. Of course, it's natural for awareness to flit away from one's interaction with the here and now. Certain categories of thought may be more likely to 'hook' your attention and lure you back into fusion with them, for example, thoughts about the future, about the task itself, or memories that involve strong feelings. Ironically, catching your attention straying can be seen as a positive opportunity to develop this underlying ability. If your mind didn't wander occasionally during meditation, you'd probably obtain relatively little benefit from doing it. In a similar manner, infallible commitment to acting in line with your personal values is very rare, perhaps impossible. However, the ability to spot yourself straying from valued living, in the here and now, and to re-commit to following your values may be more important, ultimately, than your degree of 'success' in adhering perfectly to your values. In other words, this ability to spot and 'recover' from lapses regarding mindfulness or valued living is particularly close to the heart of psychological resilience.

Mindfulness of the present moment can be learned using a variety of common techniques, many of which are derived from very ancient meditation practices. For example, it's useful, also as a form of defusion, and a way of centring, to label experiences into broad descriptive categories, such as:

- Thoughts and value-judgements
- Emotions
- Memories and images
- Physical sensations
- Urges or inclinations to do certain actions.

You might say, 'I am having the thought that my chair is too uncomfortable', 'I am noticing the urge to stretch my back', etc. This is a basic technique common to different awareness training approaches that can be used in one sitting, as a kind of meditation, but also practised regularly throughout the day for a couple of weeks. A slightly more formal version, common in ACT, involves sitting for about five minutes, picturing a flowing stream on which leaves are slowly falling and being carried past. As each thought arises just imagine it being attached to an individual leaf and slowly floating away downstream. Imagine words being written on the leaves or pictures being attached to them. In particular, notice when the stream stops flowing and you become distracted or fused with a thought, put that thought on a leaf and continue where you left off. This is mainly a way of learning to spot when you get hooked by your thoughts, something that's bound to happen even with practice.

Try it now: Noticing what you're aware of

Contact with the present moment can be helped by using language in a purely *descriptive* and non-judgemental or evaluative way. Language can be used to gently control attention in this way; describing things to yourself forces you to pay attention to them more consciously and for slightly longer.

This is another basic technique derived from Gestalt Therapy, but used in some other approaches to mindfulness. Simply take a few minutes to practise completing the following sentence 'Right now I'm aware of...', and putting different endings on those words each time. Name and describe, in brief, the different sensations that you experience in the here and now. For example, 'Right now, I'm aware of pressing the keys on my computer... Now I'm aware of a slight headache I've had for a while... Now I'm aware of the sound of the central heating coming on... Now I'm aware of an urge to scratch my nose...', and so on.

Avoid value *judgements*, try to stick to *descriptions* of the basic properties of things you currently experience and thoughts, feelings and urges that pass through your awareness. Don't add or subtract anything. Over time, fade out the use of language altogether, and just pay attention silently to your experience of the present moment, 'descriptively' and non-judgementally, without saying anything.

Being centred and self-awareness

THE MYTH OF SELF-ESTEEM

One of the pioneers of cognitive therapy, Albert Ellis, wrote a book entitled *The Myth of Self-Esteem* (2005). Ellis, drawing on the earlier work of Alfred Korzybski, argued that self-esteem was invariably *conditional* upon external events that, to some extent, are bound to be in the hands of fate. Self-esteem, whether *low* or *high*, involves 'esteeming' or evaluating yourself in general terms, as if you can be summed up in a single characteristic such as 'I am stupid' or a global rating of value such as 'I am worthless'. Ellis believed this was fundamentally irrational, as nobody can be pigeon-holed this easily by means of a single attribute. He also argued it was fundamentally unhealthy, or 'neurotic' to use the old term, because it made self-worth contingent on some specific criterion or other, thereby placing it on shaky foundations if reasons ever arose to doubt it. Many people, for example, have positive self-esteem based on their material success, popularity, and appearance, etc. However, this house of cards can come tumbling down, turning into low self-esteem, as soon as these things are taken away or even put in question.

Of course, self-esteem is often based on *comparisons* with other people. Having a sports car may make me feel successful and boost my self-esteem for a while. However, what if I move to a wealthier area and find my neighbours own not only sports cars but also expensive speedboats? There's always someone better off or more successful in life and, ironically, as we succeed we're more likely to encounter such people and start comparing ourselves to them. Making 'upward comparisons' is a well-known source of emotional disturbance. People less often make 'downward comparisons', which would involve being grateful for how much better off they are than so many others. The very fact that you're reading this book suggests you're probably better off materially than most of the world's population, who live in relative poverty. However, how do you choose who to compare yourself to in life generally? The truth is that these comparisons are ultimately quite arbitrary and therefore meaningless.

Ellis suggested that the healthy alternative to conditional self-esteem was *unconditional self-acceptance* (USA). This is defined as an attitude of accepting oneself unconditionally, warts and all, without attempting to label or evaluate oneself as a whole or make arbitrary comparisons with others. This comes close to the notion of self-acceptance that's found in modern mindfulness and acceptance-based approaches. In the same way that we suspend value-judgements about our here and now experience to connect with it more fully, we can learn to suspend both positive and negative value-judgements about ourselves.

SELF AS CONTENT (CONCEPTUALIZED SELF)

Who are you? Why? Thoughts about your own sense of identity, and stories about your life history, are often among the most entangling and difficult to defuse. You can treat your self-conceptualizations, or thoughts, beliefs and stories about yourself in the same way as other problematic thoughts, by defusing them using the kind of strategies we've already discussed earlier in this book. Both positive and negative beliefs about yourself can cause problems. Having *high* self-esteem, for example, might become a rigid outlook that biases your awareness and prevents you learning from mistakes. However, most people find that when they proceed to defuse thoughts about their self-concept, their sense of identity, they begin to feel somewhat uneasy, as if their very existence is being threatened. Who are you if not who your thoughts and beliefs say you are? What are you if not your self-concept? An alternative sense of self-awareness or identity comes from learning to connect more fully with your field of *consciousness* itself rather than its contents, something called the 'observer' perspective or 'self-as-context' in ACT.

Self-assessment: Changing the dials of self-identification

Consider the following questions about your sense of identity, and try to rate how strongly you agree with each one from 0 (not at all) to 5 (completely):

- I identify with what my body looks like from the outside, in the mirror (/5)
- I am what my body feels like inside, the physical sensations I feel (/5)
- I identify with my emotions (/5)
- I am my physical actions, in the world (/5)
- I am my thoughts, the stream of consciousness that passes through my mind (/5)
- I am my underlying or long-standing beliefs, my philosophy of life (/5)

- I am my concept of myself (/5)
- I am all of the contents of my consciousness combined, thoughts, actions, feelings, etc. (/5)
- I am the conscious space within which my thoughts, actions, and feelings happen (/5)

There's no point adding up these scores. There's also not really a 'right' or 'wrong' answer. However, take a moment now to carefully imagine, as a thought-experiment, what it would be like to change those ratings, as if you were turning your sense of identification up and down on a dial. What would it be like, in particular, to increase or reduce your sense of identification with the *content* of your experience, including your concept of yourself? What would it be like to increase or reduce your sense of identity with the space, the field of consciousness, within which your experiences occur? Take time to experiment with your self-awareness and sense of identity in this way.

SELF AS PROCESS

The self can also be experienced as a stream of consciousness or 'process of ongoing self-awareness' in the here and now, from moment to moment. Instead of being summed up by broad evaluative statements, the self is experienced in terms of a flux of descriptions of concrete present-moment sensory experiences, changing naturally rather than fixed rigidly. This is the sense of self-awareness that emerges when mindfully labelling and describing concrete experiences as they happen, in the here and now, e.g., 'Now I am thinking this…', 'Now I have the urge to do that…', etc.

SELF AS CONTEXT (OBSERVER PERSPECTIVE)

When you observe your experiences, do you also observe yourself observing them and from where? ACT, in particular, emphasizes the concept of experiencing one's self as pure consciousness or the *context* of mental processes, rather than identifying with the *content* of consciousness, specific thoughts and feelings. In other words, it distinguishes between the *observing* self and the *thinking* self. This is a tricky concept at first. In the same way that thoughts can become fused with reality, your identity can also become fused with certain thoughts, if you allow yourself to become immersed in them. Hence, the only way really to grasp this is *non*-verbally. Defusing from your self-concept and becoming centred within the broader context of consciousness allows greater psychological flexibility, making unpleasant experiences less troublesome. Think of your consciousness as being like light, illuminating a room. It's easy to focus on looking at the objects in the room, like the contents of consciousness. It's harder to focus attention upon the very light that illuminates the objects because it's not a 'thing'. In a sense, you are the consciousness of your experiences, but because consciousness isn't a 'thing', it's difficult to grasp it and remain aware of its presence for more than a fleeting glimpse at a time.

The self-as-context is explained in ACT by the metaphor of a chessboard. Imagine a chessboard the size of the whole universe, stretching to infinity. The black and white pieces are eternally locked in battle against each other. Each time a game seems to be over, before long, the board is set again and the game resumes. You can think of the black pieces as being your negative thoughts and the white ones as your positive or competing thoughts. The game is like the constant struggle in the mind. Now, it might seem natural to imagine that you're the black side or the white side, but that could best be seen as a metaphor for fusion. From the perspective of self-as-context, let's say you're the chessboard itself, the context or space within which the game is played out over and over again. That would place the 'self' outside of the battle that's raging, as a detached observer, at the level of the board. In other words, are you the thoughts you have or are you the conscious space within which these and other experiences happen?

Try it now: Self-identification exercise

This contemplative exercise has been assimilated into modern mindfulness and acceptance-based approaches from an older style of psychotherapy called 'Psychosynthesis'.

1 Close your eyes and recall something that happened to you when you were a small child. (For now it's better if you choose a pleasant memory, or at least one that's not particularly distressing.) Imagine that you're there, as if it's happening right now. See what you saw... Hear what you heard... Feel what you felt... As you do so, be aware of your awareness and notice yourself as conscious observer, experiencing these things. You're the same person, even though many things may have changed. Notice the continuity between your experience of yourself then and now. You're still the same observer of your experiences, though everything else may have changed over time.

2 Now, continuing to identify with that pure consciousness, your awareness of your awareness, focus your attention on the sensations in your body, here and now. You have a body, but you are not your body. You can observe the sensations in your body from a distance, without identifying with them. Be aware of the transience of the sensations in your body, notice they change as the consciousness observing them remains the same.

3 Now, again continuing to connect with yourself as observer or pure awareness, focus on your emotions. Notice how emotions come and go while you're always the one observing them. Be aware of yourself observing your emotions. You have emotions but you are not your emotions. You're the context in which they occur, the same observer who experiences all these different feelings.

4 Now, from the same perspective, as the context of your experiences, observe your own thoughts as they pass through your mind. This is more difficult because thoughts tend sneakily to hook you in and cause you to fuse with them before you notice it's happened. Every day you have many thousands of different, transient thoughts. Throughout your life,

you've had countless millions of individual thoughts and your beliefs and attitudes have changed and evolved. Notice how transient thoughts are and that even deeper beliefs can change over time. You have thoughts but you are not your thoughts. You have beliefs but you are not your beliefs. Be aware of yourself as the observer of your thoughts, viewing them from a distance. Although your thoughts come and go, you're still the same person observing them.

5 Notice that just by observing these things you can become aware of pure consciousness as the observer of experiences, the observer is not the thing observed. You have a body, you have thoughts, actions and feelings, but you are not just these things. You can take a step back from them and become aware of yourself as the conscious observer, separate from the contents of consciousness. Don't try to change anything; don't try to stop anything from changing. Just be aware of yourself as your field of consciousness, a flexible, expansive psychological space, within which diverse experiences can freely come and go.

Getting in touch with the wider field of pure consciousness within which experiences are contained often provides a sense of stability, peace and tranquillity. From that perspective, defusion and acceptance of other experiences becomes much easier and less threatening. As the poet Emerson once said, from this perspective, you're like a 'transparent eye-ball', which is nothing except the awareness of seeing things. Your concept of yourself is just one of the many contents of consciousness you're potentially aware of. The person you normally think you are is, by nature, situated in front of your gaze rather than behind it.

This sense of self as observer is quite *unfamiliar* to most people, because their identity has become fused with the *contents* of consciousness. Although, in another sense, this pure self-awareness is the *most* familiar thing in the world because it's there in the background wherever you go and always has been your entire life. By definition, it can't be put into words, at least not very satisfactorily. It's awareness of our self as consciousness, beyond what's captured in the use of language. The self-as-context is your sense of the continuity of consciousness. Even if self-awareness can't be easily described, it can be pointed out and drawn to your attention by asking yourself the following odd-sounding questions:

- Where is 'here' for me?
- When is 'now' for me?
- Where is 'I' for me?

Defusing thoughts also tends to heighten direct awareness of where 'I', 'here' and 'now' are located by making the contents of consciousness seem more arbitrary and less of a threat to your self-concept. Curiously, psychologists have found that the ability to locate 'I' seems to be related to the ability to adopt other perspectives, including empathizing with other people and feeling compassion for them. So even exercises such as imagining being an older, wiser version of yourself in the future, giving advice to your current self, which involve adopting fantasy perspectives, can help strengthen your sense of your self-as-context. If you imagine everything about yourself and your world being different, what remains the same? You're still observing things by means of the same consciousness, which lends a continuity to your experience no matter how much the contents may change.

In patient meditation, most people become increasingly aware of a sense of detachment or distance from their own thoughts. In the same way that dreams occur automatically at night, you'll realize that many of your thoughts are reflex-like, habitual, and *automatic* rather than being *chosen* deliberately by you. This realization can also lead to a greater sense of detachment from them. Sometimes in ACT a distinction is made between 'the mind', which produces these thoughts, and the detached *consciousness* that observes them. People who meditate may increasingly talk about their mind generating thoughts, almost as if they were talking about another person. In meditation, it becomes easier to view automatic thoughts and other internal experiences as being like the 'flotsam and jetsam' of the mind, or the noise of a radio playing arbitrary snippets of conversation in the background.

There's no doubt that it can seem like a wrench to divorce your identity from the contents of your mind but this is not a novel concept. It's integral to Buddhist philosophy, which in India was known as the philosophy of 'no-self' (*anatta-vada*), and to ancient Graeco-Roman philosophies, such as Stoicism, where the essence of selfhood was described as *pneuma*, a gust of wind. In a sense, defusing your identity from the contents of consciousness can feel like sacrificing something and even the founders of ACT refer to it at times as a kind of metaphorical death or even 'conceptual suicide'. Likewise, the great Roman-Stoic philosopher Seneca once wrote: 'A person who has learned how to die has unlearned how to be a slave'. Can you sacrifice your concept of yourself, in other words, and connect instead with your actual experience of being conscious here and now? Another Stoic, Marcus Aurelius, said that when consciousness 'withdraws into itself' and finds contentment there it becomes self-contained and invulnerable, like a perfect sphere, a fortress or sanctuary. Scholars have called this special, resilient form of self-awareness the 'Inner Citadel' of Stoicism (Hadot, 1998). Hence Marcus Aurelius wrote: 'Keep your mind centred on itself'.

> ***You can get away from it all anytime you like: by going within. Nowhere you can go is more peaceful – more free of interruptions – than your own soul ... An instant's recollection and there it is: complete tranquillity. And by tranquillity I mean a kind of harmony.***
>
> ***So keep getting away from it all – like that. Renew yourself. But keep it brief and basic. A quick visit should be enough to ... send you back ready to face what awaits you.***
>
> Marcus Aurelius, *Meditations*

Key idea: Self-as-context

ACT makes a basic distinction between two radically different ways of experiencing yourself: self-as-*content* and self-as-*context*. Most people tend to identify themselves with the *contents* of consciousness observed by them: their thoughts and feelings, etc. That's bound to be threatened when key thoughts and beliefs about yourself such as 'I am stupid' are defused. However, an alternative perspective would be to identify with *consciousness* itself, with the context in which these experiences occur. I am not my thoughts, memories or feelings, in other words. I am the consciousness observing them. Taking thoughts or beliefs about yourself as literal descriptions, fused with your sense of self, can increase suffering.

Animals and infants probably have no concept of themselves in this sense; we only appear to acquire it through the use of language. However, language represents reality imperfectly and is prone to distortion, especially when it treats value-judgements as if they were literal descriptions. Value-judgements about *yourself*, such as 'I am worthless', are therefore potentially among the most troublesome forms of cognitive fusion. That may be true even of *positive* beliefs, which can also become a prison for the self if held rigidly and fused with. Defusing thoughts and accepting unpleasant experiences, in order to act in valued ways, is made easier by having a sense of self that goes beyond these things. As literal beliefs about yourself are defused, you may be left looking for a sense of self that isn't shaken by this process, one that transcends individual thoughts and feelings.

Mindfulness meditation

The different elements of both 'open' and 'centred' responding come together nicely in the practice of mindfulness meditation, which can take various forms.

Try it now: Mindful eating

The most common form of this exercise presently involves eating a raisin mindfully, which is part of several mindfulness-based approaches. However, the concept of eating with self-awareness can be found in many different therapeutic approaches, going back to the first half of the twentieth century, such as Gestalt Therapy and Progressive Relaxation, and in meditation practices that are considerably older. This offers a good illustration of the difference between mindfulness and operating on 'automatic pilot', unaware of the present moment, because we often eat quickly as a means-to-an-end rather than savouring the experience and appreciating its *intrinsic* value.

Take a raisin, or really any food that seems appropriate, and allow yourself to use all of your senses to patiently contemplate its characteristics. Look at it for a while and perhaps feel its texture in your hands, or smell it attentively, before you *slowly* put it in your mouth. Adopt a 'beginner's mind' as if you're experiencing all these things with curiosity, for the very first time. Lazily explore the taste and texture in your mouth before you begin to chew slowly and mindfully, noticing what your senses reveal is going on in your mouth. Notice also the *muscles* you're tensing or using, in your jaw, mouth, and elsewhere, such as your facial expression while chewing. Notice, in particular, how simply observing the present-moment experience more carefully can potentially transform it but also how thoughts and mental associations are easily triggered that can rapidly take you away, in your mind, from the 'here and now' experience of eating. Keep bringing yourself back to the present-moment experience, though. How do you spot when attention wanders from the experience of eating? How do you manage to return to the task-at-hand?

Try it now: Body scan

The 'body scan' exercise is also used in several approaches, particularly Mindfulness-Based Cognitive Therapy (MBCT), where a 45-minute version is one of the main initial practices. The brief version that follows will help to give you a general flavour of the exercise, though. You will probably want to lie down and close your eyes for this exercise. Take a few moments to help yourself feel comfortable and centred before you begin.

1 Breathe slowly through your nose. Don't try to change your breathing and don't try to stop it from changing either, just let go of any attempts to control it consciously, and let it do its own thing, accepting whatever it feels like.
2 Notice the sensations that accompany your breathing, the rise and fall of your belly, perhaps your rib cage expanding slightly and then relaxing. Take a moment to meditate on your breathing, while letting go, and notice even the smallest sensations, as you breathe in and out... If any thoughts occur, just acknowledge them, accept them, and gently return your attention to your breathing and your bodily sensations...
3 Now turn your attention to the soles of your feet. Scan your body from the soles of your feet up through your ankles, calves and shins, to your knees. Study the sensations on your skin and the feelings in the muscles, under the skin. Allow yourself to accept whatever you feel as it is, and let go of any attempts to change anything for the time being.
4 Now let your awareness rise up through your thighs to your hips, in the same way.
5 Now continue to scan your body up through your belly and the trunk of your body, into your chest and shoulders.
6 Now let your awareness spread from your shoulders, down through your arms, to the tips of your fingers.
7 Now scan from your shoulders up through your neck and over your head and face.
8 Take a moment to be aware of your whole body and accept the sensations you're experiencing, as you continue to focus on your breathing at the same time.
9 If you like, imagine that as you breathe naturally in and out, your breath is passing through your whole body, helping you to remain focused on accepting whatever sensations you experience.

Try it now: Sitting mindfulness meditation

This should be a central practice, if possible, which helps to bring together elements of the other mindfulness and acceptance strategies discussed in these chapters. Ideally, you should begin by meditating for about 15–20 minutes every day, or at least 2–3 times per week. The posture you sit in isn't important, as long as it's comfortable and appropriate for remaining still for this length of time. Crossing your legs or folding your arms may cause pins and needles and make you want to move. Lying down or reclining may make you sleepy. Generally, unless you're used to sitting cross-legged, the best position will be to sit upright in a chair with your back unsupported and your hands resting loosely on your lap. You can either have your eyes open, in which case you will probably want to fix your gaze gently on some point in front of you rather than looking around the room, or else close your eyes, which is perhaps most people's preferred option at first.

Then just sit and do absolutely nothing. Or rather, remain mindful and accepting, open and centred, aware of yourself as observing the present moment. You may find that focusing your attention on your breathing helps you to remain centred in the present moment. Don't try to change your breathing and don't try to stop it from changing, just accept whatever your breath does and pay attention to the sensations. If thoughts 'hook' your attention, as they inevitably will, and your mind wanders, just spot this as soon as you can and gently return your attention to your breathing. Try to remain completely present to the experience of your breathing, throughout the full length of each inhalation and exhalation. Notice the rise and fall of your belly, your ribs expanding slightly, the length of any pauses between breaths, and even the smallest sensations elsewhere in your body as you breathe.

If necessary, you can briefly use some of the defusion techniques discussed earlier in this book to disentangle your attention from your thoughts. If it helps, you might want to repeat a word in your mind on each exhalation of breath, as a 'centring device' to help anchor your attention to the present moment. Alternatively, count from ten down to zero, one number on each exhalation of breath, starting again at ten whenever you reach zero, or if your attention wanders and you lose count. Remain connected to the present moment, mindful of yourself as conscious observer of your experiences, willingly accept your stream of consciousness and let go of any effort to control your experiences.

Applying mindfulness to daily life

It's a common feature of many therapeutic approaches that longer exercises can be used to develop skill at home, during prescribed periods of meditation, for instance, while other strategies are designed to be applied in real-world settings throughout your daily routine. There are two main ways of doing this:

1 Learning to perform brief mindfulness meditation exercises frequently throughout the day, in a variety of different settings
2 Learning to integrate elements of mindfulness with ordinary tasks and activities, such as eating or walking, etc.

It's also possible to combine these, for example, by performing a brief 2–3 minute meditation exercise before and perhaps after a task such as writing a letter, which itself may be performed mindfully throughout. Both of these approaches will be found much easier, and more effective, following some initial practice with longer and more 'formal' exercises, such as the 'Body Scan', described above.

Try it now: Brief mindfulness meditation

'Mini-meditation' techniques such as the 'Three-Minute Breathing Space' (3MBS) in Mindfulness-Based Cognitive Therapy (MBCT) are employed to provide an opportunity for *rapid-frequent* practice throughout the day and in a variety of settings. We can think of this as injecting a short burst of more profound mindfulness in-between ordinary daily activities. In MBCT the aim is to do this at least three times per day, at prescribed times, or as an acceptance-based strategy when unpleasant experiences arise. However, you might choose to do it more often, perhaps even for a few minutes during every waking hour, for a couple of weeks. It's natural to think of the shift in focus of attention involved as narrowing briefly on to some anchoring point or 'centring device' such as the breath and then widening to the present moment and the task at hand, as a way of concluding the exercise and continuing, mindfully, with daily activity.

The following brief mindfulness exercise incorporates elements from several mindfulness and acceptance-based therapies:

1. Begin by stopping whatever you were doing, stepping out of 'autopilot', and becoming aware of what you're experiencing in the present moment, particularly any unpleasant thoughts or feelings you may have the urge to struggle with or avoid.
2. Gather or focus your attention on the sensations of your breathing, in the present moment, as you've done in longer mindfulness meditation exercises, while also willingly accepting any unpleasant feelings, by imagining your breath flowing through them, creating a sense of space around them and observing their properties in a detached way.

3 Conclude by expanding your awareness gradually, throughout your body as a whole, and finally back to your environment and any tasks at hand, in the present moment, before slowly and mindfully resuming any activities you're engaged in.

If it helps, give yourself verbal instructions like, 'Even though I don't like these feelings I'm going to actively accept them and observe what happens...' or 'Let go of the struggle and accept...' You may also find it helpful to repeat a short word of your choosing (e.g., 'one'), in your mind, each time you exhale. This can serve the dual purpose of acting as a 'centring device' for your attention while also functioning as a *cue-word* to help you rapidly *recall* the state of mindfulness from previous exercises.

You can practise this briefly, for about two to three minutes, or turn it into a longer meditation, perhaps lasting 10–20 minutes, if necessary. Remember, your aim isn't to get rid of the unpleasant experiences but rather to let go of the struggle and willingly accept them instead. However, people often do find, as a kind of side-effect, that unpleasant experiences may reduce as a result of acceptance strategies like this.

Mindfulness during physical activity ('meditation in motion'), such as *walking* slowly, is another practice common to different modern approaches, and to ancient Buddhist meditation. In Mindfulness-Based Cognitive Therapy (MBCT) this involves performing *hatha yoga* postures and stretches with mindfulness. It's also comparable to the practice of 'Differential Relaxation' in Progressive Relaxation training, which we will discuss in a later chapter.

Maintaining resilience through mindfulness

Some people, such as many Buddhists, practice meditation as an integral part of their way of life. Certainly this appears to be a healthy aspiration if you want to build lasting emotional resilience.

However, for many other people these strategies will be used more intermittently. Nevertheless, whether or not you decide to continue using mindfulness throughout life, you'll probably find it useful to employ it more generally for at least a couple of weeks so that you can observe what happens. As with other approaches, you may find that setting up cues to remind you to engage briefly in mindfulness strategies is important. For example, for two weeks, you might make it your goal to connect to the present moment and your sense of self-as-context for at least one minute each waking hour of the day. There's no upper limit on the duration of each mini-meditation so if you want to continue for more than a minute, that's even better. Alternatively, make a commitment to do the same thing before eating or drinking, changing tasks, leaving a room, etc. Connecting with your sense of self as observer is a way of finding sanctuary from challenging thoughts and feelings and something you can frequently return to. Although it will become more familiar, you will undoubtedly find yourself repeatedly having to defuse from thoughts and beliefs about yourself, something that never really ends, although this becomes much easier with practice.

FOCUS POINTS

The main points to remember from this chapter are:

- Awareness of the present moment and the self as observer constitute a 'centred' way of responding to experience.
- Centred responding, along with being open and engaged, completes our account of the core ingredients of *psychological flexibility* and resilience.
- Attention to the here and now helps to limit the tendency of the mind to become absorbed in morbid rumination about the past or worry about the future.
- Awareness of the self-as-context helps to overcome the problems of conditional self-esteem and to cultivate a form of unconditional self-acceptance instead.
- Meditation techniques take a variety of forms but bring neatly together the four elements of mindfulness: acceptance, defusion, and awareness of the present moment and self-as-context.

NEXT STEP

Having explored the fundamental processes and strategies of a mindfulness and acceptance-based approach to resilience, the following chapters now describe a number of additional skills and techniques derived from more traditional CBT and established resilience-building approaches.

Further reading

Harris, R. (2008). *The Happiness Trap (Based on ACT: A revolutionary mindfulness-based programme for overcoming stress, anxiety and depression)*.

Hayes, S. C. (2005). *Get Out of Your Mind and into Your Life: The New Acceptance and Commitment Therapy*.

Kabat-Zinn, J. (2004). *Full Catastrophe Living: How to Cope with Stress, Pain and Illness, using Mindfulness Meditation* (15th-anniversary edition).

7

Progressive Relaxation

In this chapter you will learn:

- *A simple, scientific approach to relaxation: Edmund Jacobson's Progressive Relaxation method (aka 'Tension Control') and the shortened procedure called 'Abbreviated Progressive Relaxation Training' (APRT)*
- *How to avoid the common 'effort error' of actively* trying *to 'relax' instead of simply letting go of tension*
- *How to improve awareness of bodily tension by 'cultivating the muscle-sense'*
- *How to let go of subtle,* residual *levels of muscle tension and relax progressively more deeply than normal, towards the 'extreme' of absolute relaxation*
- *How to quickly release muscle tension merely by recalling the sensation of letting go and using a special counting technique*
- *How to let go (metaphorically) of mental tension/worry and settle more into contented awareness of the present moment.*

> *To learn to pass from the state of tension that usually characterizes modern living into one of marked relaxation within a few minutes or less; to repeat this again and again until relaxation becomes habitual – such, from the present standpoint, are the aims of tension control.*
>
> Jacobson, *You Must Relax*

The importance of muscle tension and relaxation

People are often told that, for their health and wellbeing, they 'need to learn to relax' but are seldom actually *taught* how to do so properly. This chapter will explain how to study muscular tension and learn to control it by using a simplified version of an old and well-established technique called 'Progressive Relaxation' (PR), sometimes also known as 'Tension Control'.

In fact, the term 'Progressive Relaxation' is used to refer to a number of closely related methods derived from the original approach of that name developed by Edmund Jacobson (1888–1983) in the 1920s. Jacobson was a respected physician and physiologist who carried out a very extensive programme of research on muscular tension and relaxation. He commenced his graduate studies in 1908 at Harvard University, where his experiments demonstrated that deep muscle relaxation reduced the response to unexpected loud noise ('startle reflex'). After teaching and conducting research at Cornell and the University of Chicago, Jacobson continued research in this area from 1936 until the 1960s at the Laboratory for Clinical Physiology in Chicago. Jacobson developed a device called the 'integrating neurovoltmeter', employed in his research to measure the contraction of muscles directly. He summarized his findings and the technique he developed in the scientific text *Progressive Relaxation* (1929[1938]), later presented in the form of a shorter self-help book for the general public, *You Must Relax* (1934[1977]).

Joseph Wolpe, one of the founders of behaviour therapy, introduced a much abbreviated and simplified version of Jacobson's approach in the late 1950s (Wolpe, 1958). This method was further simplified by Bernstein, Borkovec and Hazlett-Stevens (2000) in the early 1970s. Their approach is sometimes referred to as 'Abbreviated Progressive Relaxation Training' (APRT) to distinguish it from Jacobson's original and more extensive method (Bernstein, Carlson & Schmidt, 2007). This family of techniques has been used extensively in treating clinical problems such as generalized anxiety, specific phobias, insomnia, and certain physical and psycho-somatic conditions such as headaches, bowel disorders, back pain, etc. The method described in this chapter is a further simplified and abbreviated version of APRT, adapted for resilience training.

WHAT IS PROGRESSIVE RELAXATION?

Your 'skeletal' muscles are composed of many individual fibres, about the width of a human hair. There are about 1,030 such muscles in the human body, which make up nearly half its total weight. Arguably, the only direct *voluntary* control you have over your body is through these muscles. They function simply by contracting or shortening when a nervous signal is sent from your brain, and releasing or lengthening when this signal reduces or ceases completely, which therefore constitutes the *absolute* level of muscular relaxation. When muscles contract they generate a quite vague and subtle sensation of tension or 'control signal', self-awareness of which Jacobson believed to be central to developing self-control over the body and its functions.

Some people believe they can relax very easily without training and there are many quick techniques that can indeed make people *feel* very relaxed. However, often the perception that deep relaxation can be achieved quickly is something of an illusion. It's possible (indeed common) for a person to report feeling very deeply mentally (subjectively) relaxed, while they are still visibly tensing muscles, for example, by frowning, clenching their teeth, or hunching their shoulders. Jacobson found that when people ordinarily lie down and attempt to relax there tends to be 'residual tension' in the muscles of the body. He believed that it was particularly important to learn to relax beyond this level, even to a small degree. According to his findings, relaxation of the skeletal muscles is typically followed both by *mental* relaxation, i.e., cessation of thoughts, imagery and emotions, and also relaxation of the *bodily organs*, such as lowering of the heart rate, reduction in blood pressure and relaxation of the digestive system.

Key idea: Progressive Relaxation of the muscles

It's important to understand that by 'relaxation', from a physiological perspective, Jacobson meant *muscle* relaxation, which he specifically defined as the complete absence of all contraction or 'tension', i.e., the release and lengthening of the muscles fibres.

What do we mean by 'progressive'? Jacobson described his method of relaxation as 'progressive' in three respects (1977, p. 104).

1 The individual muscles being relaxed at any given time are to be released progressively further with each minute of practice.
2 Different groups of muscles are relaxed in turn until the whole body has been progressively relaxed throughout all the main muscle groups.
3 With daily practice, the general level of tension becomes habitually lessened so that the individual becomes progressively more relaxed throughout life, during a wider range of situations and activities.

He advised those learning his method that in the initial stages of training, even when they feel completely relaxed, they can safely assume that there are probably still further 'residual' levels of tension in the muscles, which it is the goal of this method to relax progressively away.

Jacobson's method

Jacobson's original course of training in Progressive Relaxation took up to a year and involved daily sessions using many different physical 'practice positions'. However, it began with a form of awareness training, called 'cultivation of the muscle-sense', similar in some respects to mindfulness meditation, but specifically concerned with improving awareness of the body. It involved patient, systematic training in very careful self-observation of muscular ('kinaesthetic') sensations, minute feelings of muscle tension, sometimes described as 'the world beneath the skin'.

Moreover, Jacobson believed that it's particularly important to relax the region of the eyes because he found tension in this area to be closely linked to mental processes, including worry and anxiety. The proponents of Progressive Relaxation have concluded from their research, using electrodes to measure the activity of the muscles, that when the eyes are completely relaxed, mental imagery tends to cease. Learning to reduce mental activity is normally difficult at first but becomes easier with practice as the subtle bodily tensions associated with mental activity are identified.

Remember this: Progressive Relaxation takes practice

Tension control is a physical skill like learning to play tennis or ride a bicycle and, although some take to it quickly, most people require systematic perseverance. You should read this chapter carefully before beginning to try the techniques. However, it will be difficult to completely understand until you've actually started to *practise* the techniques described. To obtain the full benefit you should normally plan to dedicate at least 20 minutes to relaxation practice per day initially and training normally lasts at least three to five weeks, although the time taken to relax may reduce significantly with practice. Nevertheless, some of the ideas and techniques may be of *immediate* interest or benefit to certain people.

The 'effort error', relaxation as 'not doing'

In Progressive Relaxation training, the technique of releasing tension has been variously described as 'letting go', 'switching off the power', allowing the muscles to 'collapse' or 'go limp', etc. It's sometimes referred to as 'going in the negative direction', as opposed to going in the direction of tension, to emphasize the notion that it's simply a matter of *stopping tensing* the muscles, ceasing activity, rather than making an *effort to relax*. Jacobson referred to muscle relaxation as 'going negative' because of the absence of any positive sensation of muscle relaxation. A maxim of his approach was that effort to relax is always failure to relax.

Strictly speaking, muscle relaxation can only be experienced as the *negation* or 'letting go' of tension. Hence, muscles are first tensed, partly to raise awareness of what not to do. The instructions Jacobson gave following initial tensing and releasing of specific muscles ran as follows:

> ***Whatever it is that you do or do not do when you begin to relax that you are to continue on and on, past the point where the part seems to you perfectly relaxed!***
>
> (Jacobson, 1938, p. 50)

This is progressive relaxation beyond the normal level of residual tension towards new, more profound levels.

Remember this: 'An effort to relax is a failure to relax'

In theory, absolute relaxation, letting go of all tension, should be as easy and effortless as simply doing nothing. However, as it turns out, it's initially far from easy to do nothing when you're in the habit of doing too much, without realizing it. It takes practice to learn what it means to completely eliminate tension and effort.

When initially trying to relax, people often err by under-estimating the level of residual tension remaining in their muscles, by unwittingly tensing other muscles to try to force themselves to relax, or by tensing to try to 'hold still' or lower a raised limb, etc. Jacobson referred to this as the 'beginner's error' or 'effort error'. Hence, '*Every effort to relax is failure to relax*' (Jacobson, 1977, p. 111).

Relaxing is a special form of *inactivity*. Although there are sensations that accompany muscular relaxation, such as gentle breathing and mental calm or drowsiness, these are really consequences or side-effects. There is no positive physical sensation of muscle relaxation. There is only the sensation of muscle tension of varying degrees. You cannot focus on the *absence* of tension any more than you can focus on the absence of pain. There's nothing positive to imagine, only the absence of sensation. The brain can't actively 'do' relaxation, it can only 'stop doing' tension. To relax the body is simply to stop tensing the muscles. Relaxation is quite literally *doing nothing* but it's paradoxically very difficult to do absolutely nothing and usually requires a surprising amount of self-awareness and patient practice to get the knack.

Some criticisms and potential limitations

A possible drawback inherent in the method of studying muscle tension might be that it encourages excessive *preoccupation* with the muscles. There is some reason to believe that paying too much attention to your muscles tends to actually make them become more tense. However, Jacobson emphasized that with practice a 'happy medium' can be reached in which sensations of tension can be located more quickly and easily with the amount of attention required naturally reducing over time as relaxation becomes more of a habit. Nevertheless, this method may not suit people who tend to become overly preoccupied with their bodily sensations.

Acceptance and Applied Relaxation

Elsewhere, we've discussed the modern trend for mindfulness-based approaches to therapy, which replace experiential avoidance with the willing acceptance of unpleasant experiences, such as worry, anxiety, and tension, etc. There's some scope for debate as to whether relaxation coping skills constitute a form of experiential avoidance or not. A number of acceptance-oriented therapists have been swayed by the strength of evidence supporting Applied Relaxation to try to reconcile these two approaches. In particular, two researchers called Lizabeth Roemer and Susan Orsillo have recently developed an approach that combines elements of Acceptance and Commitment Therapy (ACT) with Applied Relaxation as a treatment for Generalized Anxiety Disorder (GAD) (Roemer & Orsillo, 2002).

Their mindfulness and acceptance-based approach to progressive muscle relaxation emphasizes developing awareness of bodily sensations during tension and relaxation, focus on the concrete present moment, and the willing acceptance of any resulting experiences. This is perhaps similar, in some ways, to Jacobson's original approach, which emphasized mindfulness of the muscle sense and learning to let go of any effort to relax, etc. The focus is not to control or eliminate internal experiences such as anxiety but rather 'to observe and allow the presence of certain internal experiences and to practice letting go of the struggle with physical sensations' (Roemer & Orsillo, 2009, p. 211).

Hence, clients are encouraged to be open to whatever experiences arise while noting that Progressive Relaxation can sometimes helpfully reduce stress and anxiety, often by reducing attempts to struggle with and change inner experience. In other words, rather than trying to 'relax away' anxiety we can perhaps think of ourselves as relaxing into *acceptance* of anxious feelings and also relaxing and 'letting go' of the struggle to control them. When people become anxious, muscular tension can be seen as an automatic *defensive* reaction, evolved over millions of years, in which the body is tensed, adopting a 'muscle set' in preparation for *fight*, *flight*, or in order to *freeze* and evade detection. Accepting automatic anxious thoughts and feelings while voluntarily letting go of muscular tension can be seen as a way of voluntarily 'dropping your guard' and abandoning the effort to cope with anxiety through physical action. In other words, it can be seen as a way of letting go and accepting unpleasant feelings more deeply, rather than trying to control them.

The founders of ACT have recently described how Progressive Relaxation can be combined with their 'psychological flexibility' model (Hayes, Strosahl & Wilson, 2012, p. 208). They argue that Progressive Relaxation can provide a way of learning to become centred and notice experiences as they occur, developing a broader and more flexible awareness of the present moment. This is done by shifting attention periodically to notice what thoughts are being experienced during relaxation before returning attention to the part of the body being relaxed.

RESEARCH AND APPLICATIONS

Jacobson himself was involved in conducting a large military study in which 100 Navy officers were trained to become teachers of Progressive Relaxation. They ran ten-week courses with up to 300 participants each, training 15,700 Navy cadets in total during a seven-month period. Evidence was found of a decrease in physical injury, anxiety and fatigue among those trained in Progressive Relaxation, as well as improved sleep, compared to other cadets. In 1951, an account of the project, entitled 'Relaxation Methods in US Navy Air Schools', was published by Commander William Neufeld in *The American Journal of Psychiatry*.

More recent reviews of the research on Progressive Relaxation methods have concluded that the evidence supports its value in the treatment of problems such as insomnia, anxiety, certain types of acute and chronic pain, and some stress-related physical conditions such as hypertension, asthma, or irritable bowel disorder (IBS), etc. (Bernstein, Carlson & Schmidt, 2007, p. 90). Moreover, it forms the basis of a subsequent behaviour therapy technique called Applied Relaxation, which, as we shall see in the next chapter, has been found effective in a range of studies for different problems. In 2008, a team of psychologists in Italy published an article entitled 'Relaxation training for anxiety: a ten-years systematic review with meta-analysis' (Manzoni, Pagnini, Castelnuovo & Molinari, 2008). Their review of 27 individual research studies, including over a thousand participants, concluded that Progressive Relaxation, Applied Relaxation, and meditation were the most effective forms of relaxation training in terms of reducing anxiety. Statistical analysis classified the overall benefit ('mean effect size') of relaxation training as 'medium' to 'high', providing strong evidence of its value in reducing different types of anxiety across different populations.

PROGRESSIVE RELAXATION AND RESILIENCE

Why wait until tension becomes a problem? Tensing muscles is obviously a matter of degree and *unnecessary* tension, where appropriate, can be released pre-emptively before it's allowed to cause harm. Although Progressive Relaxation has often been used *therapeutically*, to address *existing* problems such as anxiety disorders or stress-related illness, it was also intended to be used *preventatively*. In particular, Jacobson's method of 'Differential Relaxation', which you will learn later, involves controlling muscular tension throughout the day, during different tasks and situations, in the service of developing a generally more relaxed lifestyle over the long term. This type of relaxation can also help you become more 'centred' in the present moment allowing you to act more fully in accord with your values, which is central to our definition of resilience.

There's a lack of direct research on Progressive Relaxation as a form of resilience-building, although it is one component of the *Penn Resiliency Programme*, used to prevent anxiety and depression (Reivich & Shatté, 2002, pp. 193–196). However, Jacobson also reported from his clinical experience that Differential Relaxation could help people to withstand many *physical* ailments, by conserving energy and allowing the body to function more resiliently. Moreover, experts in this area have reported that even students who do not suffer from any specific medical or psychiatric problems tend to describe a greater sense of general wellbeing and improved ability to cope with minor stressors ('daily hassles') following training in Progressive Relaxation. As one of Jacobson's closest followers put it, learning Progressive Relaxation can be 'like money in the bank', by providing a way of preparing to cope resiliently in the future with adversity (McGuigan, 1981, p. 208).

Precautions for Progressive Relaxation techniques

Experts on Progressive Relaxation have claimed there are no significant risks or 'contraindications' to its use. McGuigan, one of the leading experts on Jacobson's method, joked that the only potential harm from muscle relaxation would be if you were to relax in front of an oncoming truck (McGuigan, 1981, p. 217). However, there are probably some precautions we should mention before continuing.

A small minority people report experiencing negative reactions to very deep relaxation, such as nausea, headaches, disorientation or anxiety, although research suggests these reactions are normally transient and harmless. They also tend to diminish with practice.

People who are prone to 'panic attacks' sometimes experience them in response to relaxation, probably because the natural feelings of drowsiness and disorientation trigger fears of 'losing control'. If you are prone to panic attacks, you should proceed slowly and carefully with progressive relaxation, but realize that the sensations caused are normal and harmless. They're similar to those experienced when falling asleep at night.

If you have any medical conditions that might in any way be aggravated or triggered by tensing muscles or deep relaxation you should, of course, refrain from using these techniques without the approval of your medical doctor. In particular, tensing certain muscles may be inappropriate if you have certain types of *physical injury* or *cardio-vascular problems*, such as a heart or circulatory condition. You should always check with your doctor if in any doubt.

Assessing your tension

We know that muscle relaxation tends to have beneficial effects, although there are different ways of understanding the reasons for this. Jacobson emphasized the concept that residual levels of muscular tension tend to increase vulnerability to stress in response to certain events. He illustrated this by analogy with his early research on the startle reflex, which found that unexpected loud noises automatically gave *more* of a fright to individuals who tensed their muscles than those who were relaxed. Relaxed individuals were more resilient to the effect of loud noises, startling less and recovering more quickly.

Jacobson describes carefully learning to spot the tension signal and using it as a criterion for spotting future tension in a way that

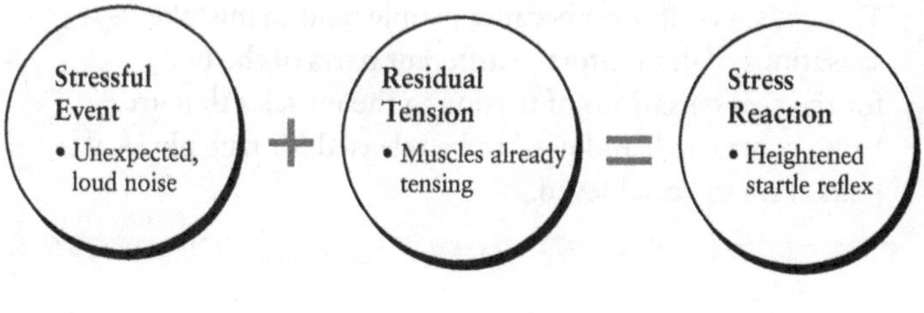

Figure 7.1

resembles a shopper taking a colour sample or swatch with them to a store to help identify the material they are looking for. The sensation of tension is often quite vague and faint: 'Tenseness, when moderate, is neither agreeable nor disagreeable but is particularly indistinct and characterless' (Jacobson, 1977, p. 109). One reason for initially holding tension for 1–2 minutes in his original approach was that it may help to identify the location of muscular tension, especially if the muscle starts to feel slightly fatigued.

Try it now: Initial tension-release experiment (bending wrist)

Keep your arm still and raise your right hand by bending it back at the wrist as far as possible, so that it is almost at a right angle to your forearm. Hold it in that position for about 30 seconds, unless it's too uncomfortable. Where do you feel the most tension as you hold that position? Where are the strongest sensations? Jacobson used this technique to introduce patients to muscle relaxation.

When asked to indicate where they feel tension, many people will point to their *wrist*. Jacobson said this would be better described as 'strain' on the joint, which is a consequence or side-effect of tension. The real sensation of tension (muscular contraction) is in the *back of the forearm*, as this is where the main muscle being used is located. Notice that the sensation of 'tension', in the muscle, is usually more faint and subtle, than the sensations of 'strain' or discomfort in the wrist.

This causes confusion because people tend to mistake sensations of discomfort in different parts of the body for the real sensations of tension in the muscles that are being contracted, and need to be released for true physical relaxation to be achieved.

We're going to use a self-rating scale to help you assess and cultivate awareness of your tension levels. This isn't necessarily going to be highly *accurate* to begin with, until you've cultivated the ability to spot tension. However, using the scale regularly, along with the other exercises, will help you to become more aware of the actual signs of tension in your body. Let's say that 100% on the scale denotes absolute physical tension, the most tense you could possibly imagine being. By contrast, 0% denotes absolute relaxation, the most physically relaxed you could possibly imagine being. Jacobson's measurements suggested that most people are far from being completely free of tension even when they lie down and feel that they are quite physically relaxed. So let's assume that your tension level is unlikely to be 0% at the outset of training.

Remember this: Rate your tension levels (0–100%)

To self-rate tension, close your eyes for a moment and scan your whole body for even the slightest sensations of muscles tensing, contracting, pulling, etc. Don't try to change anything. Don't try to relax at this stage. Just self-rate your level of tension on a scale of 0–100%. Once you've picked a number to represent your tension level, try to write down a brief list of the specific sensations that you based your rating upon.

Try to rate your tension levels frequently. Do so before and after using specific relaxation exercises. However, also do so when you notice yourself becoming tense or distressed or during challenging situations. Moreover, pause frequently throughout the day, perhaps once per hour, to rate your current tension level. Keep a record of the specific sensations you use to arrive at each rating, where possible. Your aim in doing so is to cultivate more awareness of your muscular tension and to anticipate the typical feelings that occur, especially subtle or faint sensations which you may have originally overlooked.

Once the basic rationale is understood, standard Progressive Relaxation training in behaviour therapy begins by tensing and releasing the muscles in *16* different regions of the body. We're not going to work on these muscle groups individually but it might help you to begin by scanning your body using these groups, for convenience, as a guide to help identify tension 'hot spots'.

Self-assessment: Tension across 16 muscle groups

Take a moment to rate your tension level in each of the following muscle groups right now, on a scale of 0–100%:

1 Right hand and forearm (%)
2 Right biceps and/or triceps (%)
3 Left hand and forearm (%)
4 Left biceps and/or triceps (%)
5 Forehead, upper face (%)
6 Upper cheeks, eyes, and nose, mid face (%)
7 Lower cheeks and jaws, lower face (%)
8 Neck and throat (%)
9 Chest, shoulders, and upper back (%)
10 Abdominal region (%)
11 Right thigh (%)
12 Right calf (%)
13 Right foot (%)
14 Left thigh (%)
15 Left calf (%)
16 Left foot (%)

These will only be very *rough* estimates until you learn to further cultivate your muscle sense. However, you might want to repeat this exercise periodically throughout the day to help pinpoint areas of tension that arise at different times in different situations, building a mental-map of how tension is distributed through different regions of your body. In addition to learning to relax generally, you might want to specifically focus additional time on tensing and releasing problem areas identified in this way.

Try that now: Tense the muscle group with the highest rating for at least ten seconds and then progressively relax it, keep letting go more deeply for at least 30 seconds. Repeat this about three times in total and then re-rate your tension level in that part of the body.

In addition, we will be using a slightly modified version of the practice record used in Applied Relaxation (see next chapter) to assess progress in using all of the subsequent relaxation coping skills learned (Öst, 1987, p. 400).

Practice record for relaxation coping skills

Date/ Time	*Skills practised*	*Tension before (%)*	*Tension after (%)*	*Duration (Minutes)*	*Comments (Problems? Insights?)*

You should start using this record right away to assess your new skills and monitoring your progress. Relaxation skills covered in this and the next chapter, which might be recorded on the practice sheet, include tension-release (seven groups), tension-release (four groups), relaxation-by-recall, relaxation-by-counting, differential relaxation, and cue-controlled relaxation.

Progressive Relaxation training

Abbreviated methods of Progressive Relaxation Training normally require daily practice for up to *ten weeks* (Bernstein, Carlson & Schmidt, 2007, p. 115). However, this is reduced to three to five weeks when used as a prelude to Applied Relaxation. Hence, the simplified self-help approach described here is based on a *five-week*

Week(s)	*Procedures*
1–2	Seven Muscle-Group Tension-Release
3	Four Muscle-Group Tension-Release
4–5	Relaxation by Recall and Counting Only

Optionally: Followed by Differential and Applied Relaxation methods described later.

programme of daily practice in Progressive Relaxation designed to help build resilience by learning *general* tension control. Later, you will learn how to transfer these skills to different situations and activities through Differential Relaxation and to relax quickly in the face of adversity through Applied Relaxation.

PREPARATION

Ideally, you should be lying down, or at least reclining so that your head is supported, allowing you to completely relax your neck muscles. However, lying in bed, under the covers, late at night, with the lights turned off, is not recommended during relaxation training unless you want to fall asleep! Remove your shoes and make sure your clothing is loose enough to be comfortable. If you wear spectacles then remove them. Switch off any telephones, close the doors, and make arrangements for any possible disturbances to be prevented or reduced to a minimum. Dim the lights during your initial sessions, if you feel that helps. Crossing your arms or legs, or resting your arm on the armrest of a chair, during deep relaxation, for a prolonged period, can cause pins and needles by restricting the circulation. It's best therefore to place your feet side-by-side, with your legs straight, and your hands by your sides, if lying down flat, or your feet flat on the floor and hands on your lap, if seated. You should normally have your eyes closed during relaxation exercises.

Remember this: Lie down, be quiet, and stop fidgeting!

As this procedure specifically involves relaxation of the muscles, which requires complete letting go and inaction, it is best if you try to keep any physical movement to an absolute minimum. However, if you *really do* need to move, for example, you have an itch on your nose that you have to scratch, try to do so with the minimum of disruption to your relaxation. Keep any movements brief, make yourself comfortable, but try to only use the muscles necessary and leave the rest of the body relaxed.

TENSION-RELEASE RELAXATION (CULTIVATION OF THE MUSCLE SENSE)

Although daily practice for 50 minutes was recommended by Jacobson, in modern approaches Abbreviated Progressive Relaxation Training requires about 15–20 minutes of practice about twice per day at first, perhaps reducing to once per day later. However, the procedure always begins with some form of 'tension-release cycles' to help cultivate the muscle-sense through repeated observation of the contrast between tensing and letting go.

Key idea: Voluntarily tensing muscles

Why tense muscles in order to relax? There are two main explanations. Jacobson trained individuals to study the specific sensations of tension in different muscles, by deliberately tensing them, several times, for 1–2 minutes at a time – which *feels* longer than it *sounds*! The original aim was to become much more conscious of how you are using your muscles by spotting faint signs of tension you normally overlook, hence a form of physical self-awareness training, called 'cultivating the muscle-sense'.

In addition, behaviour therapists later argued that tensing muscles first and then releasing them tends to lead to deeper-than-normal relaxation, explained by the analogy with a 'pendulum' swing, moving first in the direction of tension to build up greater 'momentum' for a swing back in the direction of relaxation. Those emphasizing this rationale, the basis of APRT, tend to recommend much briefer periods of tension, typically just 5–7 seconds. (Jacobson himself wasn't very keen on this way of presenting things.)

Either way, the assumption is that tensing first helps people learn to spot and eliminate tension more fully and to progressively relax *beyond* their normal ability, achieving a much more profound and complete state of relaxation. In my experience, there's some validity to both perspectives and tensing muscles probably serves a dual purpose. Although, we're focusing here on the abbreviated approach, some individuals may want to borrow elements of Jacobson's original method and tense individual muscles for longer to help study tension and learn to develop deeper physical self-awareness and perhaps greater muscular self-control.

This chapter will teach you how to do a much abbreviated version of the standard progressive muscle relaxation approach used in behaviour therapy. Most progressive muscle relaxation approaches begin with training in tensing and releasing *16* different muscle

Sixteen groups	*Seven groups*	*Four groups*	*General Relaxation*
Dominant hand and forearm	Dominant hand and arm	Both hands and arms	Whole body, using cue-word or counting
Dominant biceps and/or triceps			
Non-dominant hand and forearm	Non-dominant hand and arm		
Non-dominant biceps and/or triceps			
Forehead (upper face)	Face and jaws	Face, jaw and neck	
Upper cheeks, eyes, and nose (mid face)			
Lower cheeks and jaws (lower face)			
Neck and throat	Neck and throat		
Chest, shoulders and upper back	Chest, back and abdomen	Chest, back and abdomen	
Abdominal region			
Dominant thigh	Dominant leg and foot	Both legs and feet	
Dominant calf			
Dominant foot			
Non-dominant thigh	Non-dominant leg and foot		
Non-dominant calf			
Non-dominant foot			

groups, which initially takes about 45 minutes per session. It's a fairly rigorous procedure. Once this stage has been mastered, muscle groups are combined into *seven* groups to further abbreviate the procedure, and finally into *four* major groups, in the briefest version of the technique.

For the purposes of self-help, without the support of a therapist to train you, I would recommend missing out the first stage of relaxing 16 muscle groups. Instead, you should begin by dividing your body into the seven muscle groups as described below, to simplify the whole procedure. This will reduce the time taken during your initial practice sessions from 45 to about 20 minutes. Later practice sessions, as we will see, shall become briefer still.

Try it now: Basic tension-release procedure

Below, we'll describe a whole tension-release routine, including seven muscle groups (Bernstein, Borkovec & Hazlett-Stevens, 2000, pp. 37–38). However, to get the basic technique right, let's begin by experimenting in detail with a single group of muscles: *the right hand and arm.*

Prepare your environment and get into a suitable position to relax as described above. Take a few moments to relax and settle down before you begin. When you're ready, focus all of your attention on your right hand and arm. You're going to tense all the muscles in the right hand and arm for a few seconds by clenching your fist and trying to bend your arm and straighten it at the same time, so as to tense both your triceps and biceps, by bringing these opposing muscles into conflict. Don't tense too much; you only need a *moderate* level of tension, and it shouldn't be painful or overly-uncomfortable. Also, try to practise tensing the muscles *selectively.* Only tense the muscles being used and keep the rest of the body as relaxed and inactive as possible.

Now focus on where the muscles are *actually* contracting, as you bend your right arm slightly at the elbow, tense the muscles and clench your fist, holding the tension for about 5–7 seconds. Try to bend and straighten the arm simultaneously to call opposing muscles into action. Don't count the seconds, just estimate the passage of time roughly; you don't need to be precise. Focus all of your attention on the sensation of tension, the muscles pulling and hardening, rather than the other sensations in the body.

When the tensing time is up, just take a deep breath, hold it for a second or two, and as you exhale, let the arm relax completely. Don't try to relax slowly; just let the muscles turn immediately as limp as possible. Now continue to relax for about another 30–60 seconds. Don't concentrate *too much* on the muscles, as this can make them tense, but do keep thinking of letting tension go completely. Notice the *contrast* between the feelings of tension in the muscles being used and the subsequent feeling of progressively relaxing or letting go.

After releasing the tension, without the 'patter' of a therapist to guide you, it may help you to focus on progressively relaxing by paying attention to your breathing, allowing it to become slow, regular and automatic, and telling yourself to 'let go deeper and deeper…' of the muscles with every exhalation. Rather than count the seconds closely, you might want to simply relax for as long as it takes to breathe in-and-out about 8–15 times, by roughly counting or estimating your *exhalations*. However, Jacobson in particular believed that thinking, including instructing yourself to 'let go…', was incompatible with total relaxation, certainly with relaxation of the muscles involved in speech. So you may wish to 'fade' or gradually diminish your use of such self-instructions as your relaxation progresses to the point of mental quietude or when specifically relaxing the facial muscles, etc.

When the relaxation time is up, repeat the procedure one more time, trying to make the release of tension more complete the second time. This is an example intended to show how you should relax each of the *seven* muscle groups described in the procedure below.

It's particularly important that when tensing and releasing muscles, throughout any of these exercises, you bear in mind that you're working towards being able to 'relax by recall' only. So you should begin with the goal in mind and pay close attention to the sensation of 'letting go', as though learning what it feels like and *memorizing* it for future recall.

Remember this: The effect of practice

At first you may find it difficult to tense one group of muscles without tensing other parts of the body. However, this usually becomes easier with practice. You should always try to isolate the muscle group you're meant to be working on by tensing there while *continuing* to relax throughout the rest of the body. Keep still but don't try to 'hold still' by tensing up, just let go of any urge to move or fidget. If you have to move to remain comfortable then do so but your overall goal is to learn to make the muscles as limp and relaxed as possible for the duration of the session.

You should tailor your use of Progressive Relaxation to make it suit your needs. For example, if you find that a particular muscle group stubbornly refuses to relax, you should modify the approach to focus on this specific area more perhaps by tensing it for longer, relaxing longer, or doing so more repeatedly than with other regions.

Try it now: Initial seven muscle-group procedure

This section assumes you've read the basic procedure above and experimented with it sufficiently to remember what it entails and what the key sensations feel like. Each of the seven muscle groups below should be tensed and released *twice* before proceeding to the next group (Bernstein, Borkovec & Hazlett-Stevens, 2000, pp. 52–54). The muscles are always tensed for about 5–7 seconds before being released for about 30–60 seconds. This should take about 15–20 minutes in total.

1 **Right arm and hand.** Clench the fist, bend the arm slightly at the elbow, and tense the bicep and tricep muscles, e.g., by trying to bend and straighten the arm

simultaneously. Hold the tension for 5–7 seconds before taking a deep breath, exhaling, and letting the hand and arm become completely limp. Keep letting go of the muscles for about 30–60 seconds and then repeating this whole tension-release cycle once more before continuing.

2 **Left arm and hand.** Exactly as above, for the other hand and arm.

3 **Face and jaw.** As above but these muscles are tensed by frowning, squeezing the eyes shut, and clenching the jaw. Frown by drawing the eyebrows together, while squeezing the eyelids tightly shut, wrinkling the nose, clenching the teeth, and drawing the corners of the mouth back, as though in a grin. This will feel (and look!) as though you're 'screwing up your face' in a kind of grimace, for 5–7 seconds, before releasing all the facial muscles. When you release the jaw muscles completely, the teeth must normally part, and the lips will often part slightly, as though the mouth is hanging 'slack jawed'.

4 **Neck and throat.** These muscles are tensed by trying to lower the chin towards the chest, while simultaneously trying to raise it upward, thereby using opposing muscles to create tension, which often causes slight trembling. Trying to raise and lower your chin at the same time will help you to tense all the muscles in the neck region. The neck muscles normally remain tense, to some extent, even when the rest of the body is relaxed, to hold the head upright. You should be reclining, with your head supported, so that you're able to fully relax your neck muscles. This may mean your head rolls slightly to one side, depending on your body's position.

5 **Chest, back, shoulders and abdomen.** This group combines several groups of muscles that can be relaxed independently. However, for brevity they're combined together here. Take a deep breath this time and hold it for 5–7 seconds, while you pull your shoulder blades back and draw them together and harden your abdomen, as though preparing to take a punch in the stomach – or by trying to push the abdomen in and out simultaneously. Exhale as

you release all these muscles at once, and breathe naturally as you continue to let go.

6 **Right leg and foot.** Lift your right leg slightly while pointing your toes downward and turning your foot slightly inward, to tense these muscles.

7 **Left leg and foot.** Exactly as above, for the other leg and foot.

Finally, scan your body for any remaining sensations of tension, no matter how faint, and try to 'let go' of it more completely, repeating the tension-release cycle for that muscle group if necessary. End the session by simply continuing to relax progressively, focusing on letting go more deeply and completely, for 1–2 minutes, before slowly opening your eyes and moving. If you prefer, you can count from 1 to 5 in your mind to help you slowly 'emerge' from relaxation. You should try to 'differentially relax' as you end each exercise, though, by moving slowly at first and only using the muscles you need, almost as if only using one muscle at a time, retaining as much relaxation throughout the body as possible during subsequent activity.

You can experiment with the timing and methods of tension to arrive at an approach that works best for you. These are just standardized techniques, although they have been found to work well for most patients in clinical practice and subjects in research studies. You should resist the urge to cut corners in relaxation training. However, sometimes it will be appropriate to abbreviate the method above in a number of ways. For example, some people may find it equally beneficial at times to relax the head and trunk only, while omitting relaxation of the arms and legs. In the standard procedure, once the seven muscle groups can be adequately relaxed with ease, further combinations are made to reduce the number of muscle groups used to four.

The procedure above should be used at least once, but ideally twice, per day for about 1–2 *weeks* before proceeding to the next abbreviated form of the exercise.

Try it now: Brief four muscle-group procedure

This section assumes you've read the basic procedure and initial seven muscle-group method above and experimented with them sufficiently to continue to the next stage, abbreviating things by combining the muscles into *four* broad groups (Bernstein, Borkovec & Hazlett-Stevens 2000, pp. 54–56). Once again, each of the four muscle groups below should be tensed and released *twice* before proceeding to the next group. The muscles are always tensed for about 5–7 seconds before being released for about 30–60 seconds. This normally reduces the session time to less than *ten minutes* in total.

1. **Both arms and hands.** Both fists are clenched simultaneously and the arms are bent slightly and tensed together, using the same procedure as employed for each arm independently above.
2. **Face, jaw and neck.** As in the seven muscle-group version, but now the facial muscles are squeezed, jaw clenched, and opposing neck muscles tensed, simultaneously. This often causes minor trembling.
3. **Chest, back, shoulders and abdomen.** This is exactly as in the seven muscle-group procedure above.
4. **Both legs and feet.** Both legs are raised simultaneously and the feet pointed and turned slightly inward, using the same procedure as employed for each leg independently above.

Again, you should feel free to experiment and modify this basic procedure, in terms of the timing or tension strategies used, to find an approach that works well for you. Remember to focus on the sensation of 'letting go' in particular, as though memorizing exactly what it feels like, as you're going to recall that sensation in the future to relax even more quickly and easily.

Once the four muscle-group version has been sufficiently mastered, which normally takes daily practice for about an additional week, you should proceed to the next stage: *relaxation by recall.*

RELAXATION BY RECALL AND COUNTING

'Relaxation by recall' (or 'release only') is virtually identical to the four muscle-group tension-release exercise above, except that the tension stage is completely *omitted* from now onward. Muscles should no longer be tensed unless it proves difficult to relax them, in which case you should temporarily return to using the tension-release strategy above for the muscle group you're having problems relaxing.

Try it now: Relaxation by recall and counting

This section assumes you've mastered the tension-release methods above and experimented with them sufficiently to continue to the next stage, abbreviating things by relaxing *four* broad groups through recall only. This normally reduces the session time to about 3–4 *minutes* in total.

1. **Both arms and hands.** Focus all of your attention on the muscles of your arms and hands, noticing any sensations of tension, no matter how subtle or faint. Then progressively relax the muscles by recalling what it felt like to 'let go' of tension there in the previous exercises. Continue to let go more deeply and completely for about 30–45 seconds, or about the time it normally takes to exhale 8–12 times. If it helps, mentally instruct yourself to 'keep letting go more deeply...' with each exhalation, perhaps fading your voice to silence as you relax.
2. **Face, jaw and neck.** Exactly as above.
3. **Chest, back, shoulders and abdomen.** Exactly as above.
4. **Both legs and feet.** Exactly as above.

Optionally: Revert back to the earlier tension-release strategy for a particular muscle group if it proves difficult to relax or any noticeable tension remains.

Finally, count from ten down to zero in your mind, in time with each exhalation of breath. As you exhale and count, try to 'let go' of tension throughout the body progressively more deeply and completely. When finished, continue to progressively relax in silence for 1–2 minutes before opening your eyes slowly and emerging as normal.

Once you've learned to relax more deeply by counting, this technique may actually be used on its own to achieve relaxation quite rapidly. Jacobson recommended a similar technique for inducing sleep, which involved progressively relaxing the eyes, and subsequently the rest of the body, on each exhalation of breath.

CASE STUDY

Bruxism (teeth grinding)

Bruxism, or teeth grinding, is a good example of a very specific tension-related problem, often reported by people who suffer from chronic anxiety and worry. In an early study, using another method quite similar to Progressive Relaxation, two dentists trained a group of 14 patients to clench their teeth for five seconds and then release the muscles for five seconds. This was repeated five times in a row, and the whole routine was used six times per day for two weeks in total (McGuigan, 1981, p. 113). Within ten days eleven of the patients (79%) had stopped their teeth-grinding, and six months later they were still better.

Grinding the teeth, or just clenching or tensing the jaw is a common 'early warning sign' of mounting tension, worry and anxiety reported by many of my own clients. For example, Sue was troubled by stress at work and in her relationship. She had problems falling asleep at night because of worry and sometimes awoke during the night, feeling anxious and tense. She was aware that she tended to grind her teeth but with training also noticed that she was tensing her jaw and other muscles associated with speech when preoccupied with thinking about her problems. By using tension-release generally, and specifically focusing on her jaw-clenching, she was able to manage her worry and also to sleep more easily at night.

By controlling tension in her jaw muscles, she learned to control her worry, anxiety, and sleep in a way that helped her cope better with problems at work and at home as they arose, making her more resilient to future adversity.

Maintaining resilience through Progressive Relaxation

Differential Relaxation was the original approach adopted by Jacobson to help transfer Progressive Relaxation skills to a range of situations and activities, throughout daily life, the ultimate goal being to *habitually* notice and let go of tension all the time with minimal conscious effort: 24 hours per day, every day of your life. Differential Relaxation basically involves regular identification of any *unnecessary* tension present during daily activities, and the use of previously learned Progressive Relaxation skills to eliminate it (Jacobson, 1977, p. 131). This may involve simply relaxation-by-recall of specific muscles or the use of tension-release strategy where tension is more stubborn.

Differential Relaxation has three main advantages:

1 It increases your opportunity to practise Progressive Relaxation skills beyond the prescribed sessions, many times throughout the day.
2 It helps to reduce generalized anxiety and chronic tension, throughout the day.
3 It helps you to develop situation-specific relaxation skills, in the face of significant adversity or minor daily hassles.

Differential Relaxation may therefore particularly contribute to resilience-building because it challenges you to make your relaxation skills more generalized and long-standing, something we might expect to help bridge the gap to coping with future adversity and to serve a preventative function. Differential Relaxation is closely related to Applied Relaxation, which is covered in the following chapter, and the two are often combined.

Jacobson noted that this concept was far from novel. Speakers and singers often learn to relax while using only the relevant muscles to preserve their voice, sportsmen typically become more relaxed as they learn to use their muscles more efficiently, dancers and acrobats learn to use their muscles more selectively as they develop grace and skill. Perhaps the best example, according to McGuigan, is the long-distance runner who only uses the muscles necessary to run while conserving energy by relaxing the rest of his or her body.

Try it now: Differential relaxation positions

Begin by progressively relaxing using one of the strategies above, the quickest being simply to use relaxation-by-recall or the counting technique alone. (Alternatively, a cue-word can be used to relax rapidly, as described in the next chapter.) Revert back to using the tension-release strategy to relax stubborn muscles, if necessary.

Start by focusing on the transition from lying down or reclining to sitting upright, at the end of your relaxation session. Move slowly and focus on only using the muscles you need to tense. Once you're seated upright with your eyes open, try to release any unnecessary tension from the body, while using other muscles, for example, those around the eyes and in the neck. Spend a few minutes looking around, while trying to minimize any tension in the body, using relaxation-by-recall or other strategies.

Next, try slowly standing up, using your muscles only insofar as necessary. Stand upright for a few minutes, while you continue to relax the rest of your body, using your eye muscles and legs, etc., to remain upright, slowly looking around you.

When you've experimented with making small movements, try walking very slowly in a quiet environment, perhaps just walking around the room in a circle for a few minutes. Again, continue to progressively relax, using only the muscles you need to during the activity, and keeping tension to a minimal level throughout the body.

Finally, try relaxing while seated, and then standing up and walking, in a noisy environment, where you might normally be distracted by things around you. Try to learn to relax progressively, keeping tension minimal, in any environment, even when engaged in activity in a challenging situation.

Once you are able to minimize tension during more or less any situation or activity, you should progress to systematically learning to relax frequently throughout your day. The next step being to progressively relax, more or less all of the time, until it becomes *habitual* and *automatic* to spot tension and release it, wherever you are and whatever you are doing. For example, you might try pausing to scan your body for tension and progressively relax, for about one minute, at some point in each hour of the day. Like most things, this takes some effort at first but becomes much quicker and easier with practice.

FOCUS POINTS

The main points to remember from this chapter are:

- Progressive Relaxation is a physical skill that requires self-observation and patient, systematic practice, just like most other physical skills such as learning to dance or play tennis.
- An effort to relax is a failure to relax, insofar as effort implies physical or mental activity and therefore additional tension.
- Although Progressive Relaxation initially involves studying tension in different muscle groups, this is ultimately eliminated in favour of relaxation by recall and other briefer methods.
- Progressive Relaxation begins at home, as it were, but eventually 'Differential Relaxation' during daily activity is the goal, which lends itself to long-term physical and emotional resilience.
- Differential, or selective, Relaxation allows you to conserve energy by only using the muscles necessary during daily activity, letting go of excess tension and effort, and this provides the main way to develop a more relaxed way of life in general, and thereby build resilience.

NEXT STEP

In the next chapter, you'll learn to use a much more *rapid* form of relaxation as a 'coping skill'. This approach developed in the 1980s and has subsequently been found particularly effective in the treatment of anxiety, particularly worry and quite pervasive or generalized anxiety. Applied Relaxation actually developed largely out of Progressive Relaxation, and the content of the next chapter assumes you've read, learned, and started to master the techniques of Progressive Relaxation, especially 'relaxation by recall' and counting.

Further reading

Bernstein, Douglas A., Borkovec, Thomas D. & Hazlett-Stevens, Holly (2000). *New Directions in Progressive Relaxation Training: A Guidebook for Helping Professionals.* This is actually a manual for therapists rather than the general public but it contains the best overall account of modern progressive muscle relaxation and applied relaxation training.

Jacobson, Edmund (1976). *You must Relax.*

McGuigan,F. J. (1981). *Calm Down: A Guide to Stress and Tension Control.*

8

Applied Relaxation

In this chapter you will learn:

- *How to develop Progressive Relaxation into a more rapid and portable coping skill, an approach called 'Applied Relaxation'*
- *How to develop self-awareness by spotting 'early warning signs' of muscle tension and negative emotional 'spirals'*
- *How to use your* imagination *to let go of tension in anticipation of stressful situations by mentally rehearsing coping skills*
- *How to* apply *rapid relaxation coping skills in response to early warning signs of negative emotional spirals in real situations.*

> ***The first goal is to get relaxed at all, and learn what it feels like; the next is to perfect this much of it sufficiently that one can do it easily and quickly under non-stressful circumstances. Then comes the matter of being able to relax under mild stress, then under greater stress, and finally to reach the point where a relaxed state is the customary one and tension a rare one.***
>
> Haugen et al., *A Therapy for Anxiety Tension Reactions*, 1958

> ***We have seen that frowning is the natural expression of some difficulty encountered, or of something disagreeable experienced either in thought or action, and he whose mind is often and readily affected in this way, will be apt to be ill-tempered, or slightly angry, or peevish, and will commonly show it by frowning.***
>
> Charles Darwin, *The Expression of the Emotions in Man and Animals, 1872*

The importance of Applied Relaxation

WHAT IS APPLIED RELAXATION?

Applied Relaxation was developed in 1978 by Prof. Lars-Göran Öst at the Psychiatric Research Centre of the University of Uppsala in Sweden. It has also been developed, particularly in relation to generalized anxiety and worry, by Tom Borkovec, a professor of psychology at Pennsylvania State University in the USA. It's derived from a group of closely related approaches, all emphasizing the rehearsal of relaxation and other coping skills, which were developed by behaviour therapists in the 1970s, called things like *Self-Control Desensitization*, *Anxiety Management Training* and *Stress-Inoculation Training*. More recently, elements of Progressive and Applied Relaxation have been combined with mindfulness and acceptance-based approaches to therapy, of the kind which form the basis of earlier chapters in this book (Roemer & Orsillo, 2009).

CASE STUDY

My daughter, Poppy's birth!

I nearly overlooked this example when writing the chapter but... my own daughter was born about eight months ago, using Applied Relaxation. Mandy, my wife, was expecting her first baby and decided to give birth at home without using any medication for pain relief, before, during or after the delivery – not even a single Paracetamol pill!

The 'preparation stage' for giving birth is usually quite long, *about nine months*! That gives plenty of opportunity to develop relaxation skills by coping with daily hassles, minor pain and discomfort, and anxiety and worry in anticipation of the 'big day'. Mandy wanted to experiment with different techniques during her pregnancy and ended up listening quite regularly to an Applied Relaxation CD that I designed for use with my therapy clients, which includes training in the use of a relaxation 'cue-word' that she often repeated while mentally rehearsing the process of childbirth.

Poppy's birth went well except that Mandy had a 'back labour', which is normally very painful indeed. Mandy did experience some pain but was able to cope with it by using relaxation and breathing coping skills. She had a 'critical point' where she felt quite overwhelmed but I helped her cope by focusing on her breathing and relaxation. She closed her eyes and became very tranquil and deeply engrossed in her internal experiences for a very long time, while we waited for the midwives to arrive. In fact, she barely reacted to the noise they were making as they talked loudly and unpacked their medical gear in our kitchen.

Mandy's labour was quite short, about six hours, which has been widely reported as a benefit of relaxation and self-hypnosis in research studies, and is considered better for the mother and baby. Perhaps because her birth was very natural and relaxed, Poppy is a very happy, healthy and contented baby indeed. I like to think she's our personal evidence of the merits of Applied Relaxation. There are many older studies describing positive data from research on similar self-hypnosis techniques for childbirth. I only discovered after Poppy's birth that back in 2005 a team of researchers in Iran (Bastani, Hidarnia, Kazemnejad, Vafaei & Kashanian, 2005) had conducted a clinical trial with 110 women that provided clear scientific evidence of a reduction in stress and anxiety following Applied Relaxation training during pregnancy. In fact, they reported reductions of almost 40 per cent in their current anxiety levels following training and their overall stress levels *reduced* while those of the untrained women *increased*.

In brief, Applied Relaxation involves carefully self-monitoring and recording subtle 'early warning signs' of tension, negative emotion (anger, anxiety) or worry and learning to immediately 'let go' of these, voluntarily interrupting the habitual spiral, by using very rapid relaxation techniques, particularly the use of a 'cue-word' associated with deep relaxation. However, the whole approach is divided into a number of stages, which usually begin with abbreviated Progressive Relaxation training of the kind covered in the previous chapter.

Key idea: Stages of Applied Relaxation

Applied Relaxation normally consists of a number of different stages, which for the purposes of self-help and resilience-building we might summarize as follows:

- ▶ **Self-assessment and preparation**
  1 Education about the nature of stress
  2 Self-monitoring of early warning signs
- ▶ **Learning and rehearsal of coping skills**
  3 Progressive Relaxation: Tense-Release Cycles
  4 Progressive Relaxation: Relaxation by Recall (Release Only)
  5 Cue-controlled (Conditioned) Relaxation Training
- ▶ **Application and maintenance of coping skills**
  6 Differential Relaxation Training
  7 Rapid-Frequent Relaxation ('Cue-controlled Relaxation')
  8 Application of Coping Skills to Specific Imagined Situations ('Self-control Desensitization')
  9 Application to Specific Real-world Stressful Situations
  10 Long-term Maintenance (and General Resilience-building)

Differential and Rapid-Frequent Relaxation involve becoming *generally* more relaxed, continuously throughout the day, during various activities and situations. By contrast, real-world or imagined use of Applied Relaxation typically involves coping with *specific* situations that are more stressful or challenging.

Remember this: Applied Relaxation presupposes Progressive Relaxation training

This chapter builds on the preceding one and assumes that you have already spent time successfully acquiring the basic skills of Progressive Relaxation, including cultivation of the muscle-sense. You could try using some of the techniques without relaxation training but you're more likely to succeed if you first make certain you can spot muscular tension and relax very effectively.

RESEARCH AND APPLICATIONS

Applied Relaxation was originally developed as a technique for treating clinically severe generalized anxiety and specific phobias. However, it has also been found effective for a range of stress and anxiety-related problems such as insomnia, panic attacks, social phobia, claustrophobia, agoraphobia, blood phobia, dental phobia, headaches, back pain, epilepsy, tinnitus, etc. (Öst, 1987, p. 404). At the present moment, the strongest evidence for Applied Relaxation is in the treatment of Generalized Anxiety Disorder (GAD), which involves chronic worry and severe anxiety about a variety of topics.

Key idea: Resilience and general-purpose coping skills

The coping skills in Applied Relaxation are designed to be as general-purpose as possible, so that they can be transferred to a wide range of situations and events. Indeed, relaxation has been described as the 'Aspirin' of stress management, although there's now more caution about ensuring that it's not sometimes misused as a form of excessive experiential avoidance.

Applied Relaxation is derived from an approach developed in the 1970s by Prof. Donald Meichenbaum, called 'Stress-Inoculation Training' (SIT). It involves repeatedly confronting stressful situations in reality or in imagination as a way of developing coping skills and building resilience to stress in general, based upon the analogy with being 'inoculated' against a virus. The point is that you should try to face your fears systematically, in *gradual doses*, usually starting with the easier ones, and rehearsing using your coping skills to master each situation on your 'hierarchy' in turn (see below). By learning to use relaxation and other skills in a wide range of *different* situations people tend to become more self-confident and capable of coping with stress in general. This takes patient practice, however.

APPLIED RELAXATION AND RESILIENCE

The use of Applied Relaxation techniques for resilience-building resembles the clinical treatment of generalized anxiety and worry about multiple topics. Resilience-building typically involves learning to cope with lots of small daily hassles and also preparing to cope with a range of more serious adversities, including both real and hypothetical scenarios. This is typically done by mentally rehearsing the use of coping skills, like carrying out a kind of 'mental fire-drill' for coping with future misfortunes.

According to Öst, 90–95 per cent of the patients trained by him and his colleagues were able to acquire the skill of Applied Relaxation satisfactorily (Öst, 1987, p. 403). Although relaxation techniques often produce rapid improvements, the long-term benefits have sometimes been questioned. However, Öst reviewed 12 research studies in which patients were followed up an average of 11 months after Applied Relaxation training was completed, for a range of problems. Not only did findings show that the beneficial effects were maintained long term but in 75 per cent of the studies symptoms of stress, etc., continued to decrease long after the initial treatment programme was completed (Öst, 1987, p. 407). This suggests that Applied Relaxation can improve a wide range of common problems in a relatively short space of time and that the benefits very often continue to grow over the long term. Learning Applied Relaxation appears to be a good investment and an obvious way to build emotional resilience and improve coping with a range of stressful future adversities.

Remember this: Severe anxiety may require a therapist

This section discusses how you might apply relaxation coping skills in imagination or in reality to highly stressful situations of the sort you might otherwise have the urge to avoid. However, if anxiety is particularly severe, you may require the support of a professional therapist to do this. You should seek advice from your medical doctor if in any doubt.

Self-assessment and monitoring your early warning signs

The first stage of Applied Relaxation consists of self-assessing your current reactions and simultaneously training yourself to develop more physical and mental self-awareness. Cultivating awareness of subtle muscular tension is part of all Progressive Relaxation training but Applied Relaxation tends to cast the net slightly wider, looking for any thoughts or feelings, etc., that might signal the onset of excessive stress, worried thinking, or negative emotions such as anger or anxiety. Applied Relaxation places particular emphasis on spotting 'early warning signs'. The *earlier* you spot episodes or 'spirals' of stressful thoughts and feelings, the more effective your coping skills will be at 'nipping it in the bud'.

EXTERNAL TRIGGERS AND HIERARCHY CONSTRUCTION

One of the first tasks in learning to control negative emotion consists in identifying the range of events that typically trigger the problem, and spotting common themes between them. The most important triggers may be 'high-risk situations' that it's important for you to anticipate in the future so that you can develop emotional resilience. You should create a list of stressful situations that you can rate in terms of how tense you feel when you imagine them occurring and place them in rank order, accordingly. In part this may come from keeping a record (see below) of situations in which you actually experience stress, but it may also include situations you worry about, avoid, or anticipate being a problem in the future.

Key idea: Hierarchy of stressful situations

Drawing up a list of key problem situations or events will help you notice when you need to be on the lookout for stress reactions and use your coping skills. It also forms the basis of a systematic approach to applying coping skills, in imagination and in reality, to stressful events in a 'graduated' or stepwise manner, starting with the 'easier' ones. Applied Relaxation sometimes takes a simpler approach than other forms of behaviour therapy and combines different problems into a single list, rating them simply as 'mild', 'moderate' or 'severe.' For example:

- Mild stress
  - Working in a project that's falling behind in terms of deadline
  - Telephoning customers
- Moderate stress
  - Speaking during small team meetings at work
  - Dealing with angry customers
- Severe stress
  - Giving a speech at a friend's wedding in January
  - Coping with possible redundancy

INGREDIENTS OF STRESS SPIRALS

People often take it for granted that negative emotion defies analysis and talk or think about it as being some vague event that comes out

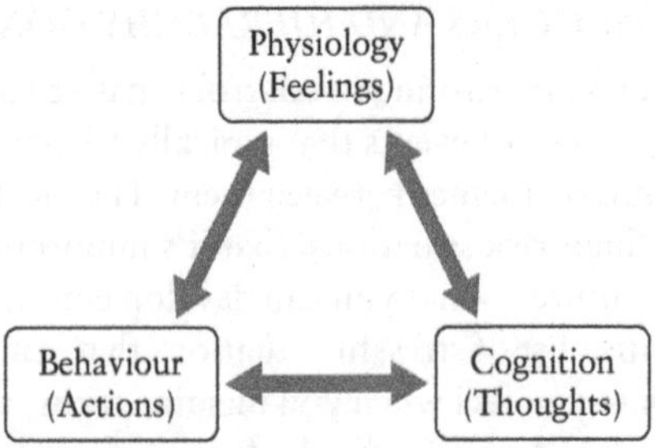

Figure 8.1 Ingredients of stress spirals.

of the blue, which psychologists sometimes call the naïve 'lump' model of emotion. It's more helpful, though, to distinguish between the different *ingredients* that make up emotions and to think in terms of a *sequence* of reactions, often referred to as an escalating 'spiral' model. The most common way to do this involves making a basic distinction between thoughts ('cognitions'), actions ('behaviour') and feelings ('physiological sensations'). Stress and negative emotions can therefore be viewed as the *reciprocal inter-action* between certain thoughts, actions and feelings, which may tend to escalate over time or even seem to 'spiral' out of control and become overwhelming.

EARLY WARNING SIGNS

Applied Relaxation places particular emphasis on identifying the *very earliest signs* of a negative spiral beginning, the 'early warning signs' of negative emotion. People almost always fail to consciously notice these early signs but react to them automatically, only noticing their distress once it's escalated to the point where it's more difficult to control. The rationale for learning to spot early warning signs is therefore very simple: It's much easier to stop a negative reaction the sooner you catch it. When people struggle and fail to control worry, anxiety or anger, their attempts to cope are very often doomed because they're 'too little, too late'. As the saying goes, 'A stitch in time saves nine', which could refer to coping with stress as well as mending clothes. Applied Relaxation involves learning to let go of stressful reactions before they've really started to escalate, the sooner the better.

The strength of these components varies between patients, but previous research has found that most people experience some physiological change, followed by a negative thought, which increases the physiological reaction, and so on in a vicious circle.

(Öst, 1987, p. 398)

Hence, Applied Relaxation particularly focuses on early *physical* reactions, including physiological sensations and muscular tension, and attempts to relax and let go of them, as in Progressive Relaxation training. However, early thoughts, images, and other feelings, or the initial signs of *worry*, may be 'let go' in the same way. In addition to spotting the early warning signs, try to notice the specific sequence of thoughts, actions and feelings that occur in stressful situations or during episodes of worry so that you can learn to 'break the chain' at different points.

Self-assessment: Example early warning signs

Typical early warning signs of stress or anxiety are listed below. Try to roughly self-rate how frequently you notice yourself exhibiting the following reactions when experiencing moderate or high levels of stress. Rate the frequency on a scale of 0–100%, e.g., where 100% means you always fidget when stressed, and 50% means you do it about half the time.

- Fidgeting, such as twisting your hair, biting your nails, tapping your feet, or drumming your fingers, etc. (%)
- Moving or walking more quickly, acting 'agitated', or pacing up and down, etc. (%)
- Talking more quickly, speaking in a more tense tone of voice, pausing less between sentences, changing the pitch or volume of the voice, etc. (%)
- Changes in breathing, often corresponding with changes in the sound of your voice, such as breathing more rapidly, higher in the chest, breathing in an irregular way, holding your breath, or heaving sighs, etc. (%)

- Changes in facial expression, particularly frowning, scowling, squinting, staring, etc. (%)
- Tensing other parts of the body, particularly clenching the jaw or grinding the teeth, tensing the neck or hunching the shoulders, clenching the hands, etc. (%)
- Physiological sensations such as increased heart rate, trembling, sweating, nausea, butterflies in the stomach, choking, a dry mouth, a lump in the throat, hot flushes, blushing, dizziness, etc. (%)
- Worry, such as thoughts or images about things going wrong (catastrophes) or about your inability to cope, etc. (%)

Be on the lookout for these and other early warning signs occurring. Watching your experience in this way can be seen as a form of self-awareness training, similar to mindfulness meditation practice.

'Worrying' is arguably a special case and consists of a sequence of fearful thoughts, and sometimes images, and unproductive attempts to prepare or solve problems, which tends to go on for some time. (See the chapter on worry for more details.)

CHRONOLOGICAL PHASES OF DISTRESS (BEFORE, DURING, AFTER)

It's also useful in some cases to distinguish between the broad *chronological stages* that occur before, during and after an individual episode or spiral of negative emotion. There are several ways to do this but one common distinction is simply between the 'before', 'during', and 'after' stages of a stressful incident:

1. *Before*: Anticipation or preparation, before a stressful situation or event.
2. *During*: Confrontation with, 'exposure' to, a stressful situation or event.
3. *After*: Recovery from stressful situations and reflection, afterwards, on what happened; it's also when you might reward (or 'reinforce') yourself for trying to use your coping strategies.

Often this can be supplemented by distinguishing between your immediate reaction when confronted with a stressful situation and what sometimes happens a few moments later if feelings escalate to a *critical point* during the event. This is often the point at which you may feel the urge to act in unhelpful ways, for example, by fleeing, freezing-up, or becoming aggressive, etc.

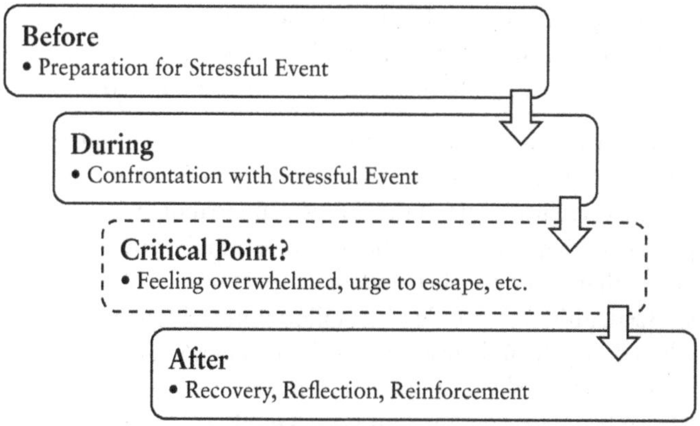

Figure 8.2 Chronological phases of distress.

Sometimes Applied Relaxation coping skills can be used before, during and after specific stressful events. It's most obviously useful to let go of tension when exposed to a stressful situation. However, it may also be important to relax *pre-emptively*, immediately beforehand, in anticipation of entering a stressful or 'high-risk' situation or when worrying about it further in advance. Likewise, relaxation can be used afterwards to minimize the 'post-mortem' or morbid rumination, dwelling on what happened in unhelpful ways and perhaps instead to recover and reflect on things in a more relaxed and constructive frame of mind. As well as using relaxation before, during and after real-life stressful situations, it can often be helpful to approach mental rehearsal of Applied Relaxation in the same way and to *imagine* using relaxation coping skills before, during and after anticipated or hypothetical situations.

Try it now: List signs of stress

Take a moment to list the typical *external* signs of stress that you might observe in other people, trying to brainstorm as many specific things as possible. What might you see or hear in their reaction that would tell you that they're becoming stressed? To this list of observable external signs, add what you suppose they might be experiencing *internally* that would be a sign to them that they're becoming stressed.

Now draw up a second list, this time of your own internal and external signs of stress. Consider whether you may also do or experience some of the things you attributed to other people, perhaps without noticing. For example, you may notice that other people frown or raise their voice when stressed, although people often fail to notice these things when doing them themselves. As the saying goes, it's far easier to spot a sliver of wood in someone else's eye than a great beam of wood in your own. Here's a clue, you're likely to notice changes in other people's voices and facial expressions but do you notice as soon as your own face begins to change or your voice alters?

IMAGERY RECALL FOR SELF-ASSESSMENT

A technique commonly used to identify early warning signs involves mentally reviewing a recent, typical example of a stressful situation, as if it's happening now, particularly trying to focus on the very earliest part of the sequence of internal reactions that occurred. This is also preparation for the use of Applied Relaxation coping skills in imagination, which we will discuss below.

Try it now: Imagery recall and questions about early warning signs

1 Practise self-monitoring by closing your eyes and picturing a situation now that makes you feel tense or anxious.

2 Once you're able to imagine the situation reaching its peak, rate your stress or tension 0–100%. Note what sensations you based the rating on.
3 Now imagine going back to the point in the situation when you first notice becoming tense or upset. In fact, go back a few minutes prior to this point, before you even noticed any distress. Next, go through what actually happens in slow motion, noting the very earliest signs of tension or distress and the sequence of internal events that follows: bodily sensations, thoughts and images, and your physical behaviour, etc.
4 You might want to review the sequence of events in your imagination about 3–4 times. Then try to write down the sequence of reactions that you experienced as accurately as possible. Look out for similar reactions in other situations in the future, and continue to self-monitor, developing a record of your typical trigger situations and early warning signs.
5 Try to maintain a brief running log of your most common early warning signs. At the end of each day, review your self-monitoring by asking yourself 'What new early warning signs did I spot?' and record these in your log.

When asked to do this people sometimes report thoughts or images but most often the early warning signs they notice are physical sensations, particularly symptoms of bodily tension. Physical actions often tend to be reported as coming slightly later in the sequence.

SELF-MONITORING RECORDS

Get into the habit of frequently rating your tension (or stress) on a rough 0–100% scale. Don't expect this to be very accurate at first but it will become more so with practice. More importantly the *attempt* to self-rate will force you to pay more attention to what you're actually experiencing. Once you've picked a percentage rating, ask yourself why you chose that number. Think carefully and note down what exactly you took as evidence of tension or stress. Four important opportunities for regular and frequent self-monitoring, which can act as reminders or cues, are as follows:

1 *Stressful feelings*. Pause and observe what's just happened whenever you begin to notice yourself feeling more negative, tense or distressed, etc.
2 *Hourly practice*. Stop and 'check in' with yourself at least once an hour throughout the day, scanning your body for any signs of tension, and noting any other early warning signs that may be present.
3 *Changing tasks*. Pause and check your body and mind for early warning signs whenever you change tasks or locations, e.g., leaving a room or starting a piece of work, etc.
4 *Stressful situations*. Check yourself for subtle signs of tension before, during and after typical stressful situations or events that you find yourself encountering.

Your goal is to learn to spot early warning signs whenever and wherever they occur, even ones you'd normally overlook. As you'll see below, these reminders can also be used as opportunities to practise frequent, rapid relaxation coping skills throughout the day.

Remember this: Frequent opportunities for self-monitoring and relaxation practice

To begin with, you should frequently scan your body for subtle evidence of stress or tension. Don't do this *continually*, just for a few moments at frequent intervals. In so doing, try to turn a vague sense of tension into something more specific, which is a form of self-awareness training. This will help you to further identify early warning signs.

Try to keep a written record of particularly stressful events or episodes of worry, as below.

Most people find it difficult at first to record information on their reactions when they happen. However, when records are filled out retrospectively, for example, at the end of a week, they've been found to correspond poorly with information recorded immediately,

Self-monitoring record for early warning signs (Applied Relaxation)

Date/ Situation	*Reaction (Feelings)(Focus on the earliest signs)*	*Intensity (0–100%)*	*Action (What did you do?)*

when negative feelings happen. So it's important to make an effort to complete records as soon as possible after a stressful event, particularly to record early warning signs.

However, perhaps more importantly, the (small) time and effort required to write the information down often tends to create a shift in attention so that you're more likely to notice things in the future that might otherwise have been overlooked. Increasing self-awareness in this way, over time, tends to lead to more control over your reactions, as spotting early warning signs makes it easier to nip spirals of negative emotion in the bud.

Remember this: The value of self-monitoring and increasing self-awareness

Writing down information on a self-monitoring record might seem tedious at first but it's often one of the most valuable exercises. The information gathered will become useful if it helps you to spot recurring patterns and common factors in the type of situations that are found stressful or your initial reactions and ways of coping.

Relaxation coping skills training

ABBREVIATED PROGRESSIVE RELAXATION TRAINING

See the preceding chapter for a detailed discussion of Abbreviated Progressive Relaxation Training (APRT), covering the basic skills you will need before proceeding to the later stages of Applied Relaxation.

Progressive Relaxation is either used alone or developed into Applied Relaxation, in which case it is usually further abbreviated.

You should continue to use the practice record to rate stress or tension before and after using more rapid relaxation coping skills, as a measure of their effectiveness and progress in acquiring the practical skill of relaxation.

Practice record for relaxation coping skills

Date/ Time	*Skills practised*	*Tension before (%)*	*Tension after (%)*	*Duration (Minutes)*	*Comments (Problems? Insights?)*

There are essentially two main ways of applying muscular relaxation skills to the body:

1. Local or 'differential' relaxation, in which the specific muscles being tensed are spotted and selectively relaxed, e.g., if you note that you tend to frown or hunch your shoulders, etc., and specifically tense and release those muscles or just relax them by recall.
2. General ('catch-all') relaxation, in which the whole body is relaxed rapidly, as far as possible, typically by using the counting technique or a cue-word, which can be applied to a wider range of situations.

The tense-and-release and relaxation-by-recall strategies you learned when practising Progressive Relaxation can be used when specific regions of the body are particularly tense. However, for the most part Applied Relaxation tends to use rapid general relaxation throughout the body. You've actually already learned a relaxation coping strategy that can be used to do this quite quickly in some situations: the 'counting technique' used in the previous chapter. However, you'll now learn how to relax even more quickly by using a 'cue-word' to recall what general relaxation feels like, i.e., the sensation of letting go throughout the body and mind that you've experienced in Progressive Relaxation training.

CUE-CONTROLLED RELAXATION (CONDITIONING)

Following initial training in abbreviated Progressive and Differential Relaxation, the next step is to learn to relax *quickly and easily* whenever you give yourself a signal, such as the phrase 'LET GO'.

Key idea: Learning a relaxation cue-word

One of the quickest ways to relax in different situations is to learn, through repeated practice, to associate a cue-word (or short phrase) such as 'RELAX' or 'PEACE' with the state of deep relaxation. (However, perhaps 'RELEASE' or 'LET GO' would better symbolize the correct response, and avoid the 'effort error', as described by Jacobson.) This is a simple coping skill, often referred to as 'cue-controlled relaxation'.

In adult humans this 'conditioning' process is seldom completely 'automatic' so it may be best to think of the cue-word as a command given to yourself ('self-instruction'), which becomes more meaningful as you repeatedly associate it with deep relaxation. Hence, you should consciously try to recall the feelings and not expect the cue-word to work completely automatically, 'as if by magic', although with practice it will begin to feel gradually more automatic. The more often you consciously associate the word with the experience of deep relaxation, the easier it will be to recall those sensations at another time, even, albeit perhaps to a lesser degree, during a particularly challenging or stressful situation.

You should begin by progressively relaxing as deeply as possible, usually by using the relaxation-by-recall technique and counting. Once relaxed, you should focus on your breathing and the idea of repeatedly making an association between your chosen cue-word and the feelings of relaxation attained. You can safeguard against the misuse of relaxation as a form of experiential avoidance, to some extent. Focus on accepting any feelings of tension and let go of any struggle with them, while continuing to accept any residual tense or unpleasant feelings that remain afterwards. In other words, don't try to force yourself to relax but accept your feelings and just let go of any tension that's under voluntary control, which you'll be able to do more and more completely with practice.

Try it now: Conditioning a relaxation cue-word

Before you even start, pick a 'cue-word' that you can use to signal relaxation to yourself, such as, 'RELAX', 'LET GO', etc. You're going to learn to associate that word with relaxation and thereby to recall feelings of relaxation more quickly (Bernstein, Borkovec, & Hazlett-Stevens, 2000, p. 67). Begin by relaxing as deeply as possible using one of the Progressive Relaxation strategies you've previously learned. For example, you might relax the four broad muscle groups by recall and use the counting technique (see previous chapter).

Next, while remaining deeply relaxed with your eyes closed, mentally repeat your chosen cue-word each time you *exhale*. It may help to remember that your breathing cycle mainly consists of automatically *tensing* muscles to inhale and then *releasing* them to exhale. Repeat the cue-word each time you exhale and release your muscles about 20 times in total, which should take about a minute and a half. Focus on the idea of using the word to symbolize the feelings of deep relaxation, and the goal of being able to recall them by using the word in the future. Repeat this every day, following Progressive Relaxation, for at least one week to build a stronger association between the cue-word and the state of deep relaxation.

You can then begin to test out your ability to rapidly recall general relaxation by using a cue-word. Close your eyes and imagine something that makes you moderately tense. Notice where the tension actually occurs in your body in response to the stressful image. Take a moment to fully experience the tension, and accept its presence. Now continue to think of the image that's making you tense. Take a deep breath, hold it for a few seconds, and exhale slowly as you repeat the cue-word in your mind and recall the feelings of complete relaxation you associated it with. Repeat this three times in total. You should be able to relax away some, or even all, of the tension. (If this is difficult, you may need to spend more time building the association between the cue-word and the feelings, or developing your ability to progressively relax more deeply.) Bear in mind that relaxation is not entirely under voluntary control so focus on the *process* rather than the *outcome*. Try to let go of as much tension as possible, while calmly accepting any feelings that remain.

Once you have learned to associate deep relaxation with your cue-word, you should begin to practise relaxing quickly just by using your cue-word three times, with your eyes closed at first and later with them open. You might want to time yourself doing this, as many people over-estimate how much time it takes, and are surprised to learn that, having followed the previous steps, they can relax deeply in less than a minute.

Learning to use a cue-word to relax quickly, as a rapid coping skill, will tend to increase your confidence in your ability to cope with stress in general. That sense of confidence, just knowing that you have a coping strategy to fall back on that works, will often increase resilience in the face of stressful events, whether or not you actually use the technique itself.

RAPID/FREQUENT RELAXATION

By deliberately relaxing frequently during a variety of *non-stressful* situations, you will encourage yourself to progressively relax more habitually, in general, throughout the day. The emphasis in this stage is twofold:

1 Minimizing the amount of time taken to relax deeply
2 Learning to relax frequently throughout the day in a wide variety of environments.

The goal in standard Applied Relaxation is to use your cue-controlled relaxation technique to relax rapidly about 15–20 times each day, for 1–2 weeks.

It's helpful to realize that Applied Relaxation involves learning to relax both *generally* and in *specific* stressful situations:

1 *Generalized relaxation* involves relaxing more or less *continuously*, throughout the whole day, and even being more relaxed when asleep.
2 *Situation-specific relaxation* involves relaxing in response to a specific situation, usually one that is particularly stressful and challenging.

The main challenge in developing generalized relaxation is how to *remind* yourself to relax *frequently* enough and in a wide enough *variety* of settings. However, the cues and reminders we described above in relation to frequent self-monitoring will help you to do this. For example, you should aim to briefly scan your body for tension and rapidly relax at least once each waking hour of the day, to do so whenever you consciously notice early warning signs of tension, or when changing tasks, or encountering typical stressful situations, etc. In fact, you should practise rapid relaxation whether or not you actually feel tense or stressed at the time, to help rehearse and develop your skills.

Try it now: Learning cue-controlled relaxation

Try to do the following frequently each day for a few weeks, perhaps 10–20 times or more, to develop your relaxation skills, using the cues or reminders described above.

1 Pause what you're doing right now, close your eyes if you like, and take a moment to roughly rate your tension level on a scale of 0–100%. Now scan your whole body more carefully and notice what the specific sensations or mental experiences were that you based your rating upon. Notice any other subtle sensations of tension as you do so. Take a moment to acknowledge and accept these feelings, experiencing them fully.

2 Now take a deep breath in and hold it for as long as is comfortable. Notice the feelings of tension in your chest and elsewhere as you hold your breath. Then exhale slowly, repeating your cue-word ('LET GO') as you focus on letting go of the tension in your chest and throughout the whole of your body. Really try to recall what it feels like to let go of all the muscles in your body as you use your cue-word and especially to let go of any tense sensations or thoughts that you noticed earlier. Repeat this about three times in total, letting go of any tension or struggle with the feelings, as much as possible, each time. In other words, let go of any tension under voluntary control, and accept whatever tense or unpleasant feelings remain.

3 Breathe naturally for about 30 seconds more as you let go more deeply and completely with each exhalation of breath. If you like, use the counting technique, by counting from five down to zero, timed with your exhalations, progressively letting go more deeply on each number.

4 Now re-rate your current tension level 0–100%. Record the date and time of this exercise in your practice record along with before and after ratings of tension and any problems encountered or observations you can learn from.

5 Optionally, you may want to conclude this exercise, as Borkovec suggests, by integrating mindfulness and acceptance-based strategies, e.g., focusing your attention on the present moment and connecting your actions in the here and now to your values.

At first, your aim is simply to relax in a variety of different environments, etc. However, you will inevitably find yourself increasingly using your relaxation coping skills to eliminate early warning signs of stress, before, during or after challenging or stressful situations. This leads naturally in to the 'application' stage proper, the systematic use of relaxation coping skills to reduce stress in response to particularly difficult thoughts or situations, which we will turn to next.

Remember this: Relaxation means letting go and doing nothing

When relaxation is used as a coping skill in response to early warning signs, it's important that you think of this in terms of 'letting go' of the distressing thoughts and feelings, etc., rather than trying to force them away or suppress them. During your previous Progressive Relaxation training you learned about the 'effort error' and to think of relaxation as 'not doing' tension rather than as a kind of activity itself.

Learn to accept early warning signs and the sequence of reactions that occurs in a spiral of worry or negative emotion and progressively let go of the components, rather than using relaxation defensively, to block distressing thoughts or feelings. Focus on the *process* of relaxing rather than the *outcome*. Let go of any tension under voluntary control, while actively accepting any tense or unpleasant feelings that remain.

Applying relaxation coping skills

The next stage of Applied Relaxation training involves systematically applying your coping skills to more challenging situations. Relaxation can be applied in a situation-specific way by presenting events in two different manners:

1 In imagination, by mentally picturing the specific stressful situation (therapists call this 'imaginal' exposure)
2 In reality, by actually facing specific stressful situations (called 'in vivo' or 'real-world' exposure).

Rehearsing coping skills in imagination allows you to prepare in advance for stressful situations you're planning to face in reality (e.g., asking someone out on a date), which might occur if you're unlucky (e.g., getting a rejected on a date), or which are distant or just *hypothetical* worries (e.g., worry about never getting a date and growing old alone). Indeed, the majority of stressful events are only ever encountered in imagination.

APPLIED RELAXATION IN REALITY

In behaviour therapy for phobias and similar problems greater emphasis is placed on actual confrontation of specific feared situations, for example, someone with a phobia of cats might be helped to apply their relaxation coping skills while a cat is brought progressively closer to them. However, for the purposes of resilience-building and self-help, the focus is naturally upon learning to cope with everyday occurrences, often labelled 'daily hassles', and the anticipation of more stressful situations in the future. Moreover, the wider the range of situations that you learn to cope with in this way, the more you are likely to develop a general resilience to stress and anxiety, even in novel or unanticipated situations.

When severe phobias are treated in behaviour therapy, 'exposure' to the feared situation is usually quite *prolonged*, perhaps lasting up to 1–2 hours at a time. It's well established that even severe anxiety tends to reduce during prolonged exposure, if certain basic principles are followed, and with repetition this reduction becomes permanent. However, when coping skills such as relaxation are used, the amount of time taken for anxiety to reduce is typically only about 10–15 minutes, although it may need to be repeated more often for improvement to be permanent. However, learning coping skills may sometimes lead to a more general sense of confidence and the ability to endure a wider range of stressful situations than prolonged exposure alone.

Coping skills should be used to relax before, during and after stressful situations if possible. At first, you should be satisfied if your relaxation skills are sufficient to manage or partially reduce stress or anxiety in difficult real-world situations. However, with perseverance you may find that you can eliminate quite severe tension and anxiety or at least reduce it substantially. In doing so, it's better if you can also develop acceptance of anxious feelings and an ability to tolerate them where necessary, while continuing to act in accord with your values and without avoidance.

APPLIED RELAXATION IN IMAGINATION

The use of Applied Relaxation in imagination amounts to the same thing as an early behaviour therapy technique called 'Self-Control Desensitization', which Borkovec also refers to as 'Imagery Rehearsal of Coping Strategies'. This method is particularly important to resilience-building as it allows you to anticipate a wide range of potential future stressors and rehearse coping with them effectively. As soon as you're ready to do so, you should begin adding the mental rehearsal procedure to the end of your existing Progressive Relaxation practice sessions.

Key idea: Mental rehearsal, almost as good as the real thing

Physiological reactions to *imagined* events are often indistinguishable from those to real events, except perhaps that they're typically less severe. Learning to cope with stress reactions to imagined situations therefore tends to promote resilience in the face of similar events in reality but also a more general ability to cope with stress reactions across different situations.

The benefits of mental rehearsal in sports psychology have been well-documented and supported by many studies. Visualizing a sporting performance tends to improve the *real* performance, building skills and confidence. Coping skills can be improved by using the imagination to rehearse them in much the same way as sport-related skills.

The use of Applied Relaxation in imagination can be seen as a way of mentally rehearsing how you plan to use your coping skills in reality, although it also tends to have the benefit itself of generally reducing anxiety and improving confidence in your coping ability. One potential problem with coping skills like those in Applied Relaxation is that you'll simply *forget* to use them. Mental rehearsal also has the benefit of making it more likely you'll automatically remember to use your strategies in real-life stressful situations.

Jacobson and his followers adapted the original version of Progressive Relaxation for use in reducing tension and anxiety in response to feared situations by imagining them. The procedure simply involves imagining progressively more anxiety-provoking versions of the feared situation or event, while observing very closely the sensations in the body, particularly any muscles being automatically tensed. While continuing to imagine the scene, these specific muscles are simply released voluntarily. People tend to tense different parts of their body when anxious, so the individual needs to learn to observe tension first and then 'let go' specifically where it is occurring. However, Jacobson and others reported early on that subtle tension of the small muscles around the eyes, and often in the forehead, neck and throat, tend to accompany anxiety in most cases (McGuigan, 1981, pp. 101–107).

Mental rehearsal of coping skills requires that you first relax and then visualize stressful situations repeatedly, including the various internal reactions that form your negative spiral. Once you're able to feel tense or anxious in your imagination you immediately respond by using your rapid relaxation coping skills to eliminate the stress reaction and relax away any bodily tension under voluntarily control.

Try it now: Applied Relaxation in imagination

You're going to mentally rehearse using your relaxation coping skills to reduce tension and negative emotions *before, during and after* a stressful situation, much as you would in real life (Bernstein, Borkovec & Hazlett-Stevens, 2000, pp. 111–114).

1 Begin by progressively relaxing as deeply as possible, using one of the strategies previously learned. For example, use relaxation-by-recall of four main muscle groups followed by the counting technique.
2 Picture the scene you've chosen and try to evoke mild–moderate feelings of tension or negative emotions in response, allow yourself to react by becoming tense and imagine thoughts and feelings of distress, which typically takes about 15–30 seconds. Acknowledge and accept these feelings, allowing yourself to fully experience them.

3 As soon as you're able to evoke feelings of tension, use your relaxation coping skills, e.g., take three deep breaths and on each exhalation use your cue-word ('LET GO') to rapidly relax away any tension under voluntary control, and to let go of distressing thoughts and feelings. Continue to progressively release tension, while you imagine coping with the same situation for about 20 seconds more.
4 Now continue to imagine being in the scene but completely letting go of any tension or struggle, having now mastered the situation and your feelings of tension, for about 20 seconds more. Allow yourself to fully accept any unpleasant or tense feelings that do remain.
5 Set the imagery aside and just focus on your breathing, and your bodily sensations in the 'here and now'. Progressively relax your whole body further, e.g., by briefly counting down from five to zero as you let go more deeply and completely, for about another 20 seconds.
6 Repeat this about 3–4 times or until your tension has reduced considerably, e.g. by at least half.

Maintaining resilience through relaxed living

Once cue-controlled techniques are learned they are used frequently to help cultivate a more generally relaxed way of living, over the long term. Indeed, Borkovec refers to *frequently* inducing calm and tranquil states of relaxation throughout the day in order to cultivate a 'relaxed lifestyle in general' by treating any sign of *departure* from that baseline level of tranquillity as itself an early warning sign and responding with relaxation coping skills.

However, relaxation coping skills tend to become 'rusty' over time so it's important to keep up some kind of long-term routine of practice if you want to maintain your emotional resilience in this way. Fortunately, once acquired, *keeping* relaxation skills intact tends to require much less time and effort. Get into the habit of scanning your body for tension about once per day and quickly relaxing away any tension. You should also continue to practise cue-controlled relaxation or differential relaxation a couple of times each week.

FOCUS POINTS

The main points to remember from this chapter are:

- Remember to identify early warning signs of stress or tension, in your muscles and in your mind.
- Treat these early signs as 'cues to cope', like a green traffic light signalling that you should respond immediately with your relaxation skills.
- Remember to relax frequently throughout the day to develop a more relaxed lifestyle in general.
- Identify specific 'high-risk' stressful situations and tackle them in a gradual step-by-step manner, starting with the easiest ones, rehearsing your coping skills first in imagination and then in reality.
- Don't turn relaxation into experiential avoidance: radically accept your anxious or tense feelings, let go of any tension or struggle under voluntary control, while continuing to accept any residual tension or unpleasant feelings that may remain.

NEXT STEP

In the following chapters, you'll learn how to postpone worry when it occurs, to reduce its frequency and duration by confining it to a specified time and place and also how to deal with anxiety by facing your fears in your imagination and countering catastrophic thinking.

Further reading

Bernstein, Douglas A., Borkovec, Thomas D. and Hazlett-Stevens, Holly (2000). *New Directions in Progressive Relaxation Training: A Guidebook for Helping Professionals*. This is actually a manual for therapists rather than the general public but it contains the best overall account of modern progressive muscle relaxation and applied relaxation training.

Davis, Martha A., Eshelman, Elizabeth Robbins and McKay, Matthew (1995). *The Relaxation and Stress Reduction Workbook*. The chapter on 'Applied Relaxation' is one of the few descriptions of this method as a self-help strategy for stress management.

9

Worry postponement

In this chapter you will learn:

- *That 'worry' refers to a specific form of prolonged verbal thinking about future problems and threats ('What if?' thinking), which is associated with anxious feelings*
- *About the modern 'cognitive avoidance' theory of worry, which suggests that worry is actually a subtle way of avoiding hypothetical catastrophes and the experience of unpleasant feelings*
- *About the basic 'Stimulus Control' strategy for managing worry, a form of behaviour therapy that involves postponing worry until a specified time and place*
- *How to distinguish between* unhelpful *worry and rational problem-solving and how to recognize early warning signs of worry, so you can nip the worry spiral in the bud*
- *How to* acknowledge *negative thoughts without worrying about them unnecessarily and* postpone *thinking about them further to a more appropriate time and place*
- *Why postponing worry and planning to think about worry later is often a better strategy than trying not to think about it ('suppression')*
- *How to use a specified* worry-time *to respond more appropriately to problems instead of worrying about them unproductively.*

And thus the native hue of resolution
Is sicklied o'er with the pale cast of thought;

And enterprises of great pith and moment:
With this regard, their currents turn awry:
And lose the name of action.

William Shakespeare, *Hamlet*

Fear keeps pace with hope. Nor does their so moving together surprise me; both belong to a mind in suspense, to a mind in a state of anxiety through looking into the future. Both are mainly due to projecting our thoughts far ahead of us instead of adapting ourselves to the present. Thus it is that foresight, the greatest blessing humanity has been given, is transformed into a curse. Wild animals run from the dangers they actually see, and once they have escaped them worry no more. We however are tormented alike by what is past and what is to come. A number of our blessings do us harm, for memory brings back the agony of fear while foresight brings it on prematurely. No one confines his unhappiness to the present.

Seneca, *Letters to Lucilius*

The importance of controlling worry

WHAT IS WORRY?

The term 'worry' has acquired a specific meaning among psychologists. It refers to a *process* of prolonged thinking about feared catastrophes, things going wrong in the *future* and frustrated attempts at problem-solving, and is associated with feelings of anxiety. Some people are probably inherently more prone to worry and anxiety than others. However, everyone can learn to *manage* worry better, in order to become more resilient to stressful events. Over the past few decades, research on worry has burgeoned, leading to some changes in the way certain clinical problems are treated. Although worry is common to most forms of anxiety and depression, it's particularly central to Generalized Anxiety Disorder (GAD), a form of severe anxiety about multiple issues, that's characterized by *chronic and severe worry* that feels *difficult to control*. However, less severe worry about everyday problems is so common as to be *the norm*, and learning to cope with it is therefore probably a key emotional resilience skill.

One of the world's leading authorities on the psychology and treatment of worry, Borkovec, has defined worry as 'a chain of thoughts and images', focusing on verbal thoughts, and associated with anxiety (and some depression), which appears 'relatively uncontrollable' and involves 'an attempt to engage in mental problem-solving on an issue whose outcome is uncertain' (Sibrava & Borkovec, 2006). Worry often consists of repeatedly posing and trying to answer questions such as 'What if something bad happens?' and 'How will I cope?'

Ironically, worry is characterized by prolonged, abstract, internal, verbal thinking – mankind's finest achievement! It usually develops when an initial *automatic* anxious reaction occurs and is followed by more *voluntary* attempts to cope through prolonged worried thinking. More severe worry is often followed by attempts to suppress upsetting thoughts and feelings, which unfortunately tend to make anxiety worse and fuel worry. Although the initial anxious thoughts and feelings may appear disturbing, it's really what happens next, 'our reaction to the reaction', that escalates anxiety into a more serious problem.

Borkovec proposed the influential but paradoxical-sounding 'cognitive avoidance theory of worry', which sees *worrying itself as a form of avoidance*. When we worry, we perceive danger, feel anxious, and naturally try to problem-solve in order to remove the perceived threat and achieve a sense of safety. As long as we believe future problems are threatening and remain unsolved there's a tendency for our attention to automatically return to them as 'unfinished business', which partially explains why worry episodes tend to keep recurring. Worry can therefore be seen as a failed attempt to avoid future dangers by mentally problem-solving and preparing to cope with them. Hence, people often feel reluctant to stop worrying because at some level they assume it helps to protect them against looming threats by giving them an opportunity to problem-solve and rehearse coping strategies, although it seldom does so very effectively and normally causes anxiety to escalate instead.

We talked earlier about the unworkable nature of many attempts to control anxious thoughts and feelings, called 'experiential avoidance'. Worry also seems to function as a way of avoiding internal experiences of anxiety by replacing concrete images and sensations with more vague, abstract, and verbal thinking processes. Worry is also typically associated with *intolerance of uncertainty* and a sense of *urgency* about trying to solve 'looming' problems – even late at night, in bed!

Worry postponement may offer an alternative way of responding by accepting initial automatic thoughts, or thoughts that have already occurred, while voluntarily postponing any subsequent worry by not continuing the train of thought, insofar as that is under your control. Rather than simply trying to avoid worry, this allows the topic of worry and associated feelings to be experienced with acceptance albeit after a delay.

Key idea: Worry as 'cognitive avoidance'

Worry, often described as 'What if?' thinking, tends focus on future catastrophes and one's perceived inability to cope. Research suggests that worry is primarily a *verbal* rather than *visual* process. Borkovec's influential 'cognitive avoidance' theory suggests that worry is actually a subtle attempt to *avoid* more acute anxiety. In part, worry involves trying to plan ways to avoid hypothetical problems. However, it is also avoidant in a more subtle way.

When problems are visualized concretely this allows natural emotional-processing, by allowing anxiety to peak but then reduce properly over time. By contrast, *worry* involves thinking about things in a vague, abstract way, skipping from one topic to another, and posing unanswerable questions. This keeps anxiety at a lower level by shifting attention away from anxiety-provoking images but also prevents anxious feelings from running their course and abating naturally (Sibrava & Borkovec, 2006). Worry itself may therefore be a form of 'experiential avoidance', as described in earlier chapters.

Remember this: Distinguishing worry from rumination

Worry and rumination are similar processes and sometimes the terms are used interchangeably. Both describe *prolonged thinking processes* associated with emotional distress. However, recently psychologists have distinguished more clearly between them. Essentially, 'worry' is more associated with feeling *anxious*, whereas 'rumination' is linked to *depressed* mood and sometimes brooding *anger*. Rumination can be spotted and postponed in a similar way to worry, although other strategies like relaxation and exposure may be less appropriate than mindfulness and acceptance-based responses. In fact, Borkovec's original experiments asked participants to consider postponing attention to *any* unhelpful or unpleasant thoughts, including both worry and rumination.

WHAT IS WORRY POSTPONEMENT?

After initial experiments showing that a simple behaviour therapy technique called 'stimulus control' could be used to manage worry, Borkovec developed a more sophisticated form of Cognitive-Behavioural Therapy (CBT) for GAD using Applied Relaxation. His approach was originally combined with standard cognitive therapy but has more recently been integrated with mindfulness and acceptance-based approaches.

This chapter draws mainly upon Borkovec's treatment for worry, particularly the basic 'stimulus control' method, which essentially involves managing the environment in which worry habitually occurs. The basic 'stimulus control' method for managing worry, or 'worry postponement', is usually defined in terms of a few brief instructions (Borkovec & Sharpless, 2004, p. 226). The three steps below are explained in this chapter:

1. **Worry recognition,** which involves developing more awareness of the early warning signs of worry, using self-monitoring records, and distinguishing unhelpful worry from helpful thinking, so the 'worry spiral' can be interrupted at the earliest possible stage before it escalates.
2. **Worry postponement**, which means immediately preventing responses that might prolong worry and delaying further worry or thinking about the problem until a more suitable time; attention is then focused on concrete present-moment experience and any task-at-hand.
3. **Worry time**, which usually takes place at the same specified time and place each day and may just involve expressing worries to yourself, although a variety of other CBT strategies are sometimes used at this stage, particularly problem-solving and mental imagery techniques.

There's a time and a place for everything, including thinking through problems. The most obvious time when worry is inappropriate is late at night, when you're trying to fall asleep. Virtually no problems are solved by worrying in bed, when trying to sleep; however, certain problems are definitely *caused* in this way. Indeed, it's a good idea to postpone worry whenever it's interfering with your quality of life or ability to pursue valued goals, etc., particularly if basic 'acceptance' and 'defusion' techniques don't prevent it from recurring. Hence, people often feel reluctant to stop worrying because at some level they assume it helps to protect them against looming threats by giving them an opportunity to problem-solve and rehearse coping strategies, although it seldom does so very effectively and normally causes anxiety to escalate instead.

Remember this: Abandon worry suppression

It's essential to understand the fact that worry *postponement* is not the same as worry *suppression*, and shouldn't be misused as a form of *experiential avoidance*. For that reason, it's sometimes helpful to make sure you actually do use your worry time initially, so that you're clear that worries set aside will definitely be returned to properly later. Anxious avoidance will tend to contribute to the sense that you're unable to cope with worry, whereas prescribed worry time is designed to help you build confidence in your ability to cope with worry more constructively.

Borkovec's CBT approach to treating worry and generalized anxiety has already been integrated with Acceptance and Commitment Therapy (ACT) (Roemer & Orsillo, 2002). Worry can be understood as a form of 'experiential avoidance' of the kind ACT aims to undermine and replace with mindful acceptance and valued action. However, the 'stimulus control' method (postponement) offers an alternative, but compatible, way of preventing worry from spiralling in response to initial unpleasant thoughts and feelings.

Consider this analogy: during mindfulness meditation practice, if you were to think of a problem that demands your attention, rather than worry about it, you might say to yourself, 'This isn't the right time to think about it but I will come back to this and deal with it later, when I've finished meditating'. It would be quite natural to postpone thinking about problems in many other situations, particularly when worries occur late at night and threaten to stop you getting to sleep.

APPLICATIONS AND RESEARCH

Borkovec's initial experiments found that among college students who suffered from worry, using the most basic form of the 'stimulus control' method for four weeks led to the percentage of time spent worrying reducing by almost half. They also reported significant reductions in associated muscular tension as well as the frequency of *unrealistic* fears. Although everyone worries, more severe worry is a common feature of both depression and anxiety disorders. As mentioned earlier, Generalized Anxiety Disorder (GAD) is the clinical problem most associated with chronic, severe worry. Many research studies have shown that CBT, including Borkovec's approach, which generally includes some form of worry postponement, can be of benefit to people suffering from GAD.

WORRY AND RESILIENCE

Established resilience-building approaches like the Penn Resiliency Programme (PRP) use traditional CBT techniques to manage negative emotions by challenging negative automatic thoughts, as *prevention* for more severe anxiety and depression. However, modern CBT has increasingly focused on the *process* of negative thinking as well as the *content* of individual thoughts. As worry is a distressing part of normal life, it might stand to reason that everyone else can benefit from learning to handle it in much the same way as individuals suffering from diagnosable emotional disorders. Indeed, the basic 'stimulus control' method has been used successfully with both mild (non-clinical) and severe (clinical) worry, from college students who suffer from ordinary stress to patients diagnosed with full-blown GAD.

Moreover, according to Borkovec, research suggests GAD may be the most 'basic' emotional disorder among adults and that understanding how to treat worry, its core feature, may provide the key to more general prevention and treatment strategies for other forms of clinical anxiety and depression (Borkovec & Sharpless, 2004, p. 209). For example, GAD typically occurs alongside other mental health problems and when it is treated first, by reducing worry, they generally improve as a result. Worry is a rigid, habitual style of responding to problems, overcoming which may lead to greater psychological flexibility and resilience. Borkovec specifically contrasts the rigid, 'stuck' nature of worry with research showing the value of more *flexible* coping styles in the stress literature. He also points to the role of mental flexibility among *resilient* children who cope well with subsequent trauma, and its correlation with playfulness, optimism and humour.

CASE STUDY

Postponing worry

Alec was prone to worry about a variety of subjects, which made him generally feel quite anxious, although his symptoms weren't quite severe enough to meet the criteria for diagnosing Generalized Anxiety Disorder (GAD). He worried about his health, his relationships, his family, and his studies and work, and also about minor daily hassles such as being late for meetings, etc. After we first met, he began keeping a simple record of his worry episodes and their duration. He immediately recognized that he was spending an unnecessary and excessive amount of time worrying about things, although he often described this as 'planning' or 'thinking things through'. It was nevertheless clear that he had a tendency to focus on the worst-case scenario and his perceived inability to cope with problems, which escalated rapidly into unrealistic, catastrophic fears.

When he realized how much time he was wasting on pointless worry, he immediately wanted to reduce its frequency and duration. He'd also been spotting 'early warning signs', in particular noticing that he tended to glaze over or stare at a spot, and tense his shoulders, as episodes of worry began to take hold. He was seldom at home in the evenings and so we agreed that it might be more practical to mark his worry time by holding an object of his choosing, a special stone, at 7pm each day, to signal he was doing worry time. At all other times, he watched for early signs of worry and postponed it. Although this seemed hard at first, he kept a simple log that showed the frequency and duration of his worry halved within 1–2 weeks and this was closely followed by a reduction in his overall level of anxiety, and other symptoms.

Assessment and worry recognition

UNHELPFUL WORRY VERSUS HELPFUL THINKING

In order to spot worry, it helps to be able to recognize the differences between worry and more productive types of thinking. Some psychologists talk about 'productive' (*helpful*) versus 'unproductive' (*unhelpful*) worry. Others prefer to assume that 'worry' is, by definition, pretty unhelpful and to be *contrasted* with terms like 'problem-solving' or 'constructive thinking'. For the sake of clarity, in this chapter we'll adopt the latter terminology, so here 'worry' will mean something generally *unhelpful* compared to rational problem-solving.

The psychologist Robert Leahy has written an excellent CBT self-help book called *The Worry Cure* (2005), which contains a very useful chapter describing the difference between 'unproductive' worry and so-called 'productive' worry, such as rational problem-solving. The sections below combine some of Leahy's observations with some additional points to look out for:

Unhelpful worry

- Focus on imponderable, vague, or unanswerable ('What if?', 'How will I cope?') questions that go round in circles.
- Turns into a chain-reaction of escalating worries about numerous different things.
- Intolerance of risk and uncertainty: Solutions have to be perfect, certain to work, or they're discounted.
- You keep on worrying because you feel it's not absolutely safe to stop until your anxiety reduces.
- You worry about things that can't be changed or aren't under your control.
- Your worry is vague and abstract, mainly consisting of self-talk.
- You become engrossed in your worries, lose track of time, and react as if the worst-case scenario is imminent and looming.
- You become focused on the *possibility* of various worst-case scenarios, regardless of their (lack of) *probability*.

Rational problem-solving ('helpful worry')

- Specific questions are posed and answered more conclusively.
- Focused on addressing one single, specific event at a time.
- Solutions just have to be good enough to probably be worth trying, and a degree of risk and uncertainty is tolerable.
- Even if you're still anxious, you cease thinking things over when it's no longer necessary or helpful.
- You accept things that can't be changed and focus on changing things that are under your control.
- You picture the problem in concrete, detailed terms, using mental imagery.
- You retain awareness of worry as a mental process, how much time it takes, and how 'urgent' various problems really are.
- You focus on the *probability* of things happening and how you plan to cope with the *most-likely* scenario.

Self-assessment: Distinguishing helpful from unhelpful worry

Use the questions below to help evaluate your typical experience of worry over the past couple of weeks, rating how strongly you agree with each statement from 0 (not at all) to 5 (agree completely):

1 My worries are focused on one specific, clearly defined, issue at a time (/5)
2 When I worry I'm looking for solutions that are good enough to be worth trying rather than the perfect solution (/5)
3 Even if I still feel anxious, I stop worrying when I stop making progress towards a solution (/5)
4 My thinking is focused on what's under my control to change and I'm able to accept things that are outside my power (/5)
5 I'm aware of how long I spend worrying rather than losing track of time (/5)
6 I focus on what's probable, the likely-case scenario, rather than what's merely possible, such as the worst-case scenario (/5)

Again, rather than totalling your scores, look at your individual responses. How could you change your attitude and behaviour to get your scores closer to five on each item? What would be the consequences if you did?

Remember this: Recognizing unhelpful worry

People often don't realize that what they're doing is unproductive worry and talk instead about trying to 'solve problems', 'plan how to cope', 'analyse things', 'dwelling on what can go wrong', 'focusing on the worst-case scenario', etc. These are potentially just different ways of describing worry, though. Watch out in general for prolonged periods of time spent thinking about future or potential problems, resulting in greater anxiety – that may just be *worry*.

SPOTTING EARLY WARNING SIGNS OF WORRY

We've already looked in some detail at the process of self-monitoring and spotting 'early warning signs' of emotional distress in the chapter on Applied Relaxation. Because worry entails focusing attention on future catastrophes, etc., that often means a lack of awareness of the 'here and now', in terms of bodily sensations and the external situation, *what* you're doing and *where* you are. Hence, it often takes practice to spot the early stages of worry before being swept along by the spiral of anxious thoughts and feelings. For instance, frowning is a common sign of worry, as are other muscular tensions like teeth-clenching and hunching the shoulders, or movements such as fidgeting with the hands, etc.

As worry tends to involve prolonged mental abstraction, it's also often associated with the eyes defocusing, gazing into the distance, or even closing. These are all potentially warning signs to look out for. A typical self-monitoring record for worry might include the headings in the table below (Newman & Borkovec, 2002, p. 153). Recording the *duration* of episodes of worry can help draw attention to the desirability of interrupting them, rather than losing track of time and allowing worry to spiral freely.

Date/ Time	*Early warning signs*	*Worry topic*	*Anxiety (%)*	*Duration (Min.)*

Try it now: 'How do you worry?' (Imagery-recall exercise)

Close your eyes for a few minutes and try to reproduce what happens when you worry. Think of it as a sequence of events, perhaps even going through the stages several times in slow motion. If it helps, try to identify the earliest thoughts that start the chain-reaction of worry, and also the earliest sensations you feel, and how changes in your behaviour or facial expression begin. Notice, for instance, if you tend to pose questions such as 'What if something bad happens?' or 'How will I cope?'

You might think of worry as having a *beginning*, *middle* and *end*, although the end, the underlying fear, is seldom arrived at but may lurk in the background. What's the thought you start with? What's the worst-case scenario or your greatest fear in relation to these worries? What specific thoughts and questions come in-between, forming the escalating spiral of prolonged worry? Do you ever really confront the worst-case scenario or just skirt around it? How realistic is it? So what if it *did* happen? Could you cope with and survive even that?

Worry-postponement strategies

The first thing to realize about postponement of worry is that most people report that, with practice and when approached in the right way, doing it is easier than they presupposed. As worry is often very clearly unhelpful, simply *spotting it early* can lead you to interrupt the spiral by choosing not to spend time dwelling on it further. It often helps to write down the topic of the worry on a self-monitoring record (see above). This should just be one or two words, to avoid dwelling on it for longer: 'Work', 'Relationship', 'Health', 'Financial problems', etc. Writing the topic down, and then putting the form away, can be seen as a gesture emphasizing to yourself that you're postponing the worry and returning your attention to the present moment instead.

It's also important to realize that you will usually need to postpone worry *repeatedly*. After deciding to postpone worry, especially at first, it's fairly normal to catch yourself beginning to worry again a few moments later. Just keep postponing it each time it returns, no matter how often. This will become much easier with practice. Remember that postponement shouldn't feel like an attempt to avoid or suppress unpleasant experiences, though. You must intend to return to the subject you're worrying about at a later time. Worry can often be postponed relatively easily, with practice, if a later time has been set aside to return to it. However, there are also some strategies, discussed below, which may help you to let go of your worries and set the problem aside.

Key idea: Postponement and worry time

Your specified worry period should ideally be at the same time, and in the same place, each day, to develop an automatic psychological *association* between worry and that setting. This will also progressively help you to break the association with other times and places, as you increasingly confine your worry within certain bounds. For example, worry time might be sitting in a specific chair at home from 7–7.30pm each evening. You should *always* postpone worry that arises at inappropriate times and places, such as when lying in bed trying to fall asleep at night.

If you do find yourself struggling to postpone worry at any time then you should go straight to your worry place to worry for a limited time, if possible. For example, while trying to get to sleep at night, if you find yourself unable to stop worrying after about 15–20 minutes of repeated attempts at postponement then it's better to just get out of bed, go to your worry place, and focus on your worries, using the worry-time approach below, until you're bored with worrying and ready to sleep. Of course, there will be times where you may find it difficult to postpone worry and a realistic 'hit rate' to aim for at first might be to spot and postpone worry at least 75 per cent of the time it arises. Recommendations for worry time vary but it's common to pick the same specific time and place every day.

Remember this: Adapt worry time to fit your life

If it's difficult to do it in the same place then try introducing a more portable 'cue', for example, holding a particular object, such as a pebble, keyring or tennis ball. This can function as a signal that you're doing your specified worry time, and postponing worry whenever you're not holding the object.

If worry is very frequent, and difficult to confine, as Borkovec suggests, it's sometimes easier to plan 'worry-free zones' instead. That entails banning (postponing) worry at certain times or places ('zones') and only allowing yourself to worry for up to 30 minutes at other times. For instance, you might initially designate driving to work or lying in bed at night as worry-free zones. Gradually more times and places are declared 'worry-free', and worry becomes progressively confined, until it's limited to a specific 30-minute worry time.

SELF-INSTRUCTION

Making a brief verbal statement ('self-instruction') to yourself may help you focus on your decision to postpone worry (Newman & Borkovec, 2002, p. 154). For example, as soon as you notice early warning signs of worry, or high-risk situations, you might take that as a signal to respond immediately by confidently instructing yourself:

> ***'I know I usually tend to worry in bed at night and I notice I'm starting to tense my shoulders and think about problems at work... Now isn't the right time to think about this... I'm going to just write down the topic and I'll think about it properly later, during my specified worry time.'***

If the worry creeps back you can instruct yourself, 'It's written down in my worry record already; I'll think about it properly later.' Keep your self-instructions concise and be confident in saying them, avoid them sneakily turning into an internal monologue about coping with the worry. In fact, you should aim to 'fade' your self-instructions over time, if possible, learning to focus on the idea of postponement, in the right attitude of mind, without the effort of giving yourself any specific verbal instructions about how to do it.

PRESENT-MOMENT ATTENTION AND INTRINSIC VALUES

Worry alienates us from the reality of our present moment. Borkovec vividly describes how clients with GAD and even people with less severe worry, are unintentionally 'spending their time in an illusory world of future-oriented thoughts' full of anxiety. Anxiety in general is strongly associated with apprehensive thoughts about *future* threats. One of the most obvious characteristics of worry, in particular, is that it involves prolonged thinking about hypothetical catastrophes in the future, and how we might struggle to cope with them.

Worry is therefore also associated with a marked *inattention* to the present moment, both your environment and behaviour, i.e., *where you are and what you're doing*. While deeply absorbed in severe worry, for example, a person may not notice the telephone ring, they may not realize that they are currently grinding their teeth or chewing their nails, etc. In a sense, during worry we rehearse living an imagined life, in which we become distressed 'as if' hypothetical catastrophes were actually occurring around us. Many people mindlessly squander the best part of their lives in the 'fantasy zone' of worry, oblivious to the real world around them as life passes them by each day.

The ability to savour present-moment experience, training ourselves to pay more attention to the 'here and now' reality of our behaviour and environment, is therefore virtually the *polar opposite* of worry and can be deliberately used as an antidote to it. In Borkovec's original stimulus-control approach, attention is trained to the present-moment by closing your eyes and focusing on the smallest sensations in the body for a while, each time worry is postponed. Progressively this can be done also with the eyes still open, and during various activities, to attune to the 'here and now' more fully. As soon as worry about hypothetical future events is spotted and recorded, attention is shifted on to the reality of the present moment instead.

If you're performing some task, then present-moment attention involves giving your attention more fully to that activity, engaging your whole being with it, something Borkovec calls the 'whole-organism approach'. Moreover, it's possible to become fully present to the 'here and now' by focusing on the quality of the process you're engaged in, and its *intrinsic value*, rather than its possible outcome or consequence. Ironically, when people are focused on the process of their behaviour, and *let go* of attention to the outcome, their performance often improves and positive consequences are more likely to follow. Hence, worry postponement has been integrated with some of the mindfulness and acceptance-based strategies discussed earlier, especially becoming 'centred' in the present moment and 'engaged' with intrinsically valued action.

APPLIED RELAXATION, MINDFULNESS AND ACCEPTANCE

We've described Applied Relaxation as a general-purpose coping skill in more detail elsewhere. However, modern psychologists note that often 'trying to relax' is used in a superficial way that backfires. When using relaxation to cope with worry, it's therefore important to first accept signs of worry and then let go of any struggle or tension that's under voluntary control, continuing to accept any feelings that remain, without trying to *force* yourself to relax as a form of 'experiential avoidance'. Applied Relaxation normally employs a rapid 'cue-controlled' coping skill for general relaxation. However, Jacobson's Differential Relaxation approach can also be used by learning to selectively relax the specific muscles being tensed in the body at the outset of worry, especially those muscles associated with vision and speech. This should be thought of, as Jacobson emphasized, as 'not doing' tension, letting go and *ceasing* an activity, rather than as actively making an *effort* to relax.

Borkovec's approach, which combines Applied Relaxation with worry postponement, gradually extends the concept of 'letting go' of muscular tension to include 'letting go' also of reactions to initial anxious thoughts and feelings, particularly worry about the future.

> ***'Letting go' is described as mere observation of these internal reactions and of nonreaction to them, of detachment rather than attachment.***
>
> (Borkovec & Sharpless, 2004, p. 218).

Borkovec equates this with the strategy of willing 'acceptance' in approaches such as ACT, discussed in earlier chapters. An alternative way of 'not responding' to worry is therefore to adopt a more detached attitude to the initial thoughts, acknowledging them, mindfully, and accepting them, but neither suppressing nor worrying further about them. However, mindfulness and acceptance strategies can also be used without training in Applied Relaxation. For example, a similar method of deliberate 'non-reaction' to worries, called 'Detached Mindfulness', is described below, which resembles the 'open' response strategies of acceptance and defusion discussed in earlier chapters, as part of ACT.

Key idea: Mindfulness and acceptance of worry

Professor Adrian Wells of Manchester University has developed an influential mindfulness-based approach to the treatment of clinical anxiety and depression called Metacognitive Therapy (MCT) (Wells, 2009). Mindfulness and acceptance-based approaches are often used to deal with negative automatic thoughts in non-clinical populations, as a form of stress management. However, Wells' approach was specifically designed to be combined with *postponement* strategies used both in the treatment of depressive rumination and anxious worry and a number of initial studies have demonstrated its effectiveness. Wells' concept of 'Detached Mindfulness' has some similarities to other mindfulness and acceptance-based strategies, although there is greater emphasis on eliminating any kind of engagement with thoughts whatsoever and just 'doing nothing' in response to them, allowing them to come and go, and eventually fade naturally from awareness.

Try it now: The Tiger Task

A specific exercise, sometimes called the 'Tiger Task', is used to get an initial flavour of Detached Mindfulness.

1 First close your eyes and form an image of a tiger in your mind.

2 Now simply do nothing except observe the image for a few minutes, aware of it as an event in your mind, neither trying to change it nor stop it from changing.

You will probably find that mental images, if left alone, normally change automatically and then decay or fade from awareness. Picture your tiger and just let it have a life of its own, without trying to tell its story yourself, just let it do its own thing.

By contrast, take a few minutes to try to *suppress* the image of the tiger, avoiding thinking about it. You may find that difficult. Paradoxically, when we try 'not to think about' something, we tend to pay more attention to the very thing we're trying to suppress. Moreover, the more anxious or depressing thoughts are, the more attempts to suppress them may tend to backfire. You're not likely to be worried about tigers. However, once you have this knack of 'Detached Mindfulness' you can learn to use it instead of allowing yourself to engage in worry.

In Wells' approach, there's greater emphasis on treating initial *automatic thoughts* as the triggers for worry episodes rather than focusing on bodily sensations as early warning signs. When you spot the thoughts that tend to precede worry episodes, respond as you did with the tiger, using Detached Mindfulness, and postponing worry until a specified time and place. Wells differs slightly from others in recommending that you only actually use your worry time if you still feel the need to, and not to bother if the 'worry' no longer seems important.

Although Metacognitive Therapy is mainly a treatment for clinical anxiety and depression, Wells has also noted the relevance of his theory for emotional resilience:

> ***[Metacognitive Therapy] states that it is not the thought itself but the individual's reaction to that thought (or reaction to a belief) that determines its emotional and longer-term consequences for wellbeing. Some individuals are more resilient than others, which is probably because they are more flexible in their responses to negative thoughts and emotions.***
>
> (Fisher & Wells, 2009: 10)

Wells goes on to say, basically, that psychologically-resilient and flexible individuals are more able to cease morbid worry and rumination rather than becoming locked into patterns of prolonged negative thinking, which can cause greater emotional suffering over time.

Try it now: Practising Detached Mindfulness

Deliberately allow yourself to have the sort of thought that normally starts you worrying but practise Detached Mindfulness in response to it instead of worry:

1 Be mindful of the thought for a while, as merely an event in your mind and not the thing itself, whether or not it's true.
2 Detach your responses from the initial thought by postponing any thoughts or actions and simply doing nothing, not trying to change it in any way, or stop it from changing.

3 Take a step back and also rehearse detachment by viewing the thought as something observed, distinct from yourself, the observer, focusing on what it's like to feel a sense of distance from the thought.

It can be helpful, periodically, to allow yourself to 'free associate' and just observe your stream of consciousness in a detached and mindful way, without trying to change anything. By learning the knack of Detached Mindfulness at other times, it will help you to adopt the same attitude when worry potentially strikes.

Worry-time strategies

Now we've discussed the concept of *postponing* worry until a specified 'worry time', let's examine what to do later, when that time actually arrives. The first thing you may notice is that you will sometimes feel your worries are no longer important and choose not to think about them, in which case you may simply decide *not to use* your worry period. It's fine not to use your worry time, as long as this doesn't serve a larger pattern of experiential avoidance. If you do still feel a need to think about your worries, you may simply allow yourself to worry as normal, having confined it to your specified time and place. People often feel calmer at their worry time and therefore more able to think things through rationally and constructively. (In some cases, however, there may be reasons why you want to use your worry time more consistently, for example, if you're trying to use repeated 'worry exposure' strategies or Applied Relaxation, as discussed below.)

PROBLEM-SOLVING

Worry can often be understood as a *failed attempt at problem-solving*. This may take the form of trying to analyse a situation, plan how to cope, or prepare for adversity, but struggling to do so very *decisively*. As long as you can approach problem-solving systematically and avoid it turning into unhelpful rumination or worry, the kind of approach described in the chapter on 'problem-solving' may be very useful and can be used during worry time to develop a 'coping plan', i.e., a realistic action plan for dealing with your problems.

MINDFULNESS AND ACCEPTANCE

Of course, some worries may relate to things that are outside of your control or 'unsolvable' problems, leaving you with distressing thoughts and feelings that may be best addressed using the kind of acceptance and defusion strategies described in earlier chapters. Likewise, where problems can be solved but 'internal barriers to action' exist in the form of unpleasant thoughts and feelings, similar mindfulness and acceptance-based strategies may be appropriate.

'WORRY EXPOSURE' AND APPLIED RELAXATION USING IMAGERY

In addition to basic problem-solving and acceptance-based strategies, worry time is sometimes used as an opportunity to employ other techniques. A common strategy is to worry visually rather than verbally, picturing the worst-case scenario until your anxiety reduces by at least half. 'Worry exposure' involves facing your worst fears patiently in your imagination until your anxiety naturally reduces, simply because you get used to the experience. (Psychologists call this 'habituation' through prolonged 'imaginal exposure'.) This may require trying to uncover the core fear underlying your worry, your 'nightmare' scenario, and writing a detailed description of it. You can read this 'catastrophe script' repeatedly to help you keep picturing the worst-case vividly and long enough to allow anxiety to naturally abate.

Applied Relaxation for worry typically involves using a similar technique called 'Self-control Desensitization' during worry time, discussed in an earlier chapter. When Applied Relaxation is used in this way, in the imagination, rapid relaxation coping skills are repeatedly employed during an abbreviated form of exposure to mental imagery concerning the worst-case scenarios being worried about, which may take less than five minutes in some cases.

DECATASTROPHIZING AND GENERATION OF ALTERNATIVES

Traditional cognitive therapy employs techniques that involve disputing beliefs about the *probability* and *severity* of catastrophes worried about by evaluating the evidence relating to them. The approach we've adopted throughout this book is based on more recent, 'mindfulness and acceptance-based', approaches that evolved partly in response to the limitations of traditional cognitive therapy.

Mindfulness and acceptance-based approaches place more emphasis on the way you respond to your thoughts rather than the truth or falsehood of their content. Disputing worries can be difficult and it sometimes backfires by encouraging people to spend even more time dwelling on them and taking them seriously, or 'fusing' with their content. However, some cognitive therapy techniques can potentially help acceptance and defusion, if used in the right way.

For example, a simple technique that's sometimes used to change anxious thinking is to end your worry time by brainstorming as many *different perspectives* on the problem as you can think of. Your goal isn't necessarily to evaluate these, in terms of their truth or probability, but simply to develop an awareness of multiple perspectives on the same problem. (You'll see in the chapter on 'problem-solving' that alternative solutions to a problem are often brainstormed in this way.) These 'alternatives' may take two forms:

1 A variety of possible options or solutions, i.e., practical ways of coping.
2 Different ways of interpreting the meaning of a feared situation, e.g., in terms of the probability of harm and how severe the consequences might be.

Borkovec recommends that humour and playfulness are also used as ways of generating multiple perspectives. Just the awareness that a wide *variety* of perspectives or possible solutions exist can create greater *psychological flexibility*, which seems to be protective against further emotional disturbance. It also forces you to treat your existing viewpoint as just one of many – as a kind of *hypothesis* – and this may help you defuse it from reality and respond to it in a more detached way. As Borkovec suggests, you may naturally evaluate some perspectives as more realistic or helpful than others. It can sometimes be helpful to focus on more rational perspectives by writing them down and rehearsing them in imagination and in response to early warning signs of worry.

The term 'decatastrophizing' is used to refer to a number of different strategies used to re-evaluate a feared event that's seen in overly-catastrophic terms. Arnold Lazarus, one of the founders of behaviour therapy, said that a very simple form of decatastrophizing is to get into the habit of responding to anxious '*What if…?*' thoughts with '*So what if…?*', shifting focus on to ideas about coping emotionally or at a practical level. 'What if the sky falls on our heads?' said *Chicken Little*. 'So what if it does?', might be a rational response, 'There's nothing you can do about it so there's no point worrying.' In the Penn Resilience Programme, for example, worry is challenged using decatastrophizing strategies from traditional cognitive therapy, such as the 'worst, best, most-likely' technique below.

Try it now: Worst, best, and most-likely scenarios

Worry tends to involve focusing on the worst-case scenario, even if it's quite unlikely to happen. That not only fuels anxiety but also distracts attention from more realistic predictions and opportunities to be pursued. Sometimes it helps to explore the range of possible outcomes that can happen in a situation by carefully answering questions like the following:

1. What's the worst that you fear might happen?
2. What's the best that you hope could happen?
3. What's most likely to actually happen in reality?
4. How could you best cope with the most likely scenario?

Doing this once might be helpful but it's usually more helpful to get into a habit of doing this systematically whenever you have time to re-evaluate your worries, for example, during prescribed worry time. It may also be helpful to develop a list of steps describing how you would actually cope if the worst-case scenario actually happened, called a 'coping plan'. Sometimes you may find that the worst-case scenario you worry about isn't even realistic and is impossible or astronomically unlikely to happen. You may also find that when you think a problem through in concrete terms, particularly how you're likely to cope with the consequences over time, it may seem less catastrophic than it first appeared. Be cautious when using these techniques, though, that they don't lead into *over-analysis* of your worries and cause further fusion with your upsetting thoughts.

Maintaining resilience through worry postponement

More recently, Borkovec has described the ultimate goal of his approach to treating worry and generalized anxiety as being to fundamentally overcome rigid, 'stuck', patterns of anxious thoughts, actions and feelings. This involves living more in the present-moment, letting go of worry in general and gradually adopting a more flexible attitude he calls 'expectancy-free living', throughout the whole day (Borkovec & Sharpless, 2004, p. 227). Learning to spot unnecessary worries about the future and instead focus on the concrete present moment throughout the day may become part of your way of life, and a source of general psychological flexibility and resilience over time.

The main points to remember from this chapter are:

FOCUS POINTS

- It's perfectly natural to postpone thinking about worries at certain times, e.g., when trying to sleep or engaged in exercise or meditation, etc.
- Learning to choose when you think about worries will give you a greater sense of flexibility and allow you to become more attuned to the present moment instead.
- It can be difficult to recognize or spot worry at first but this will become easier with practice, if you keep a self-monitoring record; spotting worry early makes it easier to postpone to a specified worry time.
- Don't confuse worry *postponement* with worry *suppression*; you shouldn't let worry postponement turn into a form of experiential avoidance.
- Just thinking about problems during your worry time is sufficient for many people to manage their worry, although you may also choose to engage in more systematic problem-solving or employ other therapy strategies, such as imagined exposure, relaxation, or decastrophizing at this time.

NEXT STEP

In the next chapter, you'll learn about a methodological approach to problem-solving, which can be used instead of worrying about problems. Problem-solving modes of thinking can lead to experiential avoidance when you try to 'fix' unpleasant thoughts and feelings. Change strategies that work in the external world can backfire when applied to internal experiences. However, some of the things you worry about are likely to be practical problems, in the real world, that are best dealt with using some form of problem-solving.

Further reading

Leahy, R. L. (2005). *The Worry Cure: Stop Worrying & Start Living.*

10

Problem-Solving Training

In this chapter you will learn:

- *How to assess and improve your general problem-solving* attitude *and orientation*
- *How to* define *your problems and goals objectively, and formulate them in ways that help you find solutions*
- *How to creatively* brainstorm *a wide variety of potential solutions, including both general* strategies *and specific* tactics
- *How to evaluate your options and* make a decision *about the best solution available*
- *How to develop an* action plan *and put it into practice effectively*

> ***The important thing is not so much to know how to solve a problem as to know how to look for a solution.***
>
> Skinner, *Beyond Freedom & Dignity*

The importance of problem-solving

WHAT IS PROBLEM-SOLVING TRAINING (PST)?

Problem-Solving Therapy, or Training (PST), is the name of a specific methodology developed by the behaviour therapists D'Zurilla and Goldfried in the early 1970s to help people become more skilled and confident at solving everyday problems of living, and coping with more serious life events (D'Zurilla & Goldfried, 1971). It's a simple, pragmatic, action-oriented approach that has been used quite extensively as a way of coping with stress and both as a *prevention* and *therapy* for clinical depression, and as a major component of treatment for generalized anxiety. Sometimes it's used as a stand-alone treatment but often as a component of other common cognitive-behavioural therapies. It's likely that having a positive attitude towards problem-solving in general, and being confident and optimistic about the process, constitutes an important part of psychological resilience, helping to prevent future anxiety and depression.

The most widely used approach describes problem-solving in terms of two main ingredients:

1 'Problem orientation', whether you have a 'positive' or 'negative' attitude towards life's problems in general, which we will analyse into several components below.
2 'Problem-solving style', which can be classed as either unhelpful (termed 'impulsive/careless' or 'avoidant') or helpful (termed 'rational').

Rational and constructive problem-solving, for the purposes of training, is roughly divided into *four* basic skills and stages, which we will be exploring in more detail below:

1 'Problem definition and formulation', which refers to the process of accurately and objectively summarizing a problem and pinpointing the main obstacles to be overcome in achieving specific goals.
2 'Generation of alternatives', the process of creatively brainstorming a broad range of potential solutions, i.e., identifying a variety of options.
3 'Decision making', predicting the likely consequences of different potential solutions and evaluating them sufficiently before making a rational choice between them or arriving at a combination of them.
4 'Solution implementation and verification', which involves actually putting the appropriate steps into action and evaluating the outcome.

In the real world, problem-solving needs to be flexible and adaptive. Learning to distinguish between these ingredients and trying to improve them can be helpful, especially when first developing a more positive problem-solving attitude. However, in some situations you will need to make 'snap decisions' and solve problems more rapidly, which may also require increasing confidence in your ability to act more spontaneously. In particular, be careful not to allow problem-solving to get into rigid, stuck patterns of thinking. Try to reconcile learning a methodology with maintaining a sense of psychological flexibility.

Key idea: Problem-solving

So what do we mean by 'problem-solving'? Well, to use the standard analogy, imagine that problem-solving is like a *journey*, or the task of finding your way through 'one of life's mazes'. What we term the 'problem' is your *starting position* and so we can call your *destination* the 'goal, from A to B. By 'solutions' we mean *possible routes* through the maze, taking you from start (your problem) to destination (your goal). Solutions and goals are often confused so, to be clear, solutions are ways of achieving your goal, the means to the end. There may be several viable paths through every maze, i.e., as the saying goes: there's more than one way to skin a cat. In other words, there's usually more than one potential solution to any given problem.

We might also incorporate the notion of 'values', discussed earlier. 'Values' refer to the general *quality* or *direction* of your actions and therefore apply to each step of the 'journey', right from the outset. For example, you might define your *problem* as bullying at work, your *goal* as having the matter investigated properly, your relevant *values* being to act with integrity and courage, and possible *solutions* being to speak informally first to your boss, to write to your HR department, to email your union representative, etc. (These elements would all normally be described in slightly more detail, of course.)

The pursuit of valued living, discussed earlier, will often lead you to encounter certain *barriers to action*. You can roughly distinguish between:

1 Internal barriers to action, in the form of thoughts and feelings, such as worry and anxiety, which it may be unhelpful to try to control or avoid rather than defuse and accept
2 External barriers to action, in the form of practical or social problems to be solved, which may be more easily overcome through rational planning of actions.

Where internal, psychological barriers occur, *mindfulness* and *acceptance* strategies are the first thing you should consider, rather than trying to apply problem-solving methods of the kind that work in the external world. However, where genuine external (practical or social) problems are getting in the way of your valued goals then rational problem-solving is often more appropriate. This will help you plan different practical solutions that will allow you to achieve goals, in accord with your personal values.

RESEARCH AND APPLICATIONS

Problem-solving has been used with a wide variety of different populations and problems, both to *prevent* mental health issues and as a *therapy* for them. It's often been used to treat depression, improve coping skills, handle stressful situations, manage crises, and prevent relapse in areas like addiction. Recently, a substantial body of evidence has accumulated from clinical trials showing that it is effective as a treatment for clinical depression (Bell & D'Zurilla, 2009). It is also used as a major component of evidence-based treatment for Generalized Anxiety Disorder (GAD). However, problem-solving has often been understood as a very generic set of skills for coping with stressful life events of all kinds, which therefore lends itself to general resilience-building.

A recent review ('meta-analysis') of research on Problem-Solving Training (PST) pooled statistical data from 31 well-designed studies, involving a total of 2,895 participants (Malouff, Thorsteinsson & Schutte, 2007). The authors found that on average PST was substantially more effective than either placebo or 'treatment as usual', across a diverse range of client groups with problems such as clinical depression, childhood conduct disorder, obesity, alcoholism, substance abuse, back pain, etc.

PROBLEM-SOLVING AND RESILIENCE

Problem-Solving Training is therefore a very simple and flexible coping strategy which can be used to address a wide range of practical problems, making it an ideal method for building general resiliency. Indeed, basic research in the field of stress over the past few decades has generally shown planned problem-solving to be one of the most reliable ways of coping with challenging life events. However, the specific strategies required to cope well with stress appear to vary considerably from one person to another and one situation to another. Nevertheless, one of the strengths of PST is its flexibility in this regard. It provides an over-arching methodology for planning more specific coping strategies tailored for individual problems.

The concept of '*negative* problem-orientation', like that of 'experiential avoidance', describes a set of attitudes that appear to be correlated with severe anxiety and depression. It's likely that '*positive* problem-orientation', by contrast, may describe a construct similar to 'psychological flexibility' and *resilience*. Problem-solving training is therefore integral to several existing forms of resilience-building such as Neenan's Cognitive-Behavioural Therapy (CBT) approach (Neenan, 2009, pp. 85–87) and Seligman's Penn Resiliency Programme (Seligman, 1995, pp. 241–261). A general-purpose self-help guide has been published by the leading authorities in this area, entitled *Solving Life's Problems* (Nezu, Nezu, & D'Zurilla, 2007).

CASE STUDY

Problem-solving for bullying at work

Sarah was being bullied at work by another colleague who she believed was 'after her job'. There are several ways this problem could have been defined but Sarah chose to sum it up as follows: She had a problem being bullied at work, wanted to have the other person's behaviour investigated properly and ideally for her to be dismissed, but previous attempts to raise the matter with her boss had been ignored. This was an interpersonal problem and could have been addressed using assertiveness training but Sarah wanted to improve her confidence in her ability to tackle problems independently and problem-solving provided her with a more flexible way of approaching things. She identified a number of possible strategies and tactics, including:

- Do nothing: Just try to ignore problem, try to keep out of bully's way.
- Speak to boss again directly: Ask to discuss matter in office, send him a letter, send an email.
- Get support: Ask another witness to accompany her in making complaint, seek advice from her union representative.
- Escalate the complaint: Go above her boss's head to the regional office.

After evaluating the likely consequences of these and other options, and rating them in terms of their difficulty and likelihood of success, she decided her best option initially would be to enlist the support of another member of staff and together approach their union representative before arranging a face-to-face meeting with her boss, with others present. She also chose this plan of action because it was consistent with her values in relation to work, *integrity* and *assertiveness* being qualities she wanted to exhibit in her actions.

Sarah planned the steps and put them into action, paying particular attention to the first step in the process, which involved emailing her union representative for their initial advice. In fact, this raised some unanticipated problems, which became obstacles, but Sarah wasn't deterred and continued to apply the problem-solving approach repeatedly, until she finally succeeded in achieving her goal of having the matter investigated properly. The bully subsequently resigned and Sarah's circumstances finally improved as a result.

Assessing your problem-solving attitude

The problem-domain analysis exercise below will help you to identify specific goals in different domains of your life that you may want to address using the problem-solving exercises that follow.

Self-assessment: Problem-domain analysis

These questions are is used to help provide a comprehensive overview of problems that you face in different areas of life. They will help you to focus on the domains or areas of life that seem most problematic and clarify what you're trying to achieve, the obstacles you're facing, what you're trying to do to resolve things, and how much you worry about it.

Satisfaction and problems

How satisfied are you in each domain below (0–100%)? Why is it not 100%? What specific problems are you facing?

1. **Relationships** (children, family, partner, friends)
2. **Work and study** (career, personal development)
3. **Self-care** (mental and physical health, and general wellbeing)
4. **Lifestyle** (Leisure activities, finances, daily routine)
5. **Other** (please specify)

Values, goals and obstacles

For the domain(s) above where you're experiencing most problems, try to answer the following additional questions:

1 **Values.** What are your most important values in this domain? What sort of person do you want to be in this area of your life?
2 **Goals.** What specific goals or outcomes would serve your values in each domain? What's the best you can hope to achieve?
3 **Obstacles.** What obstacles or barriers to valued action do you face? Why haven't you achieved your goals already?
4 **Current coping.** What are you currently trying to do to solve the problem(s)? What have you tried in the past? How well does that work? How consistent is it with your values in this domain?
5 **Worries.** What do you fear might go wrong in this domain? What's the worst that could happen? How much time do you spend worrying about it?

PROBLEM-SOLVING ATTITUDE

To solve difficult or challenging problems it's essential to adopt a favourable attitude or mind-set throughout the whole process. In fact, there's some reason to believe this may be the most influential factor in problem-solving. In other words, having a favourable attitude towards solving problems may make you more resilient than following specific steps. However, there's probably a circular relationship between attitude and skills as learning a methodological approach may improve your underlying confidence and optimism, your problem-solving attitude.

'Problem-solving orientation' or attitude is defined by researchers in terms of the following key ingredients:

1 **Recognition.** *Spotting* problems early, recognizing them accurately, and treating them as cues to begin problem-solving rather than overlooking or discounting them.

2 **Attribution**. Accurately identifying the specific *causes* of a problem, the things maintaining it in the 'here and now', rather than blaming it on vague causes (including blaming yourself or others unhelpfully) or focusing too much on its historical origins.
3 **Appraisal**. Seeing problems as *challenges-to-be-met* or even *opportunities-to-be-seized* rather than *threats-to-be-avoided*, i.e., viewing them calmly rather than catastrophically.
4 **Control**. Accurately identifying the aspects of a problem that are under your control and being *confident* about finding a solution that's likely to work.
5 **Commitment**. Realistically judging the *time and effort* required and being willing to commit to action, in the service of your goals and values, in a 'timely' manner, neither rushing nor procrastinating.

Psychologists actually speak about someone's general problem-solving orientation as being positive or negative, i.e., helpful or unhelpful. Negative problem-orientation, as we've seen, appears to be associated with mental health issues like anxiety and depression. Positive problem-orientation may be an important part of psychological resilience. It's also worth comparing the concept of problem orientation to the discussion of '*productive* and *unproductive worry*' in the chapter on that subject. Unhelpful worry tends to be based upon a negative problem orientation.

Try it now: Evaluating your problem-solving attitude

Try to rate your current problem-solving attitude as honestly as possible on the questions below (0–5), after having read the descriptions above:

1 *Recognition*. How good are you at spotting problems early on and initiating a rational problem-solving response? (/5)
2 *Attribution*. How accurately do you attribute problems to the specific things that are currently maintaining them and need to be changed? (/5)

3 *Appraisal.* How realistically do you estimate in advance the relevance of problems to your personal goals and values, and the probability and severity of any harmful consequences? (/5)
4 *Control.* How well do you estimate in advance your ability to cope with problems effectively? (/5)
5 *Commitment.* How committed are you to investing sufficient time and effort in solving problems? (/5)

What could you do to try to increase all of your attitude scores so that they're closer to 5/5? Begin taking steps now, if possible. If you're stuck, then you might be able to incorporate 'improving your problem-solving orientation' into a specific problem definition and use the steps below to find a solution. (We could call that 'problem-solving squared'!)

Problem-solving methodology

DEFINING YOUR PROBLEM AND GOALS

What's the problem you're trying to solve? What are the facts? What can you realistically hope to achieve? Once you've adopted a favourable attitude, problem definition and formulation, describing your problem and identifying its causes is obviously going to be the first practical step in rational problem-solving.

Key idea: Problem definition and formulation

'A problem well-defined is half solved,' said the American philosopher John Dewey. It's quite common for people to struggle because they haven't taken time to formulate problems and goals properly, which tends to lead to confusion, mistakes or procrastination. A good problem definition is concise: a couple of sentences. It sticks to the facts, using concrete *descriptive* language rather than evaluations or inferences. Formulating your problem means explaining how it functions: what are the *current* causes? The word 'cause' is ambiguous, though. The historical *origins* probably don't matter as much as what's currently *maintaining* your problem. What barriers to action (obstacles) prevent you from achieving your goal? In other words, what's prevented you from overcoming it already?

A typical example of a problem definition might be:

I have a 3,000 word essay to write by the end of the week but I find it difficult to concentrate at home because of the noise my children make. How can I get finished on time and make it a more enjoyable learning experience?

What makes your problem *problematic*? What barriers to action stand in the way of your goal? For example, the problem-solving literature has identified the following broad categories of typical obstacles:

- Complexity of the problem
- Conflicting goals or values
- Lack of relevant skills
- Lack of appropriate resources
- Uncertainty and ambiguity
- Emotional distress such as anxiety, depression or anger.

Where thoughts or feelings are a major (internal) barrier to action, particularly 'emotional distress', you might be best to begin by considering acceptance and defusion strategies of the kind discussed in earlier chapters.

Remember this: Don't use problem-solving for 'experiential avoidance'

Focus on changing what's most under your control, which will usually be your voluntary *actions*, and accepting things that are difficult to control, such as unpleasant subjective experiences. Automatic thoughts and feelings are often best dealt with using *mindfulness* and *acceptance* strategies rather than attempts to control or avoid them. In other words, watch out that you don't try to use problem-solving as another *unworkable* form of 'experiential avoidance'.

Try it now: Define your problem and goals

Being concise, specific, objective and realistic is the key. If you're familiar with the concept of 'SMART goals', from earlier in this book, consider using that method. Follow the steps below:

My problem statement

Describe your problem in a few sentences, trying to be as specific and objective as possible, avoiding any assumptions or using value judgements or emotive language.

My goal statement

Describe your (short-term) goal briefly, being as specific and realistic as possible, and avoiding vague or idealistic outcomes – 'What's the best you can realistically hope to achieve?'

Anticipated obstacles

List the obstacles, if any, you have to overcome to solve the problem and achieve your goal – 'Why haven't you already achieved it?'

Now rate your problem definition (0–100%) in terms of how accurate and specific it is. If that was below 100%, try to revise your definition now and make it more satisfactory. You might want to repeat this process to get closer to 100%, if possible.

BRAINSTORMING ALTERNATIVE SOLUTIONS

The more alternative solutions you can identify, the more likely you are to identify the best plan of action. Also, there's some reason to believe that people who think flexibly and creatively and are conscious of a variety of perspectives (different options) tend to experience less stress.

Key idea: Brainstorming alternative solutions

The three classic principles of effective brainstorming were defined by the psychologist A.F. Osborn as follows (Osborn, 1952):

1. *Quantity* – Try to generate as many possible solutions as you can possibly think of.
2. *Variety* – Try to be as creative as possible and discount no possible solution, no matter how unsatisfactory it may appear at first, because even seemingly poor ideas can contribute to the creative search for solutions by fuelling the process and triggering other, better ideas.
3. *Suspension of judgement* – Keep listing options and don't stop to evaluate them until you've completed your initial list, because analysis can cause digression.

However, a word of warning: some people who generate high numbers of irrelevant solutions may end up feeling worse. Don't let your brainstorming go too far off track, if it doesn't seem to be helping the creative process.

General strategies and specific tactics

Sometimes, once you've exhausted your initial ideas, if you have time to go into more detail, it's useful to review your list of solutions and expand it by making a basic distinction between *general strategies* and *specific tactics*. Your initial list will probably be a mixture of solutions at different levels, some quite specific, others more general. General strategies are like broad headings, for example, 'get help from other people', 'break it into chunks', 'do some initial preparation', etc. It's useful to consider the full range of possible strategies so you're not overlooking a whole approach at this level. For example, a general strategy such as 'do nothing' should be considered for almost any problem, at least to compare it to other options. People often overlook this but in some cases, doing nothing might actually turn out to be the most sensible option!

Tactics, by contrast, are *specific examples* of how you might go about implementing different general strategies. For instance, if your problem was that you bought a second-hand washing machine from someone and couldn't plumb it in, strategies like 'obtain help from others' can be treated as broad headings under which a range of more specific solutions might be listed: 'phone my dad', 'email an expert from the internet', 'ask the guy who sold it to me', 'call the manufacturers', etc.

Try it now: Brainstorm alternative solutions

Make a list of as many possible solutions as you can think of that might help you solve your problem and achieve your goal. Don't get distracted by analysing or evaluating things: suspend that until later. Just get all the options down on paper. Be creative and aim to come up with as varied and comprehensive a list as possible. Don't exclude anything, even apparently silly ideas, at this stage. Don't stop to analyse or digress; just get a list together that's as exhaustive as possible. All ideas can help the creative process and you can screen out any *obviously* useless ones later.

When you've exhausted your creative ideas for possible solutions, you might want to review your list and improve it. Some of the things you've listed will probably be *general strategies* and others will be at the level of *specific tactics*. You can distinguish them by first making a list of the general strategies you identified. Also look at specific tactics you mentioned and consider whether they might be subsumed under a broader heading, perhaps another general strategy you've not named. Take this opportunity to consider if there are any other general strategies you're overlooking.

Now use each one of those general strategies as a heading, and list beneath it as many specific tactics as possible, drawing on your initial list of solutions but also trying to come up with more specific examples (tactics) for each heading (strategy).

If you're struggling to come up with ideas, there are several creative perspective-shifting techniques and generic solution strategies you can use to generate more potential solutions. Looking at things in different ways can help spark new ideas. Ask yourself things like:

- What's worked in the past?
- What have you never tried?
- What would you advise another person to do if faced with the same problem?
- What would other people do that might work?
- What would an expert tell you to do?
- What would you do if you were more confident, wiser, or more creative?

  Perhaps most importantly given what we've covered earlier regarding 'valued living': What would you do if you were acting more consistently with your most important personal values? If you still need inspiration, consider generic strategies like:

  - Stop trying and do nothing
  - Carry on doing what you're already doing
  - Get help from others
  - Break the task down into chunks
  - Simplify things or just focus on the first step

- Prepare by planning or rehearsing
- Improve resources by obtaining materials, acquiring skills or seeking information
- Wait for a while, start immediately, or pick a suitable time and place for action
- If appropriate, use acceptance and mindfulness, or the other strategies in this book, to deal with internal barriers to action in the form of interfering thoughts and feelings

Remember this: Creativity and flexibility strengthen resilience

If you're tempted to cut corners, remember that this process has hidden benefits, for example, flexible thinking often protects against negative emotions like anxiety and depression. When people feel they have several options, what psychologists call a 'broad repertoire of coping strategies', they tend to feel more confident and experience less stress. In the stress literature this is called improving 'appraisal of coping ability' (Lazarus, 1999). So, view this as an initial training in generating alternatives and spend some time on it. It would be appropriate to abbreviate the process for some situations and you'll become quicker at doing it over time anyway. Also remember to consider how consistent your goals are with your most important values, as we've discussed earlier in this book.

MAKING YOUR DECISION

It's obviously important to pick the best solution, although there may seldom be a 'perfect' solution to difficult or long-standing problems. Learning to accept some degree of risk or uncertainty is often part of the process. Decision-making will normally involve either:

- *Choosing* between *mutually exclusive* options from your brainstormed list of solutions
- *Merging* several *complementary* solutions together into a single, coherent plan of action.

Evaluating solutions can be a lengthy process, and where appropriate shortcuts are applied. View this as another opportunity to develop your skills through training, though. Start off by going through the steps in as much detail as seems appropriate at first and then abbreviate things later, as with other techniques, so that you can make constructive decisions more rapidly in a variety of real-world situations.

Key idea: Decision-making and predicting consequences

Decision-making is a 'science' in itself. People use different methods to make decisions, ranging from careful rational calculation based on the prediction of consequences, to rapid and spontaneous 'snap decisions'. There are many different ways to evaluate options and choose between them but one of the most common methods is simply to rate all of the main solutions in terms of how easy they would be to put into practice (how 'doable' they are) and how likely they are to actually solve the problem and achieve your goal (how 'workable' they are). If you're interested in 'valued living' then you'll probably want to add another major criterion: how consistent is each solution with your most important values in this area.

Where appropriate, it's possible to go into much more detail, for example, by evaluating the short- and long-term pros and cons of each proposed solution, or considering the personal and social consequences. The main thing is that you're satisfied you're using criteria that seem fit for purpose.

Try it now: Make your decision

To save time, you might want to do a *rough initial screening* and simply delete any proposed solutions from your list that you're sure aren't worth evaluating any further. Once you have a shortlist of the best options, you should evaluate them in terms of the following criteria, using the table below.

1 **Ease of implementation.** How *confident* are you that you could actually put the solution into practice?
2 **Effectiveness.** Assuming you did put the proposed solution into practice satisfactorily, how *likely* would it be to *work*, i.e., to solve the problem and achieve your goal?

3 **Consistency with values.** How consistent is this solution with your most important *values* in this area?
4 **Overall conclusion.** Based on these considerations, rate your overall satisfaction with the proposed solution, on a scale of 0–100% – or if you want to be quick, just give it a star-rating, from 1 to 3 stars.

If you have time, you might also consider the wider pros and cons (advantages and disadvantages) of each proposed solution, both short term and long term. You may also want to consider both the personal and *social* consequences of your actions, particularly for *interpersonal* problems. As you evaluate your initial list of proposed solutions, you may come up with new ideas, which you can add to the list and evaluate.

Finally, make a *decision* about the best overall solution or combination of solutions and prepare to formulate a plan of action. (Note that generating specific solutions that you're confident about using and that you expect to have the desired outcome will help to improve these aspects of your problem-solving attitude in general.)

Solution	*Ease*	*Effectiveness*	*Values*	*Overall*

Remember this: Don't sacrifice your values

It's important to predict the consequences of your actions accurately and to evaluate them appropriately, using criteria that seem fit for purpose. If you want to increase valued living then you should carefully consider whether your goals serve your values but also whether your proposed solutions do. In some cases you might choose a *more difficult* and potentially *less effective* solution because it's more consistent with your personal values. For example, cheating might be an easy and effective way to pass a test, if you don't get caught, but it might also be inconsistent with the value you place on things like honesty, integrity, and even love of learning. Only you can choose your own personal values, though, and decide how consistent you want to be with them.

PUTTING YOUR SOLUTION INTO ACTION

Now a plan that's not put into action generally isn't worth the paper it's written on. (Although, that said, sometimes you might reasonably plan to 'do nothing' or *reduce* some activity.) One of the biggest mistakes you can make is to spend time planning the best solution but to fall at the last hurdle and fail to put it into practice in a 'timely' manner, neither rushing nor procrastinating.

Key idea: Solution implementation and verification

Solution implementation is just a fancy way of saying 'putting your action plan into practice'. By 'verification' we just mean figuring out how it worked out for you and what to do next.

In many cases, though this comes last, it's the *most important* stage of problem-solving. We saw earlier that poor problem-solving styles are labelled 'impulsive/careless' or 'avoidant'. By the final stage, it will become more obvious if you're rushing things carelessly or being avoidant, procrastinating, and putting things off. If you've skipped things to get to this stage are you making the error of rushing and arriving at decisions, too impulsively or carelessly? If you ultimately fail to put your plans into action are you procrastinating and exhibiting an avoidant attitude toward problem-solving? Ideally now you should act in a 'timely' manner and be prepared to *re-commit* to problem-solving and valued action if you don't achieve your goal. If at first you don't succeed, try, try again. If a solution exists, you can only really 'fail' by giving up prematurely.

Try it now: Plan your actions, serving valued goals

Write down a plan of action, based on your evaluation of the proposed solutions above. Use the following criteria to guide you, and complete the table below if it helps:

1 Be as *specific* as possible about the different steps required.
2 Be particularly clear about what the *first step* will be and when you're going to do it.
3 Be clear about the *final step* needed to complete the plan and how you will *evaluate the outcome*, i.e., how well it worked in terms of *achieving* your *goal* and how *consistent* you were with your relevant *values*.
4 Consider what barriers to action you might encounter, if following your main plan of action, and include a '*Plan B*' or contingency (backup) plan, if necessary – What will you actually do if your best solution doesn't go according to plan?
5 Specify, in your plan, how you will make sure you *commit to action* and definitely follow all the steps (or your backup plan) through to completion.
6 *Now do it!* Put your plan into action, evaluate the outcome, and decide what to do next.

Solution-implementation record

My action plan		
Anticipated ratings (before)		
Ease (%)	Effectiveness (%)	Consistency with values (%)
Actual ratings (after)		
Ease (%)	Effectiveness (%)	Consistency with values (%)
Next steps		

Remember this: Commit to valued living; don't 'lose the name of action'

Finally, once you've followed-through on your plan of action, consider what you've learned from the outcome, and the whole process of problem-solving. Praise and reward yourself, not for the results, but for of your *commitment* to action in accord with your values, regardless of the outcome. If your action plan didn't solve the problem and achieve your goal this time, that's okay, just go back to the drawing board and 'recycle' things by going through the steps again, taking into account what you've learned from the outcome of your first attempt. If your commitment lapsed, don't give up, resilience means being prepared to *re-commit* to your valued actions and goals, time after time, getting back on your feet and trying again.

Maintaining resilience through problem-solving

Return to the questions at the start of this chapter after a week or two of honing your problem-solving skills and re-rate your problem-solving attitude. Consider ways you can further improve your skills and confidence. Common pitfalls that should be addressed include:

1 Not defining the problem adequately, especially the specific goal to be achieved
2 Confusing solutions and goals, e.g., if your 'goal' is just one way among several of achieving a deeper goal
3 Not anticipating major internal or external barriers to action
4 Failing to defuse and accept 'internal barriers to action', i.e., interfering thoughts and feelings, while acting despite them.
5 Allowing yourself to digress during brainstorming by evaluating or analysing your suggestions
6 Not working out the nitty-gritty of your action plan, especially the first steps required
7 Not having a backup plan prepared in case your main solution hits an impasse
8 Setting goals and planning actions *not sufficiently consistent* with your most important values.

Over time you should aim to problem-solve flexibly across different situations, particularly learning to abbreviate your skills by solving problems in 'real-time' where appropriate, more rapidly and spontaneously. While developing this skill, you might find it helpful to write instructions to yourself on a small card or sticky note, such as the following:

Cue-Card for Rapid Problem-Solving

1 *Problem.* What specifically is the problem? What specifically is your goal? What obstacles do you face?
2 *Brainstorm.* What options do you have? How many possible solutions can you think of?
3 *Decision.* What are the main consequences of each different solution? What's your best option?
4 *Action.* What specifically will you do and when? *Now do it!* What did you learn? What next?

FOCUS POINTS

The main points to remember from this chapter are:

- Problem-solving is an established methodological approach, a form of cognitive-behavioural therapy, that research has shown to be effective for a wide range of issues.
- The most important ingredient appears to be your overall 'problem-solving orientation' or attitude, which can be divided into key ingredients and improved with practice.
- The process of solving problems can be divided into four key stages, which require different skills.
- It's useful to practise these slowly and systematically at first but also to anticipate that you'll eventually need to abbreviate things and make 'snap decisions' when solving problems in 'real-time' during some stressful situations.
- Developing a positive problem-solving orientation will contribute to your general *emotional resiliency*.

NEXT STEP

Problem-solving, like valued living, is often seen as a way of planning action. However, it doesn't provide specific guidance on individual coping skills. Interpersonal problems are among the most common sources of worry whereas healthy social relationships are consistently found to correlate with psychological resilience. In the next chapter, therefore, you'll learn some additional coping strategies, social skills for interpersonal situations, including assertiveness strategies.

Further reading

Nezu, A. M., Nezu, C. M. & D'Zurilla, T. J. (2007). *Solving Life's Problems: A 5-Step Guide to Enhanced Well-Being.*

11

Assertiveness and social skills

In this chapter you will learn:
- *About assertiveness and other social skills, such as effective communication strategies*
- *The important role played by concepts such as personal 'rights' and values in thinking about your social interactions*
- *A sample of basic social strategies, such as the 'broken record' technique, 'fogging', and 'active, constructive' styles of communication, etc.*
- *The importance of social skills in developing healthy relationships, and social support, as a basis for long-term resilience.*

> *To change the way a person feels and thinks about himself, we must change the way he acts toward others...*
>
> Andrew Salter, *Conditioned Reflex Therapy, 1949*

The importance of social skills

WHAT ARE SOCIAL SKILLS?

Behaviour therapists began developing assertiveness training methods in the 1950s, following the early work of Andrew Salter, who many see as the original pioneer in this area. Over time, their emphasis expanded beyond the importance of conventional 'assertiveness' to include a much wider range of *social skills* deemed important to healthy functioning in relationships. However, by 'social skills' we mean competence in a broad range of verbal and non-verbal strategies used when interacting with other people in general. We can define 'assertiveness', the most commonly emphasized social skill, as follows:

> ***Assertiveness is the ability to exercise and defend your personal rights, and to express your needs, opinions and feelings effectively and appropriately. It also means doing so in accord with your personal values, while respecting the rights of others and without being unduly inhibited by worry or anxiety.***

It's relatively easy to learn social skills; like learning to ride a bicycle or drive a car, it just takes practice. You can plan specific examples of what to say and do in writing, rehearse strategies in response to specific situations in imagination, and test them out in reality.

Key idea: What is assertiveness?

Assertiveness was the first form of social skill to be widely studied by psychologists. It's still probably the most important, or at least most popular, social skill to develop. It was originally explained as being a more constructive alternative to both *aggressive* and *passive* (or *submissive*) styles of communication, perhaps lying somewhere between the two. Subsequently it was distinguished also from the 'passive-aggressive' style, in which hostility is denied or concealed and manifested only indirectly, through subtle forms of attack.

We can therefore distinguish between four styles of response to challenging social situations:

1. *Aggressive*, where opinions are expressed without empathy or regard for the rights of others, often fuelled by angry feelings.
2. *Passive* (submissive), where one's own needs and rights are neglected, often linked to anxious or depressed feelings.
3. *Passive-aggressive*, where a superficial *façade* of passivity conceals underlying and indirect aggression.
4. *Assertive*, where one's rights and needs are expressed confidently and effectively, in accord with one's personal values and with empathy and respect for the rights of others.

APPLICATIONS AND RESEARCH

Assertiveness training probably reached its peak of popularity in the late 1970s. It's still employed today but is normally combined with other forms of psychological therapy, especially CBT, rather than being used as a stand-alone approach. In part, this is because it was found that the social skills required by individuals tended to vary between different groups, with different problems. Also, many individuals who appear to lack social competence are simply *inhibited* by thoughts and feelings, such as social anxiety or low self-esteem, rather than actually lacking specific skills. However, there may be a *circular* relationship between emotional and social problems and training in assertiveness and other skills has been employed, for example, in treating depression and social phobia. In particular, there is some evidence that interpersonal problems may lead to feelings of depression, which in turn lead to more interpersonal difficulty, creating a 'vicious interpersonal cycle', culminating in the onset of a more severe depressive episode (Beck & Alford, 2009, p. 305). Social-skills training has therefore been employed in the treatment of clinical depression as well as social anxiety disorder and milder (subclinical) interpersonal problems.

SOCIAL SKILLS AND RESILIENCE

Research on resilience consistently points to the importance of having appropriate sources of social support in place, such as emotional support and encouragement from friends and family, etc. By contrast, studies show that the most common topics of concern for chronic worriers are interpersonal matters. From your perspective as an individual, it's therefore worth considering how to improve the quality of your relationships to increase your long-term resilience. Developing your social skills, including assertiveness, is one traditional way to improve your relationships. However, at a more general level, it may first help to clarify your most important values in terms of relationships and to set goals and commit to acting in line with them. Being the type of person you genuinely value being in your relationships may be more important to your long-term wellbeing than 'success' in achieving your social goals, i.e., getting people to respond in ways you want. Improving social skills and strengthening healthy relationships is therefore likely to provide you with resources that will help resilience in the face of future adversity.

Four-step assertiveness

CASE STUDY

Charlotte was experiencing difficulty in her relationship with her husband, who was being quite aggressive and bullying. They still lived in the same house but were in the process of separating, after he had slept with another woman. They had three children, one of whom was still at school and lived with them. Charlotte simply wanted to feel that she was being more assertive in the relationship and not allowing herself to be pushed around, although we agreed that it was best for her to avoid excessive arguments. She wanted to 'find her voice' and regain a sense of self-respect. Although, she knew that her husband would probably dig his heels in and refuse to respond to some of her requests, she felt it was important to try nevertheless and to exhibit assertiveness in the relationship.

We first of all made a list of typical conversations that she found difficult and chose disagreements over household chores as the first problem to tackle. Charlotte brainstormed a list of different things she could potentially say in the conversation and we refined this and chose the best option from the list. We then rehearsed the conversation together in role-play, with Charlotte putting her response into the four-step format below. At first this seemed slightly unnatural but with practice it quickly became more flowing and also assertive. Charlotte said, 'Look, the fact is that this chore needs to be done and you had agreed to take care of it, I understand you don't have much time available right now, however, I feel quite angry that you've not done anything about it and I think I've a right to ask you to at least make a start, even if you have to finish the task later.' To her surprise her husband actually responded for the first time by tackling the chore, and did so without an argument developing. She became very enthusiastic about this technique and even started teaching it to other people!

Assessing your relationships

Self-assessment: Relationship challenges

To begin, using the table format below, rate how *satisfied* you are with your relationships in each of these broad domains (0–100%).

1 Intimate relationships with spouse or partner, etc.
2 Relationship with your own children or children in your care.
3 Relationship with your own parents, step-parents, etc.
4 Other family members, e.g., grandparents, siblings, etc.
5 Friends and other social relationships.
6 Relationships at work, in relation to study, etc.

Next try to identify what *problems* exist that prevent you from being more satisfied. Also consider what your relevant *values* are in terms of different relationships, what type of person do you want to be? Make a list of *goals* that would solve your problems and be as consistent with your values as possible. Finally, ask yourself what you could do or say to achieve your goals and record these initial *strategies* or solutions.

This information will help provide important examples for you to bear in mind and begin working on as you read the sections below. You should come back and revise your list of solution strategies after you've finished reading this chapter as you will probably discover some other possible options.

Relationship domain	*Problems*	*Values*	*Goals*	*Strategies*
Spouse / partner Satisfaction (%)				
Children Satisfaction (%)				
Parents Satisfaction (%)				
Other family Satisfaction (%)				
Friends Satisfaction (%)				
Work Satisfaction (%)				

YOUR PERSONAL VALUES AND RIGHTS

Considering your personal values in relation to social situations, as above, can be helpful when planning how to act differently. Thinking in terms of personal values can help in two ways, as with problem-solving in general.

1 Considering what you would do differently if acting more consistently with your relevant values can help you to come up with new suggestions. For example, what would a more empathic person or a 'good friend' do in this situation?
2 Considering which strategies would be most consistent with your values, in social situations, may help you choose between different ways of responding. For example, would this course of action be consistent with the value I place on being empathic?

Likewise, in the field of assertiveness training an emphasis was introduced, over time, upon the concept of personal 'rights'. Rather than thinking in terms of rigid demands placed on yourself ('I must not show I'm upset') or other people ('People have to show me respect') it can be more helpful to think in terms of what basic rights you and others have in common. For example, perhaps both you and others have:

- The right to express opinions
- The right to make mistakes
- The right to change one's mind
- The right to express disagreement
- The right to say when one objects to something
- The right to refuse requests
- The right to ask for help.

Of course, it's a matter for you to consider what rights you feel you and others are entitled to in general and in specific situations. It's often important to consider how to 'balance' several rights, for example, your right to express your opinion with another's right to be treated with respect. Most significantly for our discussion here: *you have a basic right to assert yourself appropriately and so does everyone else.*

Key idea: Balancing rights in social situations

Pick one of the challenging relationships you've examined above. Think of a specific interpersonal situation that's causing difficulty for you. Draw up a list of the main *rights* you believe you are entitled to in this situation.

Now draw up a list of the main rights that you believe others involved in the situation are entitled to.

Are these lists *identical*? If not, why not? Are you applying a 'double standard' by attributing different rights to different people? What would happen if you made these lists more *symmetrical* by assuming that most personal rights in this situation are mutual and apply equally to all parties? For example, if you believe you have a right to be treated with respect, in practice, do you *also* extend the same right to others?

If you've revised your list of rights now briefly describe how respecting those rights, both your own and other people's, would lead you to act differently in the situation you're considering.

What do you predict the most likely consequences would be if you were to approach that situation with more attention to balancing the rights of all parties involved?

ASSESSING YOUR SOCIAL SKILLS

Now you've considered some possible problems in relationships and the role of personal values and rights, it's time to look at your current style of coping. How are your current social skills and strategies working out in practice? It's useful to begin self-monitoring your social skills and assessing them by collecting the following information:

1 The *date and time* when a challenging social situation occurred.
2 What the *situation* was and who else was present.
3 Try to record in advance your specific *goal* for the situation, what's the best response you can *realistically* hope to get?
4 Afterwards, record your '*strategy*', what you *actually did* and *said*, and rate how well you did it (0–100%), i.e., the level of social skill you exhibited.
5 Finally, briefly note the *outcome*, what *actually happened*, how the other person responded, and rate how satisfied you are (0–100%) that your specified goal has been achieved.

You might want to use a form with column-headings like the one below to record key situations where you're dealing with other people, ideally on a daily basis.

The main thing is to record information that you find useful in tracking your progress and learning from your own experience. Take time to carefully review your notes once you've recorded about 6–7 different events. Do you observe any patterns? Are your goals realistic and relevant to your fundamental values in this area of life? Are some strategies better than others? How can you improve your skill?

Assertiveness and social skills record

Date/ Time/ Situation	*Goal (Specific, Realistic)*	*Strategy & Skill Rating (%)*	*Outcome & Satisfaction (%)*

The outcome is not entirely under your control so you may need to accept that sometimes you will act with social skill and use appropriate strategies but still not get the response you're hoping for from others. Likewise, sometimes you may just be lucky and achieve your goal, or some other satisfactory outcome, despite exhibiting quite poor skills and strategies. Don't be misled by this. Look at the bigger picture: you can't assume you'll be lucky or unlucky every time. It's best to develop appropriate strategies and skills even if they're not guaranteed to achieve your goals every single time. With that in mind, ask yourself what you can learn from each encounter and what you might want to experiment with doing differently next time.

Once you've evaluated a sample of your existing social strategies in this way, you'll be in a better position to begin experimenting with some new ones. These might be solutions of your own devising or more formulaic social skills, like the four-step assertiveness method described below. Evaluate these in the same way using the record above, particularly to track your skill level in using these new strategies as it improves with practice. If it seems difficult to act in the way you'd like because unhelpful *thoughts* or *feelings* impede your social skills, refer back to the mindfulness and acceptance strategies, etc., discussed in earlier chapters for dealing with internal barriers to action.

Remember this: Assertiveness is not aggressive

People unfamiliar with the subject quite often confuse assertiveness with the aggressive style of responding. Assertiveness is typically defined as an *adaptive* form of self-expression and it therefore makes no sense to say that someone is '*too* assertive'. People who too-eagerly announce, 'Oh, *I* don't have *any* problems being assertive; if anything I'm *too* assertive!', are often actually quite aggressive, domineering or tactless and therefore *woefully non-assertive* and lacking in basic social skills.

Learning social skills

A MENU OF SOCIAL SKILLS

Below is a brief outline of some common strategies derived from assertiveness training and other social skills approaches. This list is by no means *exhaustive* but it will give you some strategies to begin experimenting with. Pick one strategy at a time and try to use it as frequently as possible (without *over*-using it) for a week or two, until it becomes quite familiar.

The broken record

The broken record is one of the most basic assertiveness strategies and it provides a good starting point that leads naturally into most of the other techniques described below. It involves calmly and patiently repeating your point as many times as necessary, like the proverbial 'broken record', without being drawn into arguments or verbal side-issues. If at first you don't succeed, *try, try, again*. Stating what you want persistently, without taking 'no' for an answer can take courage and perseverance.

A: 'I'm not happy with this; can I have my money back?'
B: 'Nobody else has complained.'
A: 'That may be true but I'm not happy; can I have my money back?'
B: 'I'll have to speak to my manager.'
A: 'That's fine, go ahead and speak to whoever you need to, but I'm not leaving here until I've got my money back.'

Difficult situations often require persistence and non-assertive individuals often either give up prematurely or else become frustrated, angry or irritated. The broken record strategy means sticking to your main point until you get an answer, without getting bogged down in discussing your *reasons* or having to justify yourself unnecessarily. Can you refuse to take 'no' for an answer without becoming irritated or raising your voice but instead persist calmly?

Time-out (thinking time)

Another very basic skill, especially when you feel yourself becoming overly angry or anxious, is to assertively state that you want to take time to think about your response. It can be difficult to do this at first but it becomes much easier with just a little practice. For example:

> ***'I'm starting to feel a bit angry about this. I think we should leave it for now and both sleep on things, so we can talk about it tomorrow more calmly.'***

Alternatively:

> ***'I don't quite know what to say; let me go away and think about it and I promise I'll get back to you later with a more considered response.'***

Taking a 'time-out' or postponing your response shouldn't turn into a habitual form of *avoidance* but it can be useful when you feel your emotions may be temporarily getting in the way of assertive behaviour or you need time to consider the best response. So these two foundational skills, the broken record and time-out, involve making a clear rational decision to either persist in the situation or postpone things until later.

Fogging

Interestingly, 'fogging' is a bit like the *interpersonal* equivalent of the mindfulness technique we described earlier called 'defusion'. It involves acknowledging criticisms made by other people, and accepting the fact they've been said, without taking them too literally. The term 'fogging' comes from the simile of responding like a bank of fog that doesn't *resist* sticks or stones thrown at it but simply allows them to pass straight through, without being particularly affected by them. So 'fogging' is a bit like 'humouring' your critics, without taking them too seriously, just allowing their words to be acknowledged and not have any real impact on you.

> ***A: 'I really thought your presentation was awful.'***

B: 'Yeah, maybe you've got a point, it wasn't perfect. Never mind, I'll do it differently next time.'

In a sense, 'fogging' refers to the art of agreeing-without-really-agreeing. That often takes the form of simply of saying 'I suppose you might be right', 'You could have a point', etc. This is often easier if you deliberately interpret others' comments as criticisms of your *behaviour*, which may or may not be true, rather than as criticisms of your *essential character*. If you've skipped things to get to this stage, are you making the error of rushing and arriving at decisions too impulsively or carelessly? If you ultimately fail to put your plans into action are you procrastinating and exhibiting an avoidant attitude toward problem-solving? Likewise, you may adopt the view that any criticism has potentially a grain of truth in it, but isn't necessarily worth taking very seriously. Does it really matter? Another strategy is to view other people's opinions for what they are, as just opinions - merely personal hypotheses rather than facts.

Negative assertion

Negative assertion is similar to fogging but involves *explicitly criticizing* your own actions, in a calm, detached and constructive manner, without necessarily apologizing. Doing so steals the other person's thunder, if they're trying to criticize you destructively. By openly acknowledging some flaw, but treating it as relatively unimportant, you make it difficult for them to create a fuss about it. For example:

'You've got a point, yes, I did make a bit of a mess of that presentation, didn't I? I should have spoken more slowly and remembered to make time for questions.'

Keep it brief and simple. Most social strategies can backfire if not used skilfully and it's particularly important to avoid turning 'negative assertion' into unnecessary or *excessive* self-criticism. Again, this is easier if you deliberately view criticisms as referring to *changeable* aspects of your *behaviour* rather than your *essential character*. So shift attention on to specific aspects of your behaviour that you can readily change to make negative assertions constructive.

Negative inquiry

Negative inquiry is similar to negative assertion but it *invites* the other person to *explicitly* elaborate on their criticisms. For example:

'Just so that I can understand better, what is it specifically about the way I handled things that you didn't like?'

You might then continue to ask 'Was there anything else?', until the other person has exhausted their criticisms. When calmly invited to express their criticisms and to do so in full, without resistance, people will often become less aggressive and criticism, when made *more specific*, will often appear *more trivial*. This also encourages the other person to be more genuinely assertive with you rather than being indirect or manipulative, which is ultimately very helpful. Fogging, negative assertion and negative inquiry all tend to involve deliberate exposure to critical comments and other unpleasant or feared experiences. However, you have some degree of control over the course of events. You also have the opportunity to 'defuse' your thoughts about what's being said and to actively accept your feelings, while doing and saying what you consider important, in accord with your personal values. The mindfulness and acceptance strategies described in previous chapters will provide an important foundation to help you accomplish this without feeling overwhelmed.

Starting conversations (small talk)

A common problem is described as anxiety and inhibition about initiating conversations with other people, or making small talk. There are many ways to start conversations with different people at different times. You'll need to consider this somewhat on an individual basis, perhaps brainstorming a list of options for specific settings. However, for example, a general-purpose strategy that I've found helpful is to ask for help making a decision.

'You know, I just can't make up my mind where to go for lunch today; how well do you know the area; is there anywhere you would recommend?'

Most people like giving advice when they think someone is struggling with a decision they can help with and this can easily lead into a longer conversation. When trying to develop skill at initiating conversations, you can make up questions and *feign* indecision about things to find a reason for asking others' advice.

Expressing praise (active, constructive responding)

Expressing and accepting praise appropriately has long been considered a basic social skill. Recently, Seligman's Positive Psychology approach has incorporated an emphasis upon *enhancing* relationships by actively celebrating the other person's positive experiences, in greater depth (Seligman, 2011, pp. 48–51). When someone tells you about something good that happened to them, instead of simply saying 'That's nice' (passive, constructive) adopt a more actively constructive response style by asking them to relive the event with you in detail ('That's great, tell me more...'). Spend more time than normal, encouraging them to elaborate on what went well, and extending the conversation by communicating your interest and enthusiasm, expressing positive feelings, asking questions, and giving praise.

A: 'Phew! I'm glad I managed to get all the shopping done.'
B: 'That's great. You're very organized! Tell me more... Where did you go? What did you get? Are you planning to cook something special? That sounds wonderful.'

This strategy is employed in Positive Psychology because research has suggested that it predicts stronger relationships, linked to improved wellbeing and therefore longer-term resilience.

FOUR-STEP ASSERTIVENESS STRATEGY

A number of more formulaic assertiveness strategies have been developed that attempt to make the difficult task of expressing disagreement and tackling a social problem easier by breaking it down into a few stages. The four-step assertiveness strategy below consists of the following ingredients:

1 *Describe* the facts of the situation objectively.
2 *Empathize* with the other person's perspective.
3 *Assert* your own opinions, rights, or feelings.
4 *Propose* a practical solution or next step.

For example, if you wanted to complain about food in a restaurant you might say something like:

1 'The fact is that there's definitely a fly in my soup, waiter... (Describe facts)
2 'I appreciate that you feel it's not your fault... (Acknowledge and empathize with other person)
3 'However, I really feel disgusted by it and I think I've got a right to send it back... (Assert feelings and rights)
4 'So what I'd propose is that you just take it away, strike it off the bill please, and I'd be quite happy to leave it at that.' (Propose solution)

Politely reflecting back your understanding of the other person's thoughts and feelings shows them that they have been heard, and also makes clear they don't need to restate their position.

Try it now: Four-step assertiveness exercise

Pick an example of a specific situation where you think the four-stage assertiveness strategy might be helpful, a time when you'd like to deal with some conflict or disagreement more assertively. First, plan in writing how you might respond, by noting what you might say under each of the four headings below:

1 Describe the facts of the situation, as objectively as possible.
'These are the basic facts of the situation, which I think everyone can agree upon...'

2 Acknowledge the other person's viewpoint, as empathically as possible.
'I understand your position is this...'

3 Assert your own feelings, opinions, and rights.
'However, this is how I feel about things...'

4 Propose a solution, if possible.
'This is what I suggest should happen next...'

Now rehearse this a few times in your imagination until you're happy with your words and feel confident you will remember what you want to say in the real situation.

Other Social Skills

Other social skills you may potentially want to develop might include:

- Empathizing with others and 'active listening'
- Pacing and timing communication, neither over-talking nor saying too little
- Using clear and concise communication, where appropriate
- Expressing love and affection
- Expressing praise and encouragement
- Starting, continuing, interrupting or ending conversations
- Expressing personal opinions or feelings
- Refusing requests or making requests
- Objecting to behaviour or disagreeing with someone's opinions
- Setting and enforcing rules (boundaries)
- Questioning the evidence for, or consistency of, other people's views
- Accepting making mistakes, such as getting a word wrong, etc.

These are just a few common examples. You will need to self-monitor your own social skills to identify other areas where practice may be required.

INTERNAL BARRIERS TO SOCIAL SKILLS

Unhelpful thoughts and feelings can often get in the way of assertiveness and other social skills. In fact, often the only reason that people appear to 'lack social skills' is that their natural ability to cope is inhibited by worry and feelings of anxiety, or other internal barriers to action. The mindfulness and acceptance strategies described in previous chapters will therefore, almost inevitably, be required at some stage in developing your social skills.

Remember this: External focus of attention

Heightened internal focus of attention, particularly attention to unpleasant bodily sensations and images of how you come across to others (from an 'observer perspective'), have consistently been found associated with social anxiety. A number of approaches therefore recommend deliberately adopting a more 'external focus', shifting your focus of attention on to the audience or individuals you're talking to. One way of doing this is to study the body language and facial expressions of others more closely, without staring, while talking to them, as if you're trying to memorize their facial appearance so that you would be able to recognize them in a crowd or even draw a picture of them later. This is helpful in reducing anxiety, but it also means you'll spot important information that should be guiding your own behaviour, for example, subtle signs of interest or boredom, signals that others want to speak, etc.

INTERPERSONAL PROBLEM-SOLVING

The problem-solving approach you learned earlier in this book is widely employed as a method of coping with interpersonal situations. There are no universally applicable assertiveness strategies, so it's important to have a flexible means of planning how to respond to challenging interpersonal situations. Also, if you employ a standard assertiveness strategy like the four-step method below and the other person doesn't respond as you'd hoped, then the problem-solving approach will typically become important as a way of developing an *alternative* way to assert yourself, by providing a backup plan.

Try it now: Interpersonal problem-solving

Think of a specific challenging social situation and complete the details below, applying a version of the problem-solving approach discussed earlier in this book.

1 *Define the social problem.* Who is involved? Where and when does the problem happen? What do you want to achieve, what's your goal, how do you want others to respond? What obstacles stand in the way?
2 *Brainstorm alternative strategies* (solutions). Try to list as many different ways of acting as possible. You can consider some of the standard strategies you've learned above but be creative and don't be limited by them.
3 *Make a decision.* For social situations, it's usually important to consider the social consequences of different proposed solutions. How do you predict others will respond? Rate each possible social strategy (0–100%) in terms of how confident you are about putting it into practice and how likely it would be to achieve your goal, for others to respond the way you desire. Also consider which possible strategies would be most consistent with your relevant values in terms of these situations and relationships.

4 *Take action*. Choose the best option or combination and develop an action plan. What's the first step? Put it into practice and evaluate the outcome. How did others actually respond?

Remember this: Consider the consequences

It's essential to consider the consequences of your actions in social situations. This is especially true when there's any risk that others will respond in *aggressive, violent* or *undesirable* ways. Try to put yourself in the shoes of others and anticipate their reactions as accurately as possible to avoid your plans backfiring or any harm being caused.

Applying social skills

PREPARING AND REHEARSING

In traditional assertiveness training and modern cognitive-behavioural therapy, role-play exercises are commonly used to rehearse social skills. When applying your chosen social strategies as part of a self-help approach, it's a good idea to begin by preparing how you would respond as follows.

1 *Writing down* a description of how you plan to act assertively in the specific situation you're preparing for
2 *Mentally rehearsing* in your imagination what you would say and do, and imagining how others are likely to respond
3 Perhaps also *physically rehearsing* (role-playing), aloud, in front of a mirror or an empty chair, if possible.

However you prepare, it's a good idea to make sure you're ready before applying the strategy in a real-world situation and practice can help improve your self-confidence. If you don't have a clear example of a problem situation to work on, you might want to practise by considering an example situation, such as one of the ones below.

1 You notice after leaving a shop that you have been short changed but the shop assistant doesn't believe you.

2 You realize that some clothing bought a few days earlier is faulty but the shop won't accept a return because you've lost the receipt.
3 Someone pushes in front of you in a queue and refuses let you regain your place.
4 You find something wrong with the food you have ordered in a restaurant but the waiter insists that it's as it should be.

Try it now: Rehearsal of assertiveness by acting 'as if'

A 'top-down' way of developing social skills involves identifying the core value you want to exhibit, such as courage or empathy, etc. You can then try writing a draft 'script' or 'plan', describing in detail how you would specifically *think, act*, and *feel* in certain situations, if acting more consistently with your chosen value. For instance, what would it *mean in practice* to act more empathically in response to a difficult situation you're facing?

Read the script aloud to yourself before rehearsing it in your imagination, trying to picture as realistically as possible how others are likely to respond. Make any adjustments to the script you feel are appropriate and repeat this process until you feel confident about putting it into practice in the real world. If it helps, you can try rehearsing your role aloud in front of a mirror or an empty chair. Finally, try to act 'as if' you possess the virtue in the real world, using your script as a guide.

APPLYING AND REVIEWING

Having monitored your existing social interactions and planned an alternative strategy to use, following preparation and rehearsal, it remains only to put things into practice in the real world. Make sure you don't bite off more than you can chew, it's best to start with smaller challenges until your confidence and skills have developed.

Continue to use the self-monitoring record above to evaluate your progress. It's important to reflect on what can be learned whether or not encounters go as you'd wished, and to remain committed to your personal values in relation to these social situations. When confronted with a difficult situation, it's often best to employ a systematic problem-solving approach of the kind described earlier. Notice when its rational to persist with something and when it would be better to postpone things and wait. Use your mindfulness and acceptance skills to remain attuned to the reality of the present moment during social situations and to defuse thoughts about other people and distance yourself from their opinions, where appropriate.

Maintaining resilience through social skills

Overcoming social problems and strengthening healthy relationships, to build social support, will increase your resilience in the long-term. The more opportunity you have to practise key social strategies, the more skilled you will become. Aim to develop a more assertive and socially-skilled way of life. You can help make your skills more general by recalling your relevant values frequently throughout the day, and trying to remain committed to them in your interactions with others. Notice when its rational to persist with something and when it would be better to postpone things and wait. Use your mindfulness and acceptance skills to remain attuned to the reality of the present moment during social situations and to defuse thoughts about other people and distance yourself from their opinions, where appropriate.

The main points to remember from this chapter are:

FOCUS POINTS

- Focus on personal *rights* and *values* can help guide you through difficult interpersonal problems.
- There are many established social skills and assertiveness strategies that you can experiment with, such as the four-step assertiveness method, and the basic skills of repetition ('broken record'), postponement ('time-out'), and distancing yourself ('fogging').
- Systematic *problem-solving* approaches provide a more flexible way of coping with a variety of social situations.
- Preventing and overcoming social problems, strengthening social skills, enhancing relationships and improving social support networks will have positive consequences for psychological resilience over the long term.

NEXT STEP

We're nearly at the end. You've covered a lot of information about building resilience and many different strategies for dealing with both internal and external problems. Hopefully, you've been carefully putting everything into practice and not just skimming the pages. Remember: practice makes perfect! The last part of the book will look at resilience from a broader perspective by linking it to the classical philosophical school of Stoicism, which was the high-point of a therapeutic system that evolved in ancient Greece and Rome based upon the thought and lifestyle of Socrates.

Further reading

Alberti, R. & Emmons, M. (2008). *Your Perfect Right: Assertiveness and Equality in Your Life and Relationships* (Ninth edition).

Bolton, R. (1979). *People Skills: How to assert yourself, listen to others, and resolve conflicts.*

12

Stoic philosophy and resilience

In this chapter you will learn:

- *About the ancient Graeco-Roman philosophy of* Stoicism, *and how it derived from the life and thought of the pre-eminent Greek sage, Socrates*
- *How Stoic practice employed training in specific psychological exercises designed to build emotional resilience*
- *How Stoic philosophy can combine with CBT and the modern psychological approach to resilience-building you've learned in previous chapters*
- *How to 'think like a Roman emperor' – one of the* good *ones, the Stoic ruler Marcus Aurelius Antoninus – by applying Stoic principles and strategies to your daily life.*

> ***Grant me the serenity to accept the things I cannot change;***
> ***Courage to change the things I can;***
> ***And wisdom to know the difference.***
>
> *The Serenity Prayer*

> ***What, then, is to be done? To make the best of what is in our power, and take the rest as it naturally happens.***
>
> Epictetus, *Discourses*

The importance of philosophy

In this, our final chapter, we broaden our perspective to examine the question: What does it mean to approach resilience-building from a *philosophical* perspective? If you look up the *adjective* 'philosophical' in a dictionary you'll most likely find it defined, among other things, as the ability to maintain a calm attitude in the face of adversity.

We might say that to be resilient is to maintain a 'philosophical attitude' in dealing with misfortune. That should, I think, strike you as odd. Most people assume that philosophy is a rather bookish and academic subject. So what's the connection with the gritty real-world domain of resilience? In fact this use of 'philosophical' as meaning *resilient* probably stems from a very ancient tradition, which reached its peak and ultimate expression in an influential Graeco-Roman philosophy, based on the teachings of Socrates, and known simply as *Stoicism*. To be 'philosophical' in the face of adversity, your dictionary may also tell you, means essentially the same thing as being 'stoical'.

WHAT IS STOICISM?

Stoicism is the school of classical philosophy most associated with what we now call psychological therapy, stress management, and resilience-building, etc. Despite its being several centuries older than Christianity, there has been a definite resurgence of interest in Stoicism over the past few decades. Stoic theory and practice has influenced modern psychological approaches to prevention and therapy, particularly cognitive-behavioural therapy (CBT). Indeed Stoicism has been described as part of the 'philosophical origins' of modern CBT by some of its founders (Robertson, 2010). The Stoic Epictetus has even been described as 'the patron saint of the resilient' (Neenan, 2009, p. 21).

Although modern readers are likely to assume that philosophy is mainly an 'academic' or 'theoretical' subject, ancient philosophy generally had a practical dimension at its core and Stoicism was the school that placed most explicit emphasis on this. Stoicism did sometimes involve theoretical debate of the kind found in modern university philosophy departments but it primarily emphasized systematic training in psychological exercises designed to help students adopt a Stoic-philosophical lifestyle and to build emotional resilience. However, before we delve further into the relevance of Stoic philosophy to modern resilience-building, it might help to explain who we actually mean when we talk about 'the Stoics'.

MEET THE STOICS...

The philosophical school of Stoicism was founded in Athens, around 300 BC, by Zeno of Citium (334–262 BC). The name 'Stoic' comes from the Greek '*Stoa Poikile*', the 'painted colonnade' decorated with frescos in the Athenian *agora*, or marketplace, where Zeno and his followers would gather to discuss philosophy in public. Hence, the connotation of

'Stoic philosophy' was arguably something along the lines of 'philosophy of the street', 'urban philosophy' or philosophy applied to the lives of the general public outside the 'ivory tower' of academia. The Stoics tried to emulate the life of the pre-eminent Greek philosopher, Socrates (469–399 BC), who had debated philosophy in the Athenian marketplace centuries earlier, and they considered themselves to be the most authentic of several competing Socratic schools of philosophy. Although Stoicism originated in ancient Greece, several centuries later it also became very influential in the Roman Empire.

The early Greek Stoics were very highly regarded and well-known philosophers who wrote many books but unfortunately most of their writings were lost or destroyed by later generations and little direct record remains of their views. Nevertheless, we do know a great deal about Stoicism from other sources, primarily through texts recording the thoughts and practices of three famous philosophers who lived in ancient Rome many centuries after Stoicism originated. Most modern psychological therapies and stress management approaches are well under a century old; modern cognitive therapy originated less than half a century ago. By contrast, Stoicism endured as an important school of philosophical resilience-training for over 500 years, and influenced a great many people, from slaves to emperors, across many different cultures and countries.

Seneca (1–65 AD) was a celebrated Stoic philosopher and influential figure in Roman politics. He personally educated the young Emperor Nero who later went bad and became a notorious tyrant, turning against his former teacher and ultimately ordering his execution. Many *Letters* written by Seneca in Latin survive to the present day. These are really short essays on Stoicism, addressed to another student called Lucilius whom he mentored in philosophy as a way of life. Seneca has been much revered throughout the ages for his common-sense approach to philosophy and his highly eloquent writing style.

Epictetus (55–135 AD) was the slave of one of Nero's associates. He was reputedly tortured and left crippled in one leg by his master, who later set him free, perhaps in remorse. Although a lowly slave, Epictetus went on to become an influential Stoic philosopher through the public lectures he gave, which in some ways resemble modern psychological self-help workshops. His lectures were written down by a faithful student called Arrian and much of them survive to this day. Arrian also compiled some of Epictetus' remarks into a small practical guide to philosophy as a way of life called the *Enchiridion*, or 'Handbook' of Stoicism.

Marcus Aurelius (121–80 AD) was a revered Roman emperor (one of the good ones, not like Nero) who was tutored from childhood in the Stoic philosophy and way of life. He appears to have been familiar with the written lectures of Epictetus, which he tried to put into practice in his own daily life. We still have his personal journal, known as the *Meditations*, which has become one of the best-known self-help books of all time. Marcus systematically recorded his use of Stoic psychological exercises, using his journal as a kind of workbook, which appears to demonstrate just how *seriously* the Stoics took the practical techniques mentioned by teachers such as Epictetus. Although arguably one of the most powerful military and political figures in world history, the emperor Marcus Aurelius therefore dedicated his life to following the teachings of a crippled Roman slave, whose example he tried to follow in his own, very different, life.

Stoic thought also permeated the arts and religion influencing classical poetry and subsequently Christian thought and practice. We can witness Stoicism in action in these different contexts and from this rich material a number of modern academic scholars have painstakingly *reconstructed* key elements of Stoic theory and practice for modern readers (Long, 2002; Hadot, 1995; Hadot, 1998). Some aspects of Stoicism have a kind of *déjà vu* quality. We still use clichés like 'know thyself', 'all things in moderation', 'seize the day' and 'live in the here and now', etc., which derive from ancient Socratic philosophies like Stoicism. In a sense, all modern Westerners live unknowingly among the cultural rubble of this once-great philosophical system, something that's always in the background when we talk about subjects like CBT and building emotional resilience.

Remember this: Stoicism as common sense

The Stoics explicitly tried to base their philosophy upon common-sense principles, deep underlying preconceptions shared by all of humanity. Many of its principles may therefore appear to be *truisms*. For example, we should not try to control things that we *cannot* control; our impressions are not the things they represent, etc. If the Stoic philosophy seems controversial at certain points, consider whether you're interpreting these remarks the way the Stoics intended, because they generally assumed they were just stating the obvious. The point is that we all too frequently ignore the practical implications of common sense and do the opposite of what should be self-evidently the right course of action.

THE ESSENCE OF STOICISM

So what practical advice do the Stoics give us about building resilience? Well, this is a philosophy that can be studied for a lifetime and more detailed accounts do exist. An excellent modern guide to Stoicism already exists in the book *A Guide to the Good Life: The Ancient Art of Stoic Joy* by Prof. William Irvine, an academic philosopher in the USA (Irvine, 2009). My own writings, especially my book *The Philosophy of Cognitive-Behavioural Therapy*, have focused on describing the relationship between Stoicism and modern psychotherapy (Robertson, 2010; Robertson, 2005).

However, although, Stoicism is a vast subject, it was based upon a handful of simple principles. Epictetus summed up the *essence* of Stoicism as 'following Nature' through the 'correct use of impressions'. By 'following Nature', the Stoics meant something twofold: accepting external events as decreed by the Nature of the universe, while acting fully in accord with your own nature as a rational human being, by living in accord with your core values. (Scholars capitalize 'Nature' when referring to the nature of the universe as a whole, whereas lower-case 'nature' means your internal human nature as an individual, including your personal values, although you are part of the whole.)

> ***Don't treat anything as important except doing what your nature demands, and accepting what Nature sends you.***
>
> *Meditations*, 12:32

> ***Reverence: so you'll accept what you're allotted. Nature intended it for you, and you for it.***
>
> ***Justice: so that you'll speak the truth, frankly and without evasions, and act as you should – and as other people deserve.***
>
> *Meditations*, 12: 1

However, the basic twofold principle 'follow Nature' leads on to an elaborate system of applied philosophy, which we will now explore in more detail.

The first few passages of the philosophical *Handbook* of Epictetus provide arguably the most authoritative summary of basic Stoic theory and practice. I've paraphrased the key statements below, to highlight the possible continuity with approaches to resilience-building discussed earlier in this book.

1 The *Handbook* begins with a very clear and simple 'common sense' declaration: Some things are under our control and others are not. Hence, this basic observation will constitute the foundation of everything else that follows.
2 Our own actions are, by definition, under our control, including our opinions and intentions (e.g., commitments to valued action), etc.
3 Everything other than our own actions is not under our direct control, particularly our health, wealth and reputation, etc. (Although, we can *influence* many external things through our actions we do not have complete or direct control over them, they do not happen simply as we will them to.)
4 Things directly under our control are, by definition, free and unimpeded, but everything else we might desire to control is hindered by external factors, i.e., partly down to fate.
5 The Stoic should continually be mindful of the fact that much emotional suffering is caused by mistakenly assuming, or acting as if, external things are directly under our control.
6 Assuming that external events are under our control also tends to mislead us into excessively blaming others and the world for our emotional suffering.
7 However, if you remember that only your own actions are truly under your control and external things are not, then you will become emotionally resilient as a result ('no one will harm you') and you may achieve a kind of profound freedom and happiness, which is part of the ultimate goal of Stoicism.
8 To really succeed in living as a Stoic, you need to be highly committed, and may need to abandon or at least temporarily postpone the pursuit of external things such as wealth or reputation, etc. (Stoics like Epictetus lived in poverty while others, like Marcus Aurelius, tried to follow the principles despite commanding great wealth and power – both were considered valid ways of living for a Stoic but Marcus perhaps believed his complex and privileged lifestyle made commitment to Stoicism more difficult at times.)
9 From the very outset, therefore, the Stoic novice should rehearse spotting unpleasant experiences ('impressions') and saying in response to them: 'You are an impression, and not at all the thing

you appear to be.' (Note how closely this resembles what we earlier called 'defusion'.)

10 After doing this, ask yourself whether the impression involves thinking about what is under your control or not; if not, then say to yourself, 'It is nothing to me.' (Meaning, it's essentially indifferent to me if it's not under my control – I just need to accept it; although the Stoics did admit that some external outcomes are naturally to be preferred, despite lacking true intrinsic value.)

The Greek word translated as 'impression' in Stoic literature is *phantasia*, which refers to more or less anything that passes through your stream of consciousness, including thoughts, feelings, images, memories, and sense perceptions. The Stoics believed that thoughts, resembling statements, lurk behind every impression, for example, when I see a tree, I simultaneously experience the verbal thought 'That is a tree over there', without necessarily being aware of the words and concepts being used. (As it happens, ACT is based on a similar set of assumptions which sees language as permeating almost all of our experience, not just the sentences we say in our minds.)

Hence, these last two points, which clearly describe some of the most basic strategies of Stoicism, can be compared to the modern 'acceptance-based' psychological skill discussed earlier, called 'cognitive defusion'. As we've seen, acceptance-based approaches like ACT emphasize the use of *experiential* strategies, such as repeating the words in a silly voice, to achieve defusion. However, it also sometimes uses verbal strategies such as prefacing a thought with the words: 'I notice I am having the thought that…' This perhaps comes closest to the Stoic method above: You are an impression ...' Epictetus follows these remarks with this further advice:

11 When we experience desire or aversion towards certain (good or bad) things, we implicitly assume that they can be controlled (approached or avoided), and failing to achieve our desires or avoid our aversions causes suffering.

12 Hence, if you attach desire or aversion to external events, outside of your control, and judge them to be inherently good or bad, by definition, you will make yourself vulnerable to suffering.

13 It is better (i.e., more resilient) to shift your efforts to controlling your own actions where you are more assured of success, although even doing this properly may require practice.

14 To help you reduce attachment to external events and therefore suffering, describe to yourself external things you desire in objective language, e.g., of your favourite cup say: 'this is a cup I am fond of', suspending any value-judgements. (A similar technique, repeating 'Right now I am aware of ...' and describing experiences without value-judgements, was touched upon earlier in the chapter on mindfulness of the present moment.)
15 When you engage in any action, therefore, do so with a 'reserve clause', reminding yourself in advance what to expect and preparing to accept external events, insofar as they are outside of your control. (We will return to the 'reserve clause' but it's like the saying, 'Do what you must; let happen what may', and can be compared to the distinction between extrinsic and intrinsic values made in the earlier chapters on valued action.)

This final point, about Stoic acceptance, is described as keeping 'your will in harmony with Nature'. In modern language, that simply means being willing to accept those things that happen outside of your control, including the outcome (success or failure) of your own actions.

Epictetus concludes this section with the famous saying, which is widely quoted as a slogan of modern CBT: 'It is not things themselves that disturb us but rather our judgements about things.' He suggests we remind ourselves that it is our judgements primarily that cause suffering by asking ourselves whether other people might respond differently to the same problems. However, it's sometimes overlooked that Stoicism attributes suffering to a particular *type* of judgement, the cardinal error of judging *external* things outside of our direct control (health, wealth, reputation, etc.) to be of *intrinsic value*, leading to a rigid set of beliefs or assumptions, demanding that they absolutely *must* be pursued or avoided.

Key idea: Stoicism

Stoicism is an ancient Graeco-Roman school of philosophy, founded in Athens by Zeno of Citium at the start of the third century BC. The central principle of Stoicism is that we should 'follow Nature' by making the correct use of our impressions. Nature is divided into the external Nature of the universe and our internal nature as rational beings, including our personal values. Stoicism claims that human suffering is essentially caused by our tendency to lose sight of the distinction between 'internal' things which are under our direct control and 'external' things which are not, by taking our initial impressions too much at face value. The Stoics aimed to take more responsibility for their own actions, making them more in accord with the cardinal virtues of wisdom, justice/integrity, courage, and self-discipline. They also tried to become more accepting of things outside their control, rather than 'banging their heads against the wall' by trying to change the unchangeable. This typically involves making a subtle distinction between your own actions, which are under your direct control, and the outcome, success or failure, which may be partly in the hands of fate.

For the Stoics, the 'philosophical attitude', the source of inner resilience, involves perpetual mindfulness of acting in accord with virtue while accepting that the outcome, including the response of others, is beyond our direct control and will not always turn out as we had hoped or intended. The essence of Stoicism is neatly captured in the well-known Christian *Serenity Prayer*: 'God, give me serenity to accept the things I cannot change; Courage to change the things I can; And wisdom to know the difference.'

RESEARCH AND APPLICATIONS

There isn't really any direct scientific research, of course, on the ancient practices of Stoic philosophy. There are countless modern research studies on CBT and related subjects that arguably provide some *indirect* support insofar as CBT was originally influenced by Stoicism and still employs similar methods (Robertson, 2010). As we've seen, the theory and practice of ACT is supported by a number of research studies. In many respects, Stoicism has even more in common with ACT than with traditional CBT.

Remember this: Stoicism itself isn't evidence-based

Although Stoicism was cited as the philosophical basis of CBT by some of its founders, and CBT has certainly accumulated strong support from research. Stoic philosophy itself has not been tested systematically in this way by modern researchers. However, its principles are consistent with the approach to resilience-building described in this book and may provide a broader philosophical framework for those interested in exploring resilience further in terms of their philosophy of life.

PHILOSOPHY AND RESILIENCE

In a sense, the very word 'stoical' has come to mean something synonymous with *resilience*. As we've seen, when we speak of someone having a 'philosophical attitude' in the face of adversity, this figure of speech, which alludes to a kind of emotional resilience, probably stems from the Stoic philosophy in particular. The literature of Stoicism is essentially all about coping with precisely the kind of adversities studied in modern research on resilience: poverty, bereavement, illness, etc. So, at least on the face of it, the connection between ancient Stoicism and modern resilience-building seems obvious.

Resilience traditionally means 'bouncing back' from adversity, or enduring hardships without succumbing to them. However, the question of how to measure it is clouded by the lack of a clear ideal of normal functioning. What is the state that we'd like to 'bounce back' *to* after a setback? In a sense, we each have our own idea of what we're trying to recover after a setback and what we cling to during ongoing adversity. We can elevate the practice of values clarification, which helps answer this question, to a more philosophical level by bringing our ideals together in the image of the perfect Sage or role-model, and making more extensive use of this concept as a guide to valued living. The Stoic philosophy explicitly encourages us to contemplate the image of the ideal Sage, to formulate our own *model* of valued living, in the form of an ideal way of life to imitate. It's time to think more deeply, like the philosophers of antiquity, about *who* you really want to be in life, *where* you take your stand, and *what* this means for you in terms of resilience in the face of adversity. Resilience means remaining committed to acting in accord with your personal values, at a practical level, despite everything life throws at you.

Remember this: Stoics are *neither* unemotional nor passive

Many people mistakenly believe that Stoicism means being unemotional. This is *completely false* and based on a crude misreading of the Stoic texts. What the Stoics actually said was that when we correct our impressions about what is under our control and what isn't, certain irrational or unhealthy emotions tend to be replaced by more healthy and adaptive emotional responses. Marcus Aurelius said that the Stoic ideal was to be free from 'passion', meaning irrational and unhealthy emotions, and yet full of love. Love is not a 'passion', in this sense, because the Greek word translated as 'passion', literally means something closer to *emotional disturbance* – which would generally be a better English translation.

Likewise, people sometimes assume that Stoic acceptance means something like passivity, giving in, or resignation in the sense of 'rolling over' and allowing things to happen that are undesirable. This is also definitely a misconception; it's virtually the polar opposite of Stoicism. The most famous Stoics were men of action, military and political leaders, such as the Emperor and general Marcus Aurelius who fought hard to defend Rome against invasion by barbarian hordes, or Cato the Younger, the iconic Roman statesman who stood by his principles and defied Julius Caesar, until he lost his life as a result.

James Stockdale in Vietnam

CASE STUDY

Perhaps the best example of Stoicism applied in the modern world is arguably provided by the senior US navy pilot James Stockdale, later a vice-admiral, who was shot down and captured in 1965 at the start of the Vietnam War. Stockdale had been introduced to the Stoics by a university lecturer and as he ejected from his plane, he recalled telling himself that he was now about to enter the world of Epictetus, as a prisoner of war. Ironically, during his capture Stockdale was badly injured and left crippled in his left leg exactly like his role-model Epictetus who refers to his lameness several times in his writings, for example, saying that being crippled was a hindrance to his leg but not to his will.

Stockdale spent over seven years as a prisoner of war in a Viet Cong torture facility nicknamed the 'Hanoi Hilton', where he was subjected to the most intense psychological and physical brutality imaginable. Throughout his experience, he fell back on his recollection of the Stoics, particularly the writings of Epictetus as inspiration, and became the leader of hundreds of men held in captivity. After he was finally freed, Stockdale lectured on Stoicism to military students and published his reflections in the book *Thoughts of a Philosophical Fighter Pilot* (1995). He felt that the classics, particularly the writings of the Stoics captured something basic and timeless about coping with adversity that modern psychology could only provide a pale imitation of.

Assessing assumptions about control

THE STOIC FORK

As we've seen, one of the fundamental principles of Stoicism is that suffering is caused primarily by placing too much value on things outside of our direct control and not enough value on things genuinely within our control. How might this basic distinction, which we can call the 'Stoic fork', be applied in resilience-building?

A crude but helpful method consists in reviewing a problematic situation using a two-column form, with one column listing aspects of the problem which are truly under your control and the other listing aspects over which you have little or no direct control. Dividing a problem into different components and sorting them into those that can be changed and those that cannot is relatively quick and easy to do.

A more sophisticated method consists in rating your perceived control (0–100%) over each aspect of the problem identified. The Stoic prescription is to learn to better accept things outside of your control by focusing instead on the areas where you can actually make a change. Ultimately, this means your own will, or your thoughts and actions. The two-column exercise often leads to a conclusion that could be summed up by writing 'my actions' in one column and 'everything else' in the other but the process of arriving at that re-appraisal of control is what matters. The questions below may also be used to help clarify your sphere of control and prepare to reformulate your problem in terms of the aspects you can actually change.

Self-assessment: Re-appraising control

Use the questions below to help you re-appraise how much control you have over different aspects of some goal you hope to achieve. Experiment with reformulating your goal in terms that make your commitment to valued action the most important thing and the outcome, success or failure, of secondary importance.

1. What's your goal?
2. What potential obstacles or barriers might prevent you achieving your goal?
3. What personal values are most relevant in choosing how you act in pursuit of this goal?
4. How much control do you have over whether you achieve that goal (0–100%)?
5. What prevents it from being 100%? What aspects are outside of your direct control?
6. What prevents it from being 0%? What aspects do you have some control over?

What would actually happen if you accepted that success or failure isn't entirely under your control and focused instead on doing what you can in accord with your personal values? What would be the advantages and disadvantages (pros and cons) of adopting this philosophical attitude?

Applying stoic practices

ACTION WITH A RESERVE CLAUSE

As mentioned earlier, the Stoics refer to acting with a 'reserve clause', which means viewing all of your actions in terms akin to the saying: 'Do what you must and let happen what may.' The Stoics expressed this by stating their intention, 'I will travel to Athens', for example, while appending the reserve clause, 'fate permitting' or 'if nothing prevents me', to remind them to acknowledge that the outcome desired, an extrinsic goal, is not under their direct control. Christians later expressed the same notion by appending 'D.V.', *Deo Volente*, meaning 'God Willing', to their letters. I'm told Muslims mean something similar by saying 'Inshallah'. A similar notion is contained in the well-known *Serenity Prayer*. This is essentially the central principle of Stoicism.

Ancient philosophers illustrated the concept of the 'reserve clause' through the analogy of an archer. The archer can notch his arrow and draw his bow with skill, to the best of his ability but once the arrow flies, what happens next is outside of his direct control, including whether or not he hits the target. A gust of wind could blow his arrow off course; the target he's shooting could move. His action is under his power but the outcome is not. Having a 'philosophical attitude' would mean the archer being satisfied if he has done his part well and accepting of whatever happens next, whether he hits or misses his target. This, of course, is a metaphor for all goal-directed human action.

Epictetus also gives the example of a lyre-player and singer who develops stage fright about his performance, a problem similar to public speaking anxiety, one of the most common modern fears. Epictetus notes that people with stage fright generally feel little or no anxiety when performing *alone* but only when before an audience. The singer perhaps feels anxious even when he knows he performs well but is unsure how the crowd will respond. As Epictetus puts it, he wants not only to sing well but to gain applause, and that lies beyond his direct control, which causes uncertainty and anxiety about the outcome. If he were able to adopt the philosophical attitude of the 'reserve clause', he would be more indifferent to the audience's reaction. Assuming that what matters most is to do what is within his control well, he should theoretically sing as he does when alone, without anxiety. If, like the Stoic archer, he focused on doing what he can in accord with his values, to the best of his ability, and completely accepted the outcome as beyond his power to control, he would perhaps suffer less. He would also become more *resilient* to negative audience reactions and other setbacks. Even William Shakespeare received some scathing reviews – one Elizabethan critic dismissed him as pretentious, an 'upstart crow'. Should Shakespeare, then, have been worried and ashamed? (As it happens, Shakespeare appears to have read Seneca and his plays exhibit Stoic influences, so perhaps he knowingly employed the 'reserve clause' when receiving negative reviews.)

Sometimes the Stoics took this point further, arguing that not our *actions* but rather our *intentions* to act are the only thing under our direct control.

> ***Remember that your intention was always to act 'with a reserve clause', for you did not desire the impossible. What, then, did you desire? Nothing other than to have such an intention; and that you have achieved.***
>
> *Meditations*, 6.50

Put crudely, this is tantamount to saying that, ultimately, all that matters in life is that you genuinely try your best to do what you believe is important, regardless of whether or not you succeed. This is a common idea in our culture, although its original and most-developed form as part of a philosophical system is found in Stoicism. Rudyard Kipling's famous poem, *If*, advises us that like the Stoics,

> ***If you can meet with Triumph and Disaster***
> ***And treat those two imposters just the same; [...]***
> ***Yours is the Earth and everything that's in it,***
> ***And – which is more – you'll be a Man, my son!***

THE VIEW FROM ABOVE

'The View from Above' is the modern name given by scholars to a very common contemplative practice found in Stoicism and other Graeco-Roman philosophical traditions. In some ways, the View from Above captures the essence of the Stoic philosophical attitude. Suppose we consider that our emotional responses may be distorted by being too close to events and not seeing the bigger picture. It's common knowledge that we often feel less upset about events after some time has passed and we can look back upon them from a different perspective, with a sense of distance. Everything fits within some context and arguably the closest we could get to absolute truth would be the whole story, placing events within the total context of all time and space. For the ancients, this would perhaps have been the perspective of the gods, something to aspire to identification with, although something mortals could never completely emulate. Nevertheless, we can all use our imaginations to widen our perspective somewhat.

According to early Greek mythology, the gods live atop Mount Olympus, from which they look down upon the world of men in a detached way. One form of the View from Above consists in visualizing a kind of Olympian perspective, imagining what it would be like simply to look down upon our current situation in life from high in the sky.

> ***Plato has a fine saying, that he who would discourse of man should survey, as from some high watchtower, the things of earth.***
>
> *Meditations*, 7: 48

This allows us to imagine taking a step back from events but also to think of our life as situated within the context of wider events, the lives of many people around us. We can widen this further into a more cosmological perspective, sometimes called 'cosmic consciousness', in which we try to imagine the totality of space and time. Obviously, that's not literally possible to visualize but we can nevertheless contemplate the concept of all space and time ('the All') in our minds.

> ***You can discard most of the junk that clutters your mind – things that exist only there – and clear out space for yourself:***
> ***...by comprehending the scale of the world.***
> ***...by contemplating infinite time.***
> ***...by thinking of the rate with which things change – each part of every thing; the short span between our birth and death; the infinite time before; the equally unlimited time that follows.***
>
> *Meditations* 9: 32, modified

Key idea: The View from Above

One of the most common recurring themes in ancient philosophical practice is the notion that by contemplating the bigger picture, current problems tend to seem more trivial and less overwhelming. Compare this to the 'cognitive defusion' strategies, from ACT, discussed in earlier chapters. The Stoics attempted to gain psychological distance and to expand their perspective through simple contemplative exercises. There are two main ways of doing this:

1 The 'Olympian' perspective, picturing the world as if seen from high above in the sky, a bird's-eye view.
2 The 'Cosmic' perspective, which involves contemplating the totality of space and time, and the minute, transient place of your current situation within it.

Try it now: The View from Above

This exercise might be practised daily or when it seems helpful to do so. It can be made as simple or elaborate as you wish. Try doing it this way to begin. Close your eyes and take a few minutes to focus your attention on the sensations in your body, to notice your breathing, and to forget about everything else for a while. Imagine taking a step back, out of your body, and looking at yourself from the outside. Next, gradually imagine that you are floating upward, while you continue to look down at your body, left behind. If you're indoors, imagine the ceiling is disappearing as you rise upwards toward the sky. As you float slowly upwards, keep widening your perspective. Contemplate yourself below for a while, just one person among all the lives going on around you.

If you like, imagine floating up into space and looking down at the planet Earth, knowing that you're down there somewhere right now. Take a moment to contemplate how small a part of the world you occupy, how many other people live in the world, and how diverse things are. Contemplate how vast the universe is compared to the planet Earth, which is just like a tiny grain of sand on a beach by comparison.

Next, contemplate the transience of things and the passage of time. Consider the 'here and now' as just a brief moment, like the turn of a screw, in the totality of your own life. Contemplate your own life as just one of countless billions on the planet and the lifespan of your own culture as just one of many on Earth. Consider the life of the human race itself as having a beginning, middle and end, and think of your small place within the history of our species. Contemplate, finally, the lifespan of the planet Earth itself, and even the universe as having a beginning and end, thinking always of how small and transient the present moment is within the vast river of cosmic time. When you're ready, simply reverse the visualization and imagine floating back down into your body, returning your focus to the here and now, but retaining a sense of the wider perspective.

CONTEMPLATION OF THE SAGE

The philosopher Aristotle once asked: 'What more accurate standard or measure of good things do we have than the Sage?' He meant, what standard do we have to measure our own conduct by except the notion of an ideal role-model, one that we can aspire to emulate? We have values, words such as 'wisdom, courage, self-mastery, and integrity'. However, what *meaning* do these words have unless we try to picture what it would be like in practice for someone to live fully in accord with the values they describe?

> ***Choose someone whose way of life as well as words, and whose very face as mirroring the character that lies behind it, have won your approval. Be always pointing him out to yourself either as your guardian or as your model. There is a need, in my view, for someone as a standard against which our characters can measure themselves. Without a ruler to do it against you won't make the crooked straight.***
>
> Seneca, *Letter XI*

As Seneca implies, this benchmark is applied simply by using the idea as an imaginary model or source of guidance and asking either:

1 'What would the Sage do?', or,
2 'What would the Sage tell me to do?'

For example, Epictetus specifically advised his young Stoic students, when facing challenging situations, to check in with their values by asking themselves what Socrates, their main role-model, would do in the same circumstances.

However, in the modern world, it may appear there's a dearth of such exemplary role-models. We have 'celebrity culture' instead of Socrates. You should think for yourself and choose your own heroes to emulate. As nobody is perfect, you may find that it also makes sense to make a distinction between the virtues you admire in real people, warts and all, and the abstract *ideal* of the ultimate Sage, who has probably never existed and never will. For instance, you may formulate the pure, abstract idea of perfect courage, although your role-models may be *imperfectly* courageous but still provide salutary examples worthy of imitation. Which qualities do you most admire in others? What sort of person, ultimately, do you want to be in life? If this is our standard then, in a sense, the concept of 'resilience' must be *subordinate* to it. 'Resilience' refers to your ability to remain committed to valued living, a life emulating your ideal, even in the face of adversity, and to re-commit to your values, getting back on course after a setback has led you temporarily astray.

Key idea: The ideal philosopher-sage

The concept of an archetypal 'Sage' (*Sophos*), or wise man, runs throughout classical literature and plays an absolutely central role in Stoicism. (Scholars use 'sage' for specific individuals and capitalized, 'Sage', for the abstract ideal.) The image of the Sage was partly based upon the living example of the most revered philosophers of antiquity, typically: Diogenes the Cynic, Zeno the Stoic, the Pre-Socratic Heraclitus, Pythagoras of Samos, and a few others. However, without doubt, the pre-eminent incarnate sage was *Socrates* himself. The Sage provides the template or standard against which the aspiring Stoic measured his own actions. Socrates was the primary role-model or ideal that the Stoics tried to live up to through emulation of his attitude and actions. Socrates provided the best embodiment of the ideal Sage and therefore of the central *values* of Stoicism, the virtues to which Stoics aspired.

Try it now: Contemplating the Sage

Take a moment to see if you can list the people you most admire in life. Include even fictional or historical characters as well as people currently alive or who you know personally. Try to include examples of people who exhibit the kind of psychological resilience you would like to emulate.

Now see if you can take the best qualities of those individuals and try to develop a written description of your ideal resilient role-model. What strengths would they possess? If this is difficult, just pick an individual to use as your example for now. If you could sum up the qualities and attitudes that make them resilient in a few words, what would they be?

Now make a list of past, present, or future problems that relate to your own life. Beside each, write down how you imagine your ideal resilient role-model would cope with them. How would their strengths help them? What attitude would they adopt? What advice would they give you about facing your own problems?

You'll probably find that in doing this you go back and forth between specific examples of coping with adversity and the general attitudes that underlie them, which should help you to clarify things progressively.

Maintaining resilience through philosophy

If you choose to employ this approach, you may want to delve further into the writings of Seneca, Epictetus and Marcus Aurelius, and modern commentators, for philosophical inspiration. Try to make philosophy part of your way of life by contemplating your values, perhaps using the image of the Sage, regularly. Contemplate the View from Above daily if you can, to help preserve a philosophical perspective on life. As the Roman poet Horace said, 'dare to be wise', aim to have the courage and resilience to live by your ideals.

FOCUS POINTS

The main points to remember from this chapter are:

- Stoicism was a practical philosophy that emphasized emotional resilience-building, in ways that resemble modern psychological approaches.
- The basic principle of Stoicism is that we should be mindful of our thoughts, avoid confusing them with reality, and check whether they relate to things under our control or not.

- The Stoics believed that emotional suffering was mainly due to placing too much value on things outside of our control and not enough on our own actions being carried out in accord with our true personal values.
- Contemplating the View from Above or our ideal resilient role-model (the Sage) are classic Stoic strategies for building emotional resilience.

NEXT STEP

Once you've read this book once, it's a good idea to go over it again. Try to prioritize the parts that seem most relevant to your own needs. Keep tracking your progress. If you do encounter setbacks, which is only human, review the *troubleshooting* guidance in the first chapter, specifically designed to help you cope resiliently with setbacks in your resilience training!

Further reading

Irvine, W. B. (2009). *A Guide to the Good Life: The Ancient Art of Stoic Joy.*

Robertson, D. J. (2010). *The Philosophy of Cognitive-Behavioural Therapy (CBT): Stoic Philosophy as Rational & Cognitive Psychotherapy.*

Stockdale, J. (1995). *Thoughts of a Philosophical Fighter Pilot.*

Bibliography

Alberti, R. & Emmons, M. (2008). *Your Perfect Right: Assertiveness and Equality in Your Life and Relationships* (Ninth edition). Impact.

Aurelius, M. (2003). *Meditations: Living, Dying and the Good Life* (G. Hays, Trans.). London: Phoenix.

Bastani, F., Hidarnia, A., Kazemnejad, A., Vafaei, M. & Kashanian, M. (2005). A Randomized Controlled Trial of the Effects of Applied Relaxation Training on Reducing Anxiety and Perceived Stress in Pregnant Women. *Journal of Midwifery and Women's Health*, 50(4), 36–40.

Baumeister, R., Campbell, J., Krueger, J. & Vohs, K. (2003). Does high self-esteem cause better performance, interpersonal success, happiness, or healthier lifestyles? *Psychological Science in the Public Interest*, (4), 1–44.

Beck, A. T. & Alford, B. A. (2009). *Depression: Causes and Treatment* (Second edition). Philadelphia: University of Pennsylvania Press.

Bell, A. C. & D'Zurilla, T. J. (2009). Problem-Solving Therapy for Depression: A Meta-Analysis. *Clinical Psychology Review*, (29), 348–353.

Bernstein, D. A., Borkovec, T. D. & Hazlett-Stevens, H. (2000). *New Directions in Progressive Relaxation Training: A Guidebook for Helping Professionals*. Westport, CT: Praeger.

Bernstein, D. A., Carlson, C. R. & Schmidt, J. E. (2007). Progressive Relaxation: Abbreviated Methods. In P. M. Lehrer, R. L. Woolfolk & W. E. Sime (Eds.), *Principles and Practice of Stress Management* (Third edition, pp. 88–122). New York: Guilford Press.

Biglan, A., Hayes, S. C. & Pistorello, J. (2008). Acceptance and Commitment: Implications for Prevention Science. *Prevention Science*, 9(3), 139–152.

Bolton, R. (1979). *People Skills: How to assert yourself, listen to others, and resolve conflicts*. New Jersey: Prentice Hall.

Borkovec, T. (2006). Applied Relaxation and Cognitive Therapy for Pathological Worry and Generalized Anxiety Disorder. In G. C. Davey & A. Wells (Eds.), *Worry & its Psychological Disorders: Theory, Assessment & Treatment*. Chichester: Wiley.

Borkovec, T. & Sharpless, B. (2004). Generalized Anxiety Disorder: Bringing Cognitive-Behavioural Therapy into the Valued Present. In S. C. Hayes, V. M. Follette & M. M. Linehan (Eds.), *Mindfulness & Acceptance: Expanding the Cognitive-Behavioral Tradition* (pp. 209–242). New York: Guilford Press.

Braid, J. (2009). *The Discovery of Hypnosis: The Complete Writings of James Braid, The Father of Hypnotherapy* (D. J. Robertson, Ed.). Studley: The National Council for Hypnotherapy (NCH).

D'Zurilla, T. J. & Goldfried, M. R. (1971). Problem Solving and Behavior Modification. *Journal of Abnormal Psychology*, 78(1), 107–126.

D'Zurilla, T. J. & Nezu, A. M. (2007). *Problem-Solving Therapy: A Positive Approach to Clinical Intervention*. New York: Springer Publishing.

Ellis, A. (2005). *The Myth of Self-Esteem*. Prometheus.

Epictetus. (1995). *The Discourses, The Handbook, Fragments* (R. Hard, Trans.). London: Everyman.

Fennell, M. J. (1999). *Overcoming Low Self-Esteem: A Self-Help Guide Using Cognitive Behavioral Techniques*. London: Robinson.

Fisher, P. & Wells, A. (2009). *Metacognitive Therapy: Distinctive Features*. London: Routledge.

Hadot, P. (1995). *Philosophy as a Way of Life* (A. I. Davidson, Ed., & M. Chase, Trans.). Malden, MA: Blackwell.

Hadot, P. (1998). *The Inner Citadel: The Meditations of Marcus Aurelius* (M. Chase, Trans.). Cambridge, MA: Harvard University Press.

Hadot, P. (2002). *What is Ancient Philosophy?* (M. Chase, Trans.). Cambridge, MA: Harvard University Press.

Harris, R. (2008). *The Happiness Trap (Based on ACT: A revolutionary mindfulness-based programme for overcoming stress, anxiety and depression)*. London: Robinson.

Hayes, S. C. (2005). *Get Out of Your Mind and into Your Life: The New Acceptance and Commitment Therapy* . New Harbinger.

Hayes, S. C., Follette, V. M. & Linehan, M. M. (Eds.). (2004). *Mindfulness and Acceptance: Expanding the Cognitive-Behavioral Tradition*. New York: Guildford Press.

Hayes, S. C., Luoma, J., Bond, F., Masuda, A. & Lillis, J. (2006). Acceptance and Commitment Therapy: Model, processses and outcomes. *Behaviour Research and Therapy*, 44, 1–25.

Hayes, S. C., Strosahl, K. D. & Wilson, K. G. (1999). *Acceptance and Commitment Therapy: An Experiential Approach to Behavior Change*. New York: Guilford.

Hayes, S. C., Strosahl, K. D. & Wilson, K. G. (2012). *Acceptance and Commitment Therapy: The Process and Practice of Mindful Change* (Second edition). New York: Guilford.

Hofmann, S., Sawyer, A., Witt, W. & Oh, D. (2010). The effect of mindfulness-based therapy on anxiety and depression: A meta-analytic review. *Journal of Consulting and Clinical Psychology*, 78, 169–183.

Irvine, W. B. (2009). *A Guide to the Good Life: The Ancient Art of Stoic Joy*. New York: Oxford University Press.

Jacobson, E. (1938). *Progressive Relaxation: A Physical and Clinical Investigation of Muscular States and Their Significance in Psychology and Medical Practice* (Second edition). Chicago: University of Chicago Press.

Jacobson, E. (1977). *You Must Relax*. London: Unwin.

Kabat-Zinn, J. (2004). *Full Catastrophe Living: How to Cope with Stress, Pain and Illness, using Mindfulness Meditation* (15th anniversary edition). London: Piatkus.

Kuyken, W., Padesky, C. A. & Dudley, R. (2009). *Collaborative Case Conceptualization: Working Effectively with Clients in Cognitive-Behavioral Therapy*. New York: Guilford.

Lazarus, R. S. (1966). *Psychological Stress and the Coping Process*. New York: McGraw-Hill.

Lazarus, R. S. (1999). *Stress and Emotion: A New Synthesis*. New York: Springer Publishing.

Lazarus, R. S. & Folkman, S. (1984). *Stress Appraisal and Coping*. New York: Springer.

Leahy, R. L. (2005). *The Worry Cure: Stop Worrying & Start Living*. London: Piatkus.

Long, A. (2002). *Epictetus: A Stoic and Socratic Guide to Life*. Oxford: Oxford University Press.

Malouff, J. M., Thorsteinsson, E. B. & Schutte, N. S. (2007). The efficacy of problem-solving therapy in reducing mental and physical health problems: A meta-analysis. *Clinical Psychology Review*, (27), 46–57.

Manzoni, G. M., Pagnini, F., Castelnuovo, G. & Molinari, E. (2008). Relaxation training for anxiety: a ten-years systematic review with meta-analysis. *BMC Psychiatry*, 8(41).

Masten, A. S., Cutuli, J., Herbers, J. E. & Reed, M.-G. J. (2009). Resilience in Development. In S. J. Lopez & C. Snyder (Eds.), *The Oxford Handbook of Positive Psychology* (Second edition, pp. 117–131). Oxford: Oxford University Press.

McGuigan, F. J. (1981). *Calm Down: A Guide to Stress and Tension Control*. London: Prentince-Hall.

McGuigan, F. & Lerher, P. M. (2007). Progressive Relaxation: Origins, Principles, and Clinical Applications. In P. M. Lehrer, R. L. Woolfolk & W. E. Sime (Eds.), *Principles and Practice of Stress Management* (Third edition, pp. 57–87). New York: Guilford Press.

Mooney, K. & Padesky, C. (2002, July). Cognitive therapy to build resilience. Notes from workshop presented at the annual meetings of British Association of Cognitive and Behavioural Psychotherapies, Warwick, UK.

Neenan, M. (2009). *Developing Resilience: A Cognitive-Behavioural Approach*. Hove: Routledge.

Newman, M. G. & Borkovec, T. D. (2002). Cognitive Behavioural Therapy for Worry and Generalised Anxiety Disorder. In G. Simos (Ed.), *Cognitive Behaviour Therapy: A Guide for the Practising Clinician* (pp. 150–172). Hove: Brunner-Routledge.

Nezu, A. M., Nezu, C. M. & D'Zurilla, T. J. (2007). *Solving Life's Problems: A 5-Step Guide to Enhanced Well-Being*. New York: Springer.

Osborn, A. (1952). *Wake up your Mind*. New York: Charles Scribner's Sons.

Öst, L.-G. (1987). Applied Relaxation: Description of a Coping Technique and Review of Controlled Studies. *Behaviour Research & Therapy*, 25(5), 397–409.

Padesky, C. A. (1994). Schema change processes in cognitive therapy. *Clinical Psychology and Psychotherapy*, 1(5), 267–278.
Reivich, K. & Shatté, A. (2002). *The Resilience Factor*. New York: Three Rivers.
Robertson, D. J. (2005, July). Stoicism: A Lurking Presence. *Counselling & Psychotherapy Journal* (CPJ).
Robertson, D. J. (2010). *The Philosophy of Cognitive-Behavioural Therapy (CBT): Stoic Philosophy as Rational & Cognitive Psychotherapy*. London: Karnac.
Roemer, L. & Orsillo, S. M. (2002). Expanding our conceptualization of and treatment for Generalized Anxiety Disorder: Integrating mindfulness/acceptance-based approaches with existing cognitive-behavioural models. *Clinical Psychology: Science & Practice*, 9(1), 54–68.
Roemer, L. & Orsillo, S. M. (2009). *Mindfulness & Acceptance-Based Behavioural Therapies in Practice*. Guilford: New York.
Salter, A. (1949). *Conditioned Reflex Therapy* (2002 Anniversary edition). Gretna: Wellness Institute Ltd.
Seligman, M. E. (1995). *The Optimistic Child: A Proven Program to Safeguard Children against Depression and Build Lifelong Resilience*. New York: Houghton Mifflin.
Seligman, M. E. (2002). *Authentic Happiness: Using the New Positive Psychology to Realize your Potential for Lasting Fulfilment*. New York: Simon & Schuster.
Seligman, M. E. (2011). *Flourish: A New Understanding of Happiness and Well-being*. Nicholas Brealey: London.
Seligman, M. E., Rashid, T. & Parks, A. C. (2006). Positive Psychotherapy. *American Psychologist*, 61(8), 774–788.
Seneca. (2004). *Letters from a Stoic* (R. Campbell, Trans.). Middlesex: Penguin.
Sibrava, N. J. & Borkovec, T. D. (2006). The Cognitive Avoidance Theory of Worry. In G. C. Davey & A. Wells (Eds.), *Worry and its Psychological Disorders: Theory, Assessment and Treatment* (pp. 239–256). Chichester: Wiley.
Simon, S. B., Howe, L. W. & Kirschenbaum, H. (1972). *Values Clarification: A Practical, Action Directed Workbook*. Warner.

Skinner, B. (1971). *Beyond Freedom & Dignity*. Cambridge, MA: Hacket.
Stockdale, J. (1995). *Thoughts of a Philosophical Fighter Pilot*. Stanford, CA: Hoover Institute Press.
Wells, A. (2009). *Metacognitive Therapy for Anxiety and Depression*. New York: Guilford.
Wolpe, J. (1958). *Psychotherapy by Reciprocal Inhibition*. Stanford, CA: Stanford University Press.

Index

Notes